A Poor Priest for the Poor

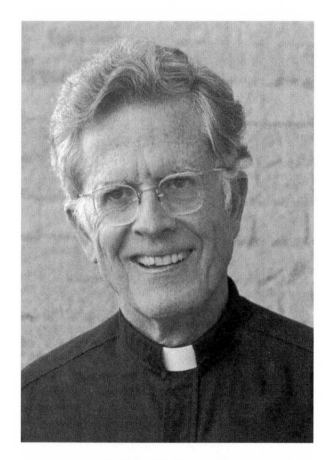

Fr. Richard M. Thomas, S.J.
1928 – 2006

A Poor Priest for the Poor

THE LIFE OF FATHER RICK THOMAS S.J.

Richard Dunstan

THE LORD'S RANCH PRESS
VADO, NM

Contents

To Lynn,
who met Father Thomas
before I met either of them

"You only go through this life once —
you might as well go 100 percent for Jesus."

FR. RICK THOMAS, S.J.

Preface

The title of this book, "A Poor Priest for the Poor," paraphrases the words spoken by Pope Francis, himself a Jesuit, to a gathering of journalists in Rome right after his election in 2013. He told them: "Some people wanted to know why the Bishop of Rome wished to be called Francis. Some thought of Francis Xavier, Francis De Sales, and also Francis of Assisi." Then he proceeded to tell the story: "During the election, I was seated next to the Archbishop Emeritus of São Paolo and Prefect Emeritus of the Congregation for the Clergy, Cardinal Claudio Hummes: a good friend, a good friend! When things were looking dangerous, he encouraged me. And when the votes reached two thirds, there was the usual applause, because the Pope had been elected. And he gave me a hug and a kiss, and said: "Don't forget the poor!" These words of Cardinal Hummes had an acute and immediate impact on the soon-to-be pope. Pope Francis recalls:

"And those words came to me: the poor, the poor. Then, right away, thinking of the poor, I thought of Francis of Assisi... That is how the name came into my heart: Francis of Assisi... *How I would like a Church which is poor and for the poor*!"

Since entering office, Pope Francis has tried to be faithful to the calling he received during the papal conclave. He has exhorted, prodded, and pleaded with the Church to be a 'poor Church for the poor'. Despite every form of reaction possible, he has remained firmly committed to bringing the vision of St. Francis of Assisi to life in the Church.

The allusion to the Francis pontificate in the title is, in my opinion, an apt one. While I do not write in any official capacity on behalf of the Society of Jesus, as you read this biography, I think you will come to agree with me that Pope Francis and Rick Thomas are kindred Jesuit spirits. First of all, both Pope Francis and the priest you will meet in these pages, Rick Thomas, are formed in the spirituality of St. Ignatius of Loyola. From this formation they learned the importance of discernment for following God's will. They are extraordinarily *flexible* men, docile to the Holy Spirit, willing to change long-held perceptions when they see that they are wrong. You will discover in this book a man who, from the moment that God called him to be a priest, never stopped changing. I have never met a man like Fr. Thomas who was willing to change so immediately and decisively when he came to know the truth. You will meet a man who, among many other positions, underwent radical shifts in his understanding of racial equality, the centrality of the poor, the importance of the Holy Spirit in the life of the Church, and the prophetic nature of the pro-life movement today.

Both are also deeply *pastoral* men entirely in communion with the teachings of the Catholic Church. Each pursues an intensely practical theology, a "theology of the people," as Pope Francis came to understand it when he was archbishop of Buenos Aires. Neither one of them has time for an academic theology that is out of touch with the real lives of the people of God. As a theologian myself, I am keenly aware of this danger. I cannot sit on the 12th floor of the library at the University of Notre Dame reading my theology homework without hearing in my head the voice of Fr. Thomas lambasting "those theologians in their ivory towers!" Fr. Thomas was not dismissing the importance of theology, but rather a *kind* of theology – and theologians – completely out of touch with the real needs of the world.

Both are invested in *the religiosity of the poor*. Fr. Thomas could always be seen 'praying the beads' whenever there was a free moment. His love for the rosary was well known. Fr. Mitch Pacwa, SJ, a renowned television host on EWTN, tells the story of visiting Rick Thomas in 1975 at the Lord's Ranch. As soon as he got into the car, Fr. Thomas announced that they would start praying the "beads for the needs." Anyone who has ever met Fr. Thomas will smile in recalling that from the moment the car started, to the moment you pulled up at your destination, you never stopped praying the rosary. Fr. Pacwa recalls that, although he knew how to pray the rosary, it had not been an important part of his life for many years. Fr. Thomas brought him back to a love for the rosary, and he has prayed a daily rosary ever since.

And finally, both are profoundly *in love with the poor*. Over and over as I was reading this book, I was choked up recalling Fr. Thomas' love for God's favorites. I grew up with this incredible man. He lived for a while in a small adobe house just a short footpath from my home. He taught me how to ride and get back on a horse, how to read and pray with the Scriptures, how to pray, how to laugh at *The Far Side* comic strip, how to be spiritually sensitive to the movements of the Holy Spirit, and especially, how to love the poor. When I first told him that I had decided to join the Jesuits, his greatest concern was that I would not be able to live the poverty and simplicity of life that I had learned growing up on the Lord's Ranch. He had come to discover what worked for him as a Jesuit: *If he wanted to be a Jesuit for the poor, then he had to be a poor Jesuit.* Not unlike Pope Francis, who moved out of his papal quarters into a simple apartment at the Casa Santa Marta, Fr. Thomas came to realize that he had to live like the people he served. This principle became the benchmark for living on the Lord's Ranch.

Fr. Thomas's witness as a 'poor Jesuit for the poor' continues to guide me today. I hear him echoed in what are for me Pope Francis' most challenging words from *Evangelii gaudium*, 201:

"No one must say that they cannot be close to the poor because their own lifestyle demands more attention to other areas. This is an excuse commonly heard in academic, business or professional, and even ecclesial circles... None of us can think we are exempt from concern for the poor and for social justice... I fear that these words too may give rise to commentary or discussion with no real practical effect."

The life of Fr. Rick Thomas is proof to me that at least one Jesuit priest that I grew up with, knew and loved, committed himself on a profound and practical level to a lifestyle of solidarity with the poor. His life remains a challenge for me as a Jesuit. I made my first version of the Spiritual Exercises as a senior at Franciscan University of Steubenville. Kneeling before the crucifix, I heard the Lord ask two things of me. First, he asked me to take a vow of poverty. That is how I knew I was supposed to be a religious and not a diocesan priest. A love for poverty – a love I am still far from effectively putting into practice – had been deeply engrained in my heart from a young age by the example of Fr. Thomas. Second, the Lord asked me to follow in the footsteps of St. Ignatius of Loyola. I had grown up with a modern St. Ignatius, and I knew that it was my time now to walk down a path similar to the one he had trod. Fr. Thomas was able to attend my first Jesuit vows in Grand Coteau, Louisiana in 2005. His tears of joy as I took my vows of poverty, chastity and obedience assured me that I was indeed doing the right thing and was, and am, exactly where I am supposed to be.

As you read this book, I hope you too will be challenged to rethink your own lifestyle and its commitment to God's favorite children. When asked by a reporter how he could manage to live so simply, Fr. Thomas answered: "I don't know that I'm living simply yet." He used to tell us regularly: "You can't preach the good news and be the bad news." The good news for the Church of today, proclaimed unequivocally by the pontificate of Pope Francis, and the example of Fr. Thomas, is that God desires a 'poor Church for the poor.' God blesses the poor, and he will bless us too if we commit ourselves to the saintly path mapped out in these pages. May each one of us learn from Fr. Rick Thomas an unwavering dedication to cultivate 'a poor Church for the poor.'

Nathan W. O'Halloran, SJ
January 6, 2018

100 Percent for Jesus

When Rick Thomas was a boy, he loved horses more than anything. He wanted to spend his whole life training horses for a living. So in hindsight, it's not really surprising that he was up to his cowboy hat in training a horse when he got a message from God. It was plenty surprising at the time, though, especially to him, and it wasn't very welcome, either. God was calling him to do something completely different, pretty much the last thing he wanted to hear. But the timing probably wasn't accidental. It was the perfect test: if he was prepared to walk away from horses to follow God's call, there wouldn't be any limit to how far he would go to follow God.

It was the summer of 1944. Rick – actually everybody called him "Dick" at the time – was 16 years old. His older brothers were away fighting the Second World War, but Dick was too young for that, so he was home on his family's ranch in Florida, waiting for his senior year in high school, and as usual, spending as much time as he could with horses. Dick liked girls well enough, and even dated them sometimes, but the pictures he pinned up on his bedroom wall weren't girls, they were horses, and he had even traveled as far as Ohio, by himself on a train at age 15, to learn more about training horses.

The particular horse he had been training that summer day was so difficult he called her "Hitler," and Dick was taking a rest from the struggle, relaxing under a hickory tree, when he heard from God. It isn't clear whether the voice was audible, but whatever the exact experience was, he had no doubt at all that it was God speaking to him. Unfortunately, the content wasn't his idea of heavenly: "I want you to be a priest."

Dick was a good Catholic teenager. He was a top student at Jesuit High School in Tampa, president and valedictorian of his graduating class, and he went to Mass every Sunday with a smile. But that was as far as it went. He wasn't especially pious, he wasn't even an altar boy, and nothing appealed to him less than the priesthood.

"I thought a priest was one dull career," he said near the end of his life. "I wanted to ride horses and look at horses and spend all my time with horses."

Well, so much for that plan. God had something different in mind. And pious or not, when he believed he was hearing God speak, Rick Thomas listened – and obeyed. Not just once, but day after day after day, moment to moment even, from teenage to old age. Whether he liked it or not, and no matter how crazy it might look, to others or even to himself.

For sure, he didn't always like it. Especially not at age 16. That call to the priesthood was something he just did not want to talk about, so he didn't tell anybody about it for months, not even his parents. They had other plans in mind for him, and they would have done their best to talk him out of it, but he never gave them the chance. The first person he did tell was his high school principal, and only because the man happened to ask. The principal was a priest himself, so he wasn't interested in talking him out of it, and he followed up by inviting young Dick to join the Society of Jesus, the Jesuits; Dick just said "OK" – he was too disgusted with the whole priesthood business to bother to check out any other options.

So in August 1945, he found himself in Louisiana, 800 miles from home, joining the Jesuit novitiate at age 17. He wisecracked his way through the whole experience, but he was bored out of his mind, and after a few weeks he asked one of the priests if he could go home. "Really?" the priest asked. "Why did you come to a seminary then?" "Because God told me to," he answered. "Then that's the best reason to stay," the priest told him. So back Dick went to his room. "Well, OK," he told God with a sigh. "Here I am." And for the rest of his life, there he was, whenever and wherever he believed God was calling him.

Rick Thomas isn't an easy man to get a handle on. Was he an old-fashioned pre-Vatican II Catholic or a radical, a *barrio* politician in a Roman collar or a supernaturalist fanatic, a slave-driver or a clown? As you read through this book, you'll find stories at one place or another to fit all those labels, but there's a common thread. Rick Thomas would go to absolutely any lengths to do what he believed God wanted him to do, and he was convinced that God had zero concern about how crazy it looked. He lived for years in an unheated office, sleeping on an army cot. (He once offered to sleep *under* the cot, so another priest could sleep *on* it, but the other man made other arrangements.) He gave away his shoes on at least one occasion, his socks on another. He blessed a whole swimming pool to turn it into holy water. He was jailed half a dozen times. He prayed for days for a dead woman to come back to life. (Spoiler alert: she didn't, but after you read some of the other stories here, you'll understand why he thought she might.) He took more advice from his friends from the shantytowns of Juárez than he did from professors, or for that matter bishops (obedience yes, advice not so much), and one time he told his entire 10-state Jesuit province it needed to repent.

"You only go through this life once," he said, "so you might as well go 100 percent for Jesus."

If that sounds a little intense – and it was! – I need to point out that he also managed to be good-humored most of the time. He went through life with a crooked grin and a self-deprecating chuckle that could turn into a mule-braying laugh, and a lot of the laughs were on himself.

I get to write this biography because I knew Father Thomas (just a little – nothing like the way his close friends and his co-workers knew him), and because I already wrote another book about the work he and his friends have done in El Paso and Ciudad Juárez, across the Rio Grande in Mexico. By the grace of God, I got to spend a lot of time with him just a few weeks before he died, and in the middle of the very last interview, it dawned on me all of a sudden that this deathly ill man across the table from me, still making the odd wisecrack in the middle of all the talk about God and the poor and the ministries, was a man my grandchildren will live to see canonized. I could be wrong about that – as his Jesuit provincial superior told me, that's for God and the Church to decide – but he certainly had a saint's attitude: 100 percent for Jesus, and zero percent for looking cool, or staying comfortable, or any of the other things that pull most of us away from that commitment.

Back when I knew him, Father Thomas didn't much like talking about himself, and he almost bragged about how bad he and his friends were at keeping track of things. Not a promising start for a biographer. But it turns out they kept pretty good track after all. There's a surprising amount of material to work with. For one thing, he left behind a lot more in writing than I would have expected. His friends found a practice sermon he wrote in seminary in 1949, his thesis for his theology degree in 1959, a diary he kept in his first few months after he began his lifetime of work in El Paso in 1964, and a personal testimony from around 1980 about some of the most important events in his ministry up to that date. He kept calendars where he wrote down important events (when he remembered, which wasn't all the time), and for more than 40 years he published a newsletter, mainly about events and projects in his ministry, but also loaded with comments on his spiritual principles and outlook.

He was interviewed by a lot of people, too, for newspaper and magazine articles and on TV and radio programs, and I have a large collection of those interviews. I also interviewed him my-self, many times, between 1989 and 2006 and especially in 1999 and 2000; those interviews were mainly for the other book, but they're a help with this one as well. Best of all, though, are his own recollections, recorded by his friends during his last illness, when he finally started to talk about himself. Thanks to his friend Michael Reuter, I have almost 24 hours' worth of CDs, ranging from early childhood to his last years. He didn't totally trust his own memory – "don't believe everything I tell is right" he warned his friends as he talked – and yes, I have found a few discrepancies, but I'm going to assume most of it *is* right, since he would know more about his own life than anybody else would.

On top of the material from Father Thomas, I have interviews with dozens of people who knew him. I talked to most of those people myself; in a few cases, other people did the interviews and recorded them for me. These sources range all the way from his older brother Bob, who remembered the day he was born, to my *de facto* editor, his longtime co-worker Ellen Hogarty, who was with him when he died. Without those interviews, this biography wouldn't be happening (see Acknowledgements and Notes on Sources for more information). But as much as I can, I'm going to tell Father Thomas's story as it comes from the man himself. I pray that I do get it right, and I take the blame for anything that ends up wrong. I know Father Thomas would forgive me, though. "God has what He wants in the Book of Life," he told his friends in those last conversations, "and that's all that counts anyhow."

CHAPTER 1

A Childhood Free to Wander

"I'd ride till I got tired. Then I'd fish till I got tired. Then I'd hunt till I got tired. Then I'd go back to riding till I got tired."

Richard Thomas grew up with plenty of elbow room. There was lots of open land in the 1930s in his part of Florida; a real estate boom had gone bust in 1926 and it would be decades before another boom would make the state what it is today. His parents' home in Seffner (pop. 301 at the time), 13 miles east of Tampa, stood on 20 acres of its own, but that was just the beginning – the property was surrounded by thousands of acres of unfenced private land operated on the "open range" principle, where livestock (and children) were free to come and go as they liked. So he had lots of freedom, with horses to ride and wild pigs to hunt, but also lots of work and responsibility. He also had some big shoes to fill – but as it turned out, not the shoes everybody was expecting.

The land, the freedom, and the big shoes all traced back to his father, Wayne Thomas Sr., a larger-than-life figure who was the center of the universe to the whole family. Wayne lived to be 96, and his descendants remember him as a talkative man with a terrific memory and insatiable curiosity, even in old age, "the most generous person you could ever imagine," according to grandson Robert Thomas. All three of his sons worshiped him, said Robert, and called him "Daddy" all his life; just mentioning him could choke Richard, his youngest son, with emotion seven decades later.

Born in Springfield, Tennessee, in 1889, Wayne lost his own father when he was a year old, and arrived in Florida with his mother in 1904, "a shoeless 14-year-old on the back of a horse-drawn wagon" Robert wrote in an account of the family background. A youth of enormous ambition, curiosity, and honor, he rushed through high school on doubled-up classes, and at age 20 he bought his first business: the weekly Plant City *Courier*, near Tampa. Running a newspaper in Plant City didn't make for a quiet life. Wayne backed the "dry" party in an ongoing battle over liquor and saloons, and pretty soon he was packing a pistol for protection from the "wet" forces in a running battle, in a town that was averaging a murder a week; one of the "wets" had threatened to shoot him on sight. At least once he had to dodge bullets in a gun battle between two other men.

As time went on he branched out into ranching, local politics, and especially real estate and prospecting, and in the 1920s he picked up the nickname "Mr. Phosphate." He also went broke at least twice, most notably in the bust of 1926; he hung on to the family home and 20-acre parcel at Seffner because his wife, Dorothy, put her foot down and wouldn't let him mortgage it. But by the mid-1930s, the deals had turned good, and he was well on his way to becoming one of the richest men in Florida, thanks mainly to his nose for phosphate, and, in the 1940s, the creation of the Port Sutton deep-water port and industrial park near Tampa.

Stories about Wayne Thomas tend to be about his honesty and his generosity. Once, running for another term on the Hillsborough County budget board, he decided not to bother campaigning; in fact, one source says he was hoping he wouldn't get re-elected. So he didn't spend any money on the campaign, but when he had to declare campaign expenses he declared the three-cent stamp for mailing in the expense report. He won the election anyway. His donations to the community included Hillsborough River State Park, a two-story brick building for a vocational school, and a 40-acre site for a Boy Scout camp for African Americans.

Wayne was a Christian believer, a Methodist Sunday school superintendent in his youth and a financial supporter of Pentecostal seminarians in later life, but most of the time he didn't actually attend church. His son Bob said Wayne simply never met anybody, Protestant or Catholic, that he could follow; "He didn't need organized religion," said grandson Robert, Bob's son. Catholicism came into the family with Dorothy, his second wife, and Wayne took a lot of criticism for marrying a Catholic, but he seems to have been happy enough to have his children raised in the Church.

Wayne married Opal Wilson in 1912; they had two children, Wayne Jr. and Opal. The elder Opal died in a flu epidemic in 1919, and Wayne Sr. married Dorothy Durand in 1921. Dorothy, born in Toronto, Canada, in 1895, was the granddaughter of a leader in the Upper Canada Rebellion of 1837. She trained as a lawyer and practiced law in Toronto, but moved to Florida in 1919 for her health. She was active in church and community projects, especially education and health. She was president of the Tampa Civic Association and the Hillsborough County Federation of Women's Clubs, and a member of the Hillsborough County welfare board. A Girl Scout camp near Tampa is named after her.

Wayne and Dorothy had three children together: Bob, then Patrick, who died shortly after birth, and finally Richard; an adopted daughter, Marion, was also part of the family.

Richard was born at home in Seffner, March 1, 1928, about two weeks overdue and weighing about 13 pounds ("and I've been late to things ever since," he often said). He was baptized at Sacred Heart Church in Tampa April 1, 1928, a month after birth, as "Richard Thomas," with no middle name; the "M" in his signature stands for Michael, his confirmation name from 1939. In childhood, everybody called him "Dick," and his surviving relatives and Jesuit colleagues still do; "Rick," the name he became famous with, didn't come into the picture until well into his 30s, when he arrived in El Paso.

Bob, just under 4 at the time, had a clear memory of his baby brother's birth; the nurse took him to see the new baby after Bob got up from his afternoon nap. The birth was good news for Bob: Dick was to be his only playmate at their rural home. Unfortunately, they didn't always get along, Bob recalled in an interview shortly before his own death in 2007 – when Bob was 7 or 8 and Dick 4 or 5 they fought on a regular basis, mainly because Bob would goad his little brother into lashing back. "My parents were quite concerned that we fought so much, and for that I have life-long sorrow," Bob said.

Bob Thomas (left) and Dick Thomas (right) as boys in Florida.

Mostly, though, they did get along. When Dick was learning to talk, Bob would translate the baby talk for the rest of the family. A couple of years later, Dick started to have nightmares and would wake up crying every night; their mother offered Bob $10 – a lot of money at the time – to cure the nightmares, and according to his last interview he did, but he didn't explain how he went about it.

Wayne Thomas Sr. was pretty much broke in 1928, and he didn't go in for wasting money at any stage of his life. The boys were raised frugally, with small allowances, cheap shoes, and no extra clothes. They had to save for anything they wanted; Dick remembered years later how disappointed he was when a Sears catalog tent he had saved up for turned out to be junk. Food was simple, too, fresh and simply prepared, and Wayne Sr. wouldn't eat any meat that had come through a public slaughterhouse.

Home was a modest but comfortable flat-topped, two-story stucco house, near Lake Weeks, where the boys fished and swam. It's still standing today, though it has changed a lot in appearance from the days when Dick and Bob lived there. The family had fruit trees, fish, cows, and chickens, and the Thomases were never short of food or medical care.

The land around Seffner was full of forests, swamps, and plains, with a few low hills, and the boys were free to wander anywhere they wanted on it, even on private property, unless it was specifically fenced off. It wasn't until the 1960s that liability lawsuits and changes in property tax brought an end to the era of open range in the area.

The Hillsborough River wasn't far away either, and Dick spent a lot of time there too, fishing and canoeing. "You could drink out of it in my day," he said. "You could see alligators if you were real quiet."

All that outdoor space suited Dick, and Bob remembered him as a loner in the best sense. As the youngest, Bob said, Dick had to learn to get along with people, so he was well-behaved, peace-loving, and good at staying out of trouble. But he also showed that single-mindedness of his adult life right from the beginning: "When he got his mind focused on something, or an idea in his head, even as a small child, he persevered in that. He was not easily swayed from anything." He also got his father's curiosity, though unfortunately not his memory, he said years later, and his friends agree, at least about the curiosity: "I always felt sorry for the person who picked us up at the airport," said Ellen Hogarty, who often travelled with him to speaking engagements in later years. "Father would ask more questions than anybody I ever met."

Dick was healthy – healthier than Bob as a child – and physically active, though he was never coordinated enough to succeed in team sports like Bob or Wayne Jr. He went in for solitary outdoor activities like fishing, and, later, training and riding horses. Whenever he went to summer camp, he'd make up for his lack of ability at team sports by doing outside projects that would score competition points for his camp "tribe."

He was shrewd, too, and not always in the best sense. At age 5, he found a way of scamming early Florida tourists, selling them baskets of "fruit" which had fruit only on the top layer, with nothing but Spanish moss farther down. "They had to send me off to grammar school because I was cheating people in business," he said. "It's a good thing God got hold of me or who knows what I would have become." On the plus side, he took the $5 his parents gave him for buying popsicles at summer camp one year, used it for capital to start a shoeshine business, and came home with $20.

Enterprises like the shoeshine scheme, and the curiosity Dick shared with his father about practically every subject, caught Wayne Sr.'s eye at an early age. Dick was Wayne's favorite – although Dick didn't know that until Bob told him many years later – and Wayne planned to have Dick take over the family businesses. Dick's vocation to the priesthood came as a rude shock, and Bob got the job instead.

Bob and Dick both went to boarding school in Tampa, Bayshore Academy, with the Sisters of the Holy Names of Jesus and Mary. They stayed in Tampa four nights a week, and they didn't like it; their own home was happy, and they wanted to be there. But it was the only way they could go to Catholic school.

Dick had problems getting along with some of his teachers in elementary school; Bob said he was glad he missed those teachers himself, but he also said the challenge probably strengthened Dick's character. He said Dick was a natural leader, solid rather than flamboyant, and firm in standing up for what he thought was right.

At the same time, Bob said, Dick was "naturally obedient to his parents, or God, or any other authority." He was always ready for Mass on Sunday; he never had to be asked twice. "There wasn't any big show about it – he'd just be there." Skipping meat on Friday was never a problem, either. Bob and Dick were both good students, so they built up collections of the holy cards, statues and prayer books the nuns at Bayshore gave away as prizes. Dick never showed any particular signs of outward piety as a child, Bob said, but he did obey the commandments – so much so that Bob was convinced Dick had never been out of a state of grace in his life. Dick made his first Holy Communion on March 31, 1935, at age 8, and he was confirmed Jan. 15, 1939, at 10½, both at Sacred Heart Church.

In the fall of 1941, Dick, age 13, was one of 43 boys who enrolled as freshmen at Jesuit High School in Tampa. Wayne Sr. bought a car for Bob, who was a senior that year, to drive the two of them to school, so the boarding school days came to an end. But it was a tough time to be a high school student. The Pearl Harbor attack came on Dec. 7 of Dick's freshman year, and by graduation time many of his fellow students were serving in the Armed Forces – along with Bob, who joined the Navy, and

Wayne Jr., who joined the Air Force. By graduation day in 1945, only 16 boys were left out of the 43.

Dick was a top student, but he didn't go out for sports or join many clubs; "he loved to go to his ranch," recalled Father Harold Rahm, who was a young teacher at Jesuit High at the time, not yet a priest. He had a few dates, too, but never a girlfriend or a real dating relationship with anyone. One date Bob remembered was a very pretty girl slightly older than Dick who had been Miss Tampa and who was planning to enter the Holy Names novitiate as a nun just a few days later.

Father Rahm, who would later found Our Lady's Youth Center in El Paso and then pick Father Thomas to replace him as its director, had young Dick as a student in Tampa, and they got to be friends; Father Rahm remembered chatting with him on a bench in the hall, or riding with him at the ranch; "He was the richest boy in the school, and as far as I was concerned, one of the best." His classmates liked and respected him too, and he graduated in 1945 as class president and valedictorian.

The class prophecy said Dick would be the 70th [*sic*] president of the U.S., because "his simplicity, humility and integrity have earned for him the highest of distinctions." Like his father, his classmates had a surprise coming.

Wayne Thomas, Sr.

CHAPTER 2

Horses at Home

One thing the Thomas family didn't have when Dick was small was a horse. But even so, he spent most of his time thinking about horses. Whenever anyone asked him where the family should go for the day, he'd suggest a visit to a family friend who did have horses. It was a 20-mile trip, so it didn't happen too often. He'd go with Bob, and Dick would get to ride first, for five or 10 minutes; then Bob would take over, for substantially longer. Dick would complain that he wasn't getting his share of riding time, but he'd be told it was perfectly fair since he got to ride when the horse was still fresh, "whatever that meant."

"I always loved horses," he said. "If I'd see a picture of a horse in a magazine, I'd cut it out. Instead of having a pinup girl, I'd have a pinup horse."

But soon enough, horses did come to the Thomas home. For one thing, the friend with the horses had promised he would give one to Wayne Sr., and eventually he did – a thoroughbred mare, "a sorry horse," Fr. Thomas said later, but pregnant with a colt. Somewhere around the same time, Wayne bought his sons a Florida cow pony named Neppy, a gentle, intelligent horse that anybody could ride. "That was one great horse," he said later. Dick was still last in line; "my brothers rode it. I didn't get to ride it except infrequently, because they were always riding it." But

Neppy stayed around for years, and as Wayne Jr. and Bob grew older and moved out, Dick finally got his chance.

By then, there were other horses at home too, as Wayne Sr. began to take an interest and started buying and selling horses for maybe $60 apiece at auctions. Wayne liked to see the horses, liked the way they ran around with their tails in the air when the barometric pressure changed and rain was threatening.

"He'd buy a horse and he didn't know anything about it, he'd just like the looks of this horse, he'd buy it, and it would turn out to be blind or whatever," said Dick. Wayne would sell the ones that didn't work out. "There were horses coming and going. I liked all that, of course. It was sort of a hobby with him. We didn't feed them. Just throw them out there, there's all the grass they can eat, and it doesn't cost you a nickel." Wayne even bought a stallion, with the intention of breeding their own horses. So finally Dick could ride to his heart's content, and ride he did. One time he even asked his mother to let him bring his horse into the kitchen, and sure enough, she said yes.

But the big moment for Dick came when that thoroughbred colt from the pregnant mare got old enough to train. Dick asked for the job. He got some books, and he took a correspondence course; "I was training, and learning, and studying, all at the same time." The correspondence course was offered by a horse trainer named Jesse Beery, of Pleasant Hill, Ohio. Beery was something of a legend. He had a gentle, non-violent, confidence-building way of training horses, and he went from town to town advertising for people to bring him "untrainable" horses, which he would have behaving in 15 minutes. "That was his claim: I can break any horse in the world and train it," Father Thomas said. "That wasn't exaggerated, either. He'd take these wild, mean horses and train them in a short time, and the people could watch it." Beery also invited questions by mail, and answered them personally.

Dick did what he could based on the books and the correspondence course, but apparently he wasn't satisfied with the results. So at age 15, he took a train to Ohio, found a ride to Pleasant Hill, and visited Beery for several days, staying at his house. The neighbors told Dorothy she should never have let a 15-year-old travel by himself or stay at a stranger's house, but it worked out fine. Beery, by then over 80 and no longer training horses himself, was kind and friendly. Dick had a long list of questions based on his own experiences and failures. "I had all these questions written out, what's this, what's that, and he answered them all very patiently. He told me 'I never had anybody ask me so many questions as you did.'" In payment, Dick gave Beery the Thomas family's sugar stamps: sugar was rationed at the time because of the Second World War, and the Thomases didn't use sugar. Beery also suggested that Dick should marry his granddaughter. "He thought I'd make a good spouse because I didn't smoke. I wasn't interested in his granddaughter; I didn't meet her."

He may not have gotten the granddaughter, but he definitely got the lessons, and he wasn't shy about putting them into practice. Coming home, he went into business. "I'd take people's horses, and train them, and charge them." "Dick indicated that he could ride any horse there was, if you let him alone and have his own way about it," Bob said. "At our ranch, when he was probably 15 or so, he rode an outlaw horse. All the cowboys were sitting around waiting for the horse to buck him off. He never bucked. Dick had him going pretty normally almost immediately."

Father Thomas rode horses all his life, but he didn't brag usually about his riding skills, especially later in life; he was better at training horses than he was at riding them. "I was not a jockey," he said. "I didn't have the disposition to be a jockey." Still, he could do what he needed to, and as a teenager he wasn't too modest to show off his courage by riding the family stallion

– especially when girls were around. "Everybody was afraid of him," he said. "I'd ride him, and let people think what a big shot I was."

One day he decided to solve the problem of the "barbecue bull," which the family was planning to butcher and eat, except that nobody could catch it. The bull would jump out of pens and disappear for days on an enormous pasture covered with trees and cypress ponds. Dick took Neppy and another horse, named Danger. He and Danger ran the bull ragged; then he switched to Neppy, who was still fresh, and roped the exhausted bull by the horns.

As a high school senior, he entered a rodeo, but that didn't work out as well. He practiced twice a day, roping speedy Brahma calves and throwing a cow by the horns, but when he and Neppy actually rode out into the ring, it turned out practice wasn't enough. "In a rodeo, you don't miss," he said. "If you miss, forget it.

"I tried to rope the calf. I chased it around a little bit. I didn't rope the calf, and I don't know if I even threw the rope. When I got finished, somebody told me, and this is a nice way of saying it, 'Man, that's a good horse you have – she really knows what she's doing.' What he was saying was the horse knows how to rope a calf, but you don't, and he was right."

Actually, Dick was always ready to give credit to the horse rather than himself, whether it was Neppy or a trick pony he had. An extremely intelligent animal, a beautiful pinto, the trick pony – actually a small horse – could lie down on command, walk calmly across a cattle guard, or even walk a fallen log in the swamp with a rider on her back.

"I had a psychology class years later and the professor said animals can't think," he said. "I thought, this guy never went to the barn."

"He had an eye for horses," Bob said. "I used to say that he talked to horses, and listened to them. Because he would go up and look at a horse, in the face, and look him over pretty much for a minute, and then he'd tell you: this horse is nine years old, he's been abused, his leg was badly injured once, and he'd go on and on about the personal details about that particular horse, that let you know that he had the talent for seeing the horse and hearing the horse silently communicate with him, his background.

"This is not a bunch of bull. He could do it."

Rick Thomas's love for horses lasted throughout his life.

CHAPTER 3

"I Want You to Be a Priest"

Different people had different ideas about what Dick should be when he grew up. His father wanted him to study engineering, and then join him in business. His mother wanted him to be a surgeon. "She had said that for years," he said. "I didn't want to be a surgeon. I said, 'well, I'll be a veterinary surgeon.' She didn't like that either." Dick himself, obviously, wanted to train horses. What nobody in the family had in mind for him was the priesthood – no matter how big a collection of holy cards he had.

"God was very important to me, and I had faith in God, but I was very worldly, in that my interest was in horses," he said.

But apparently God had a different plan from anybody else's, and He let it be known on a summer day in 1944. Dick's brothers were off fighting Hitler, and Dick, age 16, was at home fighting his own "Hitler" – his nickname for the horse he was trying to train, a tough, mean, athletic filly, one of the worst he had ever met. He tried tying up one of her legs; she chased him on the other three. "It was all I could do to get away from her."

Dick needed two or three days off to recover, and so did the horse. As usual, he relaxed outdoors, and as he sat under that hickory tree, he heard from God. "It came to me real strong: 'I want you to be a priest. You've got to be a priest.' I knew it was

God." He didn't tell that story to anybody at the time; in fact, he didn't tell anybody the part about hearing from God for decades to come. Apparently, audible voice or not, he never questioned whether it was God he was hearing from. One thing for sure, though: it wasn't wishful thinking. The whole idea made him miserable. He didn't know how to tell his parents, and he didn't even want to tell his friends.

The first to hear, many months later, was his high school principal, a good friend, Father Louis Twomey. Dick got a call to the principal's office one day and the principal asked him if he had given any thought to the priesthood. That was a fairly obvious question to ask the valedictorian in a Jesuit high school, and there's no record of whether Father Twomey was surprised when he answered yes, he had. But the principal was ready with the next step.

"He said 'we'd [Jesuits] like to have you,'" Father Thomas recalled later. "I said 'OK.' The exchange was that brief." It may have been the most sudden vocation in Jesuit history; Dick was saying "yes" to the first order that asked him because he didn't want to be a priest at all, so he hadn't done any investigating or even any thinking about what order to join.

"The whole thing was a pain in the neck," he said. "I didn't want to bother making any plans."

Father Twomey called the Jesuit provincial superior, who happened to be in town, so Dick had a chat with the provincial. Later the priests gave him an oral exam – "not nearly as penetrating as now" – and offered him a choice of dates for entering the novitiate. He could go July 31, the feast of St. Ignatius Loyola, founder of the Jesuits; or he could go Aug. 15, the feast of the Assumption. "I chose the 15th of August. That's putting off the misery for 15 days.

"I hadn't told anybody, and I told Father Twomey don't you tell anybody. I didn't tell a soul. I knew my classmates would give me the finger if they knew I was going to be a priest."

Finally he let his mother in on the secret. She was the Catholic parent, but she was still pushing him to be a surgeon. She wasn't happy to hear the news. She left a long letter under his pillow, telling him how disappointed she would be if he went ahead with his plan. The letter caused him great distress.

Next he told his father, as the two of them rode off together in a truck to see some caverns. As they drove along, Wayne asked Dick, for the last of many times, where he planned on going to college. Cornered at last, Dick told his dad he was going to be a priest. He wasn't expecting a good reaction, and he didn't get one.

"Man, the door shut," Father Thomas recalled six decades later, his voice still catching with emotion. "He didn't say a word, but the door shut. It broke his heart. He never said a word about it after that, but the door was shut, and I could feel that it was shut. We had a good relation, but not that real close relation we had before."

According to Father Thomas, he didn't tell Bob at the time, but according to Bob, he did. Bob apparently liked the idea better than his parents did, but he thought Dick was rushing things a bit. Home on leave from the Navy, Bob went to the pastor of the Jesuit parish in Tampa and suggested Dick should wait a year to enter seminary; he thought it would give him a broader outlook and make him a better priest. The pastor apparently didn't agree, and that was the end of that.

The rest of the family were still in the dark. A few days before he left for seminary in Louisiana, Dick ate dinner with his sister-in-law and his nephew Tommy (Wayne III), who was also his godchild. He didn't say anything about his plans, and after he left for seminary, they asked his mother "where's Dick?"

The seminary was in Grand Coteau, near Lafayette, Louisiana. He flew to New Orleans. "My father said you're going to have to buy your own ticket. That was his way of saying I don't approve of it. He never said anything else."

From New Orleans he took the Southern Pacific train to Lafayette, "dreading the experience." He didn't let it show, though. Another passenger on that train trip remembered a peddler who came through the train with a sales pitch for tourist photos, 25 cents for a folder full. "Dick just listened intently, with his mouth open and his eyes fixed. The salesman noticed this and asked him if he wanted to buy the pictures. He said 'no, but I'll give you a quarter if you'll give that speech again.'" The fellow passenger was Jack Deeves, another Jesuit postulant (entrant), from New Orleans. Father Deeves went on to ordination too, and the two men stayed good friends for 60 years, until Father Thomas's death. Father Deeves remembered that Dick was wearing a long-sleeved red shirt, khaki pants, and a tan cowboy hat on the train.

Dick actually entered the seminary, St. Charles College at Grand Coteau, on Aug. 14, 1945, the day of the Japanese surrender and the end of the Second World War. He did his best to keep his spirits up; Father Deeves remembered him cracking jokes, singing hillbilly songs, and complaining about the laundry. It was hot and humid, August in Louisiana, and the postulants wore ordinary clothes, working up a heavy sweat during recreation. Somebody in charge asked if he had any problems. Yes he did, he answered. "When I take off my pants they stand up in the corner."

Jokes aside, life as a postulant was "boring as it could be. There was nothing to do." He found himself asking for work to occupy his time. Postulancy lasted 10 days or two weeks. Then, after making a retreat, he came back to his room one night to find a cassock on his bed. "That means, the next day I wear my cassock. I'm a novice."

The routine was strict. Up at 5, visit to the Eucharist in the chapel at 5:25, an hour meditation in his room, Mass, thanksgiving, breakfast, 10-minute examination of conscience, then work, indoors or outdoors, all in silence. Orders were given in Latin.

The only free time was half an hour at 8 p.m. for personal chores the novices hadn't gotten done earlier in the day. After a last visit in the chapel at 9, it was bedtime.

The novices were assigned spiritual books to read. More boredom. "I wasn't interested in all that. I said, 'Lord, you'd better give me that interest, because I don't have it.' Well, He did. He answered my prayer, and I've had interest ever since."

Interest in spiritual books, yes. Interest in the priesthood, still no. After a few weeks in the novitiate he went to see his old high school religion teacher, Father Ignatius Fabacher, who was now assigned to the seminary. "I told him I've done enough penance. I'm ready to go home."

"He said 'why'd you come in the first place?' I said 'well, I thought God wanted me to be a priest.' He said 'that's the best reason of all. So go ahead and do what you think God wants you to do.' He straightened me out."

And for young Dick, it was the best answer of all – enough to last to ordination, enough to last for a lifetime in the priesthood. "Well, OK," he said. "Here I am."

CHAPTER 4

Jesuit in Training

Dick spent four years in Grand Coteau: two in the novitiate, two more in the juniorate. It doesn't sound like a high point in his life. For one thing, it was lonely. "You didn't have any close friends in the novitiate, because you weren't supposed to talk to anybody," he remembered later. Also, he had an ongoing battle with Latin and Greek; he hadn't taken either of those languages in high school, and he needed extra tutoring, along with two other students. "Dick had great difficulty with Latin," said Father Deeves.

But the novitiate was like the train trip, like the spiritual reading, like the whole call to the priesthood: he made the best of it. He was prayerful and obedient, said Father Deeves, but also the class wise guy – "eccentric, but not wildly eccentric, not eccentricity that would bother anyone. He had an unbelievable sense of humor." Father Jack Vessels, one year ahead of Dick in the novitiate, remembered him the same way: "He was always happy. He enjoyed life. He had a great sense of humor. He was always living in the moment." On the spiritual side, Father Vessels said, he showed an obvious sense of God's presence.

He also sang hilarious country songs, said Father Vessels. "He would sing those old ballads that would go on and on, and they were funny."

Dick was one of eight or 10 novices in his entry year; there were a few more in the next class up, 13 or 14. Most of them were straight out of high school, like Dick, and about three-quarters of them were from one specific high school: Jesuit High in New Orleans. That tended to bind the non-New Orleans novices together, said Father Vessels, who was from McAllen, Texas, in the Rio Grande Valley near the Mexican border.

One thing Dick liked was the farm work novices had to do at Grand Coteau. It fit in with his Seffner background. "For us city boys that was not all that much fun," said Father Vessels. Dick learned beekeeping, and, indoors, also barbering. "He was an excellent barber," Father Deeves recalled. "We cut our own hair, and he was one of the best." On Thursdays the novices would go for hikes.

He was also well-liked. "I can't remember him ever being spiteful or mean or rude," said Father Vessels. Father Vessels himself had a temper, and he lost it once with Dick; why, he couldn't remember. Dick gulped, and immediately Father Vessels was afraid he had broken the friendship, but there was no grudge held.

Despite everything that went before, it doesn't seem Dick had any trouble making up his mind when the time came. At one point in the novitiate he got a letter from a girl he knew back in Florida, who was wondering if there was any hope of a possible courtship between them. The superior opened the letter – normal procedure in the novitiate – brought it to him and asked him what he wanted to do about it. Nothing, he replied; "I'm going to be a priest." He told the superior, 'Tell her I hope to meet her in heaven someday.'" "I never sensed in Dick Thomas any doubt about his vocation," said Father Deeves. He went ahead with his vows; he also signed an act of consecration and promise of fidelity to Our Lady, along with numerous classmates.

Next he moved on to the juniorate, two more years of classics. At some point in his time at Grand Coteau, his mother brought his father to visit. "Of course, I was praying for his conversion. He only came one time to Grand Coteau." Then Dorothy fell ill, during his time in the juniorate, and Dick went home to Florida for a visit. Dorothy lingered on for several more years.

In 1949 Dick moved on from Grand Coteau to Spring Hill College, in Mobile, Alabama, for three years of philosophy. This was a much happier time in his life, and he had a long string of stories to tell his friends more than 50 years later. "I had a wonderful time at Spring Hill," he said. "It was such a big difference from Grand Coteau."

The three years started off with an enormous practical joke. The young Jesuit scholastics arrived by train at night. The next older class greeted the newcomers and escorted them to their rooms by a long and confusing route, all over the building and even out on the large balconies found on every floor; "I don't know how I ever got to breakfast or chapel or anything. Maybe I followed the crowd." When the new men finally got to breakfast, the older scholastics came up, shook hands and introduced themselves – by one another's names. "They've given you the wrong name, but with great earnestness so you wouldn't forget. 'Hi, I'm Tony. I'm glad you're here. I'm from New York.' He's not Tony and he's not from New York. They're always playing tricks on you." His own class did the same thing to the new class the next year.

Most of the Spring Hill stories are about the superior of the philosophy program, Father Joe Bogue, a gruff, beefy man usually called "the Boss" (though not to his face). The Boss was loud, unpredictable and mean-looking, but soft underneath, with a good sense of humor and a good heart. He cherished and protected his philosophy students, even from the rector of the college. "He was very protective of the philosophers. Philosophers, in general, could do no wrong."

One of the Boss's unexpected rules was that any student could take a nap whenever he needed one, without permission, even if he was supposed to be in class. "You just take a handkerchief and put it on your doorknob." Nobody ever cracked up from studying too hard while Father Bogue was superior.

The Boss also organized competitive sports every afternoon, with all the students and some of the faculty playing, a $1 prize for victory, and results in the daily one-page newsletter. "Good or bad, you played," said Father Thomas, the non-athlete. Father Bogue also brought in movies and sent the students swimming at the Gulf shore nearby.

The Boss had a collection of mannerisms – "the guys loved to imitate him" – and a totally black-and-white way of looking at everything. If anybody went to ask him for permission for anything, he'd take a long, deep breath – "he took 20 or 30 seconds to exhale," and then answer either "you do that" or "we don't do that around here." "He just gave his opinion and that was it. You wouldn't know what the heck he was going to say."

While Dick was at Spring Hill, Father Twomey, Dick's high school principal from Tampa, turned up, and Dick wanted to visit with him, but he needed permission; according to the rules, he was only allowed to talk to other scholastics or faculty. It was Father Bogue's nap time, so Dick went pacing up and down nervously outside his room, afraid to wake him. The Boss noticed and called him in.

"You must be a mind reader," Dick said.

"I am," came the booming voice of the Boss.

"May I do what's on my mind?"

"You may!"

Dick was still cutting hair at Spring Hill, usually with good-quality equipment. Once, though, he had a cheap pair of clippers. The clippers couldn't be hung on the wall, so he left them on the floor; he accidentally kicked them during a haircut and broke the casing. Dick wrote a letter to the manufacturer, all literally true but diplomatically worded, asking the company to replace the clippers.

"I was real proud of myself. Man, what a letter, what a work of art." But the Boss told him not to send it; instead, he said, "you tell them the casing broke because the clipper is utterly no good." So Dick typed out another letter, out of obedience. It didn't work; the company wrote back that Dick's reasoning wasn't valid, and that was the end of that. "I wasn't about to tell the Boss his reasoning was no good."

Dick had his problems with another professor, who taught psychology. They often clashed, and once Dick had to make a presentation in the class in his lousy Latin. The professor, who had a Ph.D. in Latin, cut him off halfway, not politely at all. Later, Father Deeves recalled, someone asked Dick how he was getting along with that professor.

"Fine," he said. "I remember him every day at Mass at the *nobis quoque peccatoribus* [to us, though sinners]."

All in all, Spring Hill sounds like a pretty cheerful place. The scholastics even put on satirical skits, for example parodies of songs from the musicals they saw during Father Bogue's movie time, singing the show tunes with lyrics filled with philosophical jargon. Dick was one of the ringleaders; he even invited the Boss to join the cast.

But none of this got in the way of Dick's spiritual life, a life that had come a long way since the days when he had to ask God to give him an interest in it. Father Deeves remembered Dick asking him about his prayer life once during a picnic – a question Father Deeves couldn't find any easy answer for. Father Deeves didn't know many details of Dick's prayer life, either, but he still remembered him praying in chapel, head slightly tilted up, eyes closed, hands not folded.

"I could see he was really into it," Father Deeves said. "Everyone became aware of that. Everyone knew it wasn't phony."

A 15-minute practice sermon Dick wrote in November 1949, two months into his time at Spring Hill, was still hidden away in a trunk at the Lord's Ranch at his death 57 years later. The topic was God's love in the Eucharist, and a call for more frequent Holy Communion. Here is a partial text:

> "By receiving Him in the Eucharist, Christ lets us become infinitely rich. The resources of Standard Oil, the finances of Wall Street and all the gold at Fort Knox fade to paltry insignificance when compared to what we possess in Holy Communion. After receiving Holy Communion, we possess God and with Him all created things. Jesus Christ owns every tree, every field, stream and mountain, all the gold, all the rubies, and every diamond. God owns the Western Hemisphere, the Atlantic and Pacific Oceans, the entire earth, all the stars and the whole universe. There is nothing, not a thing, that God does not own. And through Holy Communion we possess God the owner of all these things.

> "In Holy Communion Christ lets us possess all power. Our Lord lets us hold the whip that sends lightning cracking to earth and the authority that commands the tides of the sea. After Holy Communion, there lies within us the mighty breath that raises hurricanes and tidal waves, the voice that summons the seasons of the year, and the gentle kiss that makes a rosebud bloom. The most Blessed Sacrament of the Altar lets us possess God, Whose hand raised the sun from the east this morning, and Whose hand this evening will set it gently in the west."

He closed with this paragraph:

> "Jesus Christ—yesterday, today and the same forever— is looking from the tabernacle this morning and loving you. At this moment He sees into your heart. He is longing to come and be with you. He wants to tell you the secrets of His own Sacred Heart. But the door of your heart has the lock on the inside. He can knock, but you alone can open it."

Dick graduated from Spring Hill in 1952 with a BA in English. His transcript shows him as mainly a B student, with some As and Cs, but he got Ds in physics. Some of his family came to the graduation ceremony. "I didn't think it was a big deal at all, but they thought it was a big deal that I was going to graduate from college," he said.

CHAPTER 5

A Point of Conversion

L ooking back on the Spring Hill years, something Dick did off campus may well have meant more for the future of his priesthood than anything he learned in a classroom. Not long after he got there, he joined a team of volunteer scholastics who spent their Sundays teaching catechism on the streets of an African American neighborhood in Mobile – and not long after that he had an encounter that turned his whole attitude toward race, and social justice, upside down.

Dick Thomas was a child of the segregated South. Not that he was raised to hate black people – far from it. As a child, he called one of the few black people he knew "Uncle," and sometimes visited him in his shack on the Thomas property. But he was brought up with the understanding that black people were inferior and needed to be kept in their place. "You couldn't sit down and eat with them. They couldn't come to the front door if they had to come to your house. They had to come to the back door. You wouldn't call them Mr. and Mrs. They couldn't come to the white schools, or a hotel, or a restaurant, or any public facility that was for white people. I was brought up with that mentality. That's just the way people thought and acted. I never thought anything about it too much."

Contact with black people was near zero in his childhood. The only African Americans he knew were "Uncle," who was an elderly ex-slave, and a younger man who shared the shack. It was OK to visit, but his mother warned him never to eat anything there. That was sad for him, because the men often cooked what they called "heavy bread" on a hot plate over a wood stove. "It smelled delicious," he said. "I would like to have eaten it."

There were no black novices at Grand Coteau; the only black people at Grand Coteau worked in the kitchen, and Dick only met them when he was assigned to kitchen work.

But at Spring Hill, some of the Jesuit scholastics went to Crichton, an African American neighborhood at the edge of Mobile, walking a mile each way to teach catechism to the children. The children weren't Catholic, but their parents were open, and the scholastics would teach them right on the street, as individuals or small groups, five minutes at a time. Some Sundays they'd teach as many as 100 children.

Not long after arriving at Spring Hill in 1949, Dick volunteered for that group. "I'd just walk around and talk to each kid for five minutes, and then go on farther down the street and talk to one or two more, and spend the afternoon that way.

"I hadn't been there very long, going down on Sundays, when I met this young lady, I forget her name. When I met her, it was a point of conversion for me, because she was very refined, very polite, well-educated. When I met her, all this stuff that I'd heard in my younger life, it just disappeared, because she wasn't anything like they said black people were." He said his whole concept of race was shattered by that one conversation.

He worked in Crichton all three years he was at Spring Hill, and after a while he extended the work to the adults in the neighborhood, especially through the Crichton Recreation Association, a state-chartered non-profit corporation which he encouraged them to form. The association wanted to buy a lot to set up a community center, but the group had no money. Dick wrote an article about the work for *Jesuit Missions* magazine "and lo and behold, a guy in India sent money to pay for the property."

Retelling the stories decades later, he remembered that the Mobile train station had two water fountains, one marked "white," one marked "colored," 15 feet apart. It wasn't a big surprise; "that kind of stuff was all over the South."

"During those three years, I had a deeper and deeper conversion that these people were mistreated. I thought about what Jesus said, love your neighbor as yourself, and I could see the injustice."

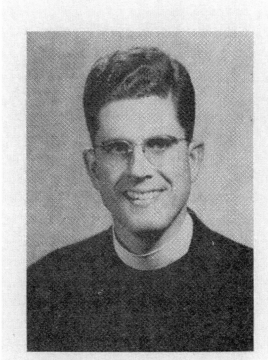

**MR. RICHARD M. THOMAS,
S.J.**
Religion, English, Latin

From 1954 Jesuit High School Dallas yearbook, faculty.

CHAPTER 6

Regency: Training for the Outside World

With Dick's degree from Spring Hill in his pocket, it was time for what Jesuits call regency. After their philosophy courses and before their theological training, Jesuit scholastics spend three years at the front end of the classroom, teaching boys in high school. It's an important part of Jesuit formation. "It gave us a much more worldly attitude when we went on to theology," said Father Vessels, who spent his own regency in the same place Dick did: Jesuit High School in Dallas. "When we went back to theology we had a more mature attitude toward what religion means to people in the world."

Dick was in Dallas from 1952 to 1955, teaching freshman classes in a building on Oaklawn Avenue formerly used by the Vincentian Fathers; Father Vessels was teaching sophomores. Dick taught English, religion, and, believe it or not, Latin. "I taught it, but I was never any good at it," he said. He was also moderator of the altar boys and assistant moderator of the probationary sodality. His brother, Bob, remembered that Dick took his work extremely seriously and expected the boys to take their assignments with the same seriousness, but he had his lighter moments too. He helped found two square dance clubs for the Catholic youth of Dallas, and according to the school yearbook, he inspired a student to invent the "Whine-o-meter" to measure excuses for late homework.

He also built a life-size Christmas crib for Immaculate Heart Grammar School, a local school for black children, but that was the least of his efforts to wake up the world, and especially his students, to racial discrimination.

First, he talked about the evils of racism in class. Then, he assigned his students an essay on "how I'd like to be treated if I were colored" (the politest of several terms in use at the time), and he sent the essays on to the National Association for the Advancement of Colored People (NAACP).

Next, he asked the NAACP to send him a cultured, articulate black speaker to give the students a better view of black people than they might have had up until then. The NAACP sent along a man in his 20s, an army pilot as Father Thomas remembered later. "He was a young guy that the students would look up to because of his education and his career. I brought him in without asking permission and I brought him in the back way so nobody would see him." Dick got a scolding from his superiors when word got out.

But bringing a black speaker into the classroom was nothing compared to his next move. He started taking his white high school freshmen to the black slums of south and west Dallas on Saturdays and Sundays. "I became friends with some of the people who lived down there. I'd take different boys on different days. They'd see how these people lived and meet with them and so on."

It couldn't last, of course. "The student counselor said the parents were complaining because the kids would go down and might catch some disease. So I had to back off from that, but the kids that went down there, they had a conversion themselves." A good number of those students went on to seminary, he said.

"As soon as you have genuine contact with the poor, you're going to have a conversion, unless you're extremely hard-hearted. You'll see they're the same as you."

Not to compare it to the slums, but the house where Dick and his fellow Jesuits lived in Dallas needed a lot of work, and that led to a classic Dick Thomas-style adventure. One morning a man came to the door asking for breakfast, and Dick got the rector's permission to feed him in return for some of the work. The man did such a good job that he got lunch, too, and at supper time Dick went back to the rector with a proposal.

"I said, 'man, this guy's a good worker, and he's willing, and we sure need the help, can we keep him around?' The rector said, 'you can keep him, but don't let the minister [the priest who served as business manager] know that he's here.'" The rector was the overall head of the residence, while the minister was in charge of material needs, so the rector was supposed to be the minister's boss, but apparently the minister had the stronger personality. So the scholastics hid the man away in one of the many unused rooms upstairs. "We kept him for several days. The minister was predictable, in that he would move in a rhythm, and one of the guys who had been teaching there before knew what his rhythm was, that at a certain time he would come out of his room and walk around, a regular path inside, and then go back to his room. We had this guy there for days and nights, and [the minister] never knew he was in the house. To me it was hilarious, to be carrying this on with the blessing of the rector, as long as we didn't let the minister know.

"The weekend came, and the rector said, 'this guy's been working all week, we'll give him $20 and let him take time off.' On Sunday night or Monday morning the phone rings, and it's the jail." The man had gotten picked up by the police, on what charge Father Thomas didn't say, and had given the Jesuit house as his address. Unfortunately the minister got the phone call, and that was the end of the arrangement. "That kind of blew our cover."

Mixed in with Father Thomas's lighthearted memories of Dallas was major loss. His mother's long illness ended when she died at home Jan. 17, 1953. Dorothy Thomas was just 57. She had been prominent in community service activities, and the Tampa *Morning Tribune* carried a 10-inch-long obituary with her picture.

CHAPTER 7

Encounter with Theology

D ick finished his regency in 1955, and it was time to study theology. He headed off to St. Mary's, in Kansas, back in the classroom as a student instead of a teacher. St. Mary's was in the Missouri province, and the Jesuits there had their own ideas about scholastics from the New Orleans province: the northerners took it for granted that the southerners were all racially prejudiced, so the atmosphere was a little chilly. Fortunately, Dick had an ace in the hole. He wrote his NAACP friends in Dallas and asked for a letter of reference. "I showed it to the guys from the Missouri province, and they backed off."

He wasn't quite so serious about another challenge at St. Mary's. He was still struggling with languages, Hebrew this time. Father Deeves, who was also back in the classroom after spending his regency in Tampa, remembered a two-week Hebrew course with a very old teacher. One day's lesson apparently involved Genesis 1:11, from the six-day creation account, describing the creation of plants "of every kind," and Dick gave the wrong answer. The professor corrected him, giving the right expression, pronounced "*le-mino*." "Well, lemme know!" Dick retorted.

On the other hand, one of the best memories of his whole seminary education came from his year at St. Mary's. He got to study moral theology with Father Gerald Kelly and Father John Ford, two men he called "the very best, best professors possible." They were both big names in their field, so much so that they were considered as a source of "probable opinions," which means support for the idea that option A is permissible even if most moral theologians would pick option B (the "safe opinion"). "If you have enough of these guys and they're weighty enough, you have a probable opinion that you can do A and don't have to do B," Father Thomas said. "You could count on what they told you."

Both men were clear teachers, practical-minded, approachable and trustworthy, he said. "Ford was a big guy physically, very sweet disposition. He was easy to talk to; you could talk to him after class. He wasn't stuck up." He even liked Dick's southern accent. "I consider it a great grace that I had him and Kelly both," Father Thomas said.

Father Ford is best known today for his support of *Humanae Vitae*, Pope Paul VI's 1968 encyclical condemning contraception. "It put him in bad with his peers," Father Thomas said. "They were all on the other side."

At the end of his year in Kansas, the students were given a choice of summer activities, and Dick picked a trip to Colorado, to work on a house for Jesuits living in Denver. "I'd never been there and they said it was very high, very beautiful," he said. It was also a chance to spend some time with his father. "I wrote my father and brother and said 'why don't you come up here and visit me in Colorado? It's beautiful.' They came, and we spent several days driving around the mountains and having a good time." Dick and Wayne Sr. hadn't lost contact; Dick visited his father in Florida every year. "It wasn't that we were fighting," he said. "It's just that there was no closeness, like there had been before."

Dick didn't return to St. Mary's in the fall of 1956. Kansas didn't agree with his health. He had severe hay fever, plus a rash from certain foods. A lot of the scholastics at St. Mary's had those problems, but Dick suffered worse than most, and the province sent him all the way to California, to Alma College in Los Gatos, south of San Francisco, in hopes he would get better there.

So off he went, but not straight west from Kansas. His route took him to El Paso, at the western tip of Texas, just across the Rio Grande from Mexico. He had somebody to visit there: Father Harold Rahm, his old high school teacher, now ordained to the priesthood and running a three-year-old ministry in the impoverished Mexican-American neighborhood of South El Paso, right up against the river. It was called Our Lady's Youth Center, and Father Rahm had founded it in 1953 to help him fight the gangs that were tearing the neighborhood apart. But it was expanding into a massive social ministry covering all age groups and nearly all the needs of the dirt-poor residents. As he looked around the operation and visited with his old friend, Dick didn't know he'd be coming back, to stay, less than a decade later.

Postcard of Alma College that Dick Thomas
saved in a box of memorabilia.

CHAPTER 8

California and Ordination

T he move to Los Gatos worked. Dick's allergies cleared up immediately, and he settled cheerfully into his theology studies.

"I think he loved California," said Father Armand Nigro, who was his classmate at Alma, two years ahead of him. The Alma campus has been shut down since Dick's time, but in 1956 it had a beautiful setting in suburban Los Gatos, south of San Jose, with a grove of California's famous redwoods, plus large ponds on either side of property for swimming and fishing.

Once, Father Nigro recalled, another student complained about the weather. "Dick said 'come to my room. I'll show you a picture and you won't complain anymore.'" It was a picture of St. Mary's in Kansas. "It was sort of a grim place," Father Nigro said.

The seminarians got to be good friends at Alma, Father Nigro said, because until ordination they could only leave the premises by permission, and only with a companion.

One of Dick's pastimes was hopping trains. He knew the schedules, and on his time off would jump aboard a freight, go sightsee somewhere that appealed to him, and come back by another train. "He called it just honking around," said Father Louis Lambert, a younger Jesuit from Tampa who had contact with him over the years, though he wasn't at Alma at the same time.

"They nicknamed him 'Honker.'" At least once, Father Lambert said, Dick was left stranded when the train schedule changed, and he had to call the rector; he got back in the small hours of morning.

Dick was "a tall, handsome, lanky guy, on the thin side even then," said Father Nigro. "He was a straight shooter. He spoke truth to you. He didn't try to hide his feelings. But he was very kind."

His classmates knew him as a prayerful man and a careful listener, "not the life of the party. He was easy to be with, to talk with, but he was quiet. He wouldn't push himself forward."

At Alma, Dick carried on with his study of theology: dogmatic and doctrinal training. He remembered one of his canon law professors with great frustration. "They called him 'Arizona,' not to his face, because he was so dry and so clear. He comes to class, no book, no notes, nothing. He said a prayer and he starts — nothing but Latin." No questions allowed, either. "He goes on and on and on and on, then he starts quoting canon law. He'd have that thing so well memorized that he'd come to the last sentence and the last period, and the bell would ring. I've never heard of a guy that could do that. He never looked at his watch.

"One day in class we had an earthquake. Wham! Like the building had been torpedoed. He stopped and said, 'What do we do now?' in English. Nobody answered him. The floor was like riding a wave. In 10 seconds or so the whole episode was over, and he continued in Latin. That's the only time in the whole course that he didn't end one second before the bell. He'd never been in an earthquake before."

"The time for the exam comes. I'll say it's the hardest exam I ever took in my life. The questions were so complex. You would have to know precisely in detail a whole bunch of canons that would influence each other to answer the question, which an ordinary canon lawyer may not know. He'd know it's complex and you have to look it up." Typical question: a priest runs off with a woman, but not intending to marry her, and flies from San Francisco to New York at 12:02 a.m. on a holy day of obligation, passing over many different dioceses where the holy day rules might be different. "What's this guy's obligation to say the breviary? Every question was liked that. There was nothing simple. It was the hardest test I ever took. I passed, which was a miracle. I didn't know anything. At least half the guys flunked."

The exam wasn't the worst thing, he said, and neither was the Latin. "What he was talking about all this time didn't have any connection to pastoral reality. What they ought to make these guys do, they need to work in a parish or a hospital and deal with people, not just spend their life in a library. Some things are important and some are not. Some cases come up all the time and some of them don't."

Fortunately, he had another canon law professor, Father Joseph O'Brien SJ, a former California provincial, who actually taught him something of value. "I'm still putting into practice things he taught us," Father Thomas said nearly 50 years later. "He knew what an ordinary person had to deal with."

Dick wasn't too happy with some of his moral theology teachers, either. He said he learned more about the morality of an obscure sexual practice that he never heard of again, than he did about the First Commandment, which grew to be at the heart of his ministry in his mature years.

In 1958, 13 years after he entered Grand Coteau, the time for ordination came at last. There was only one problem: nobody seemed to know – or care – what the plans were for ordaining Dick Thomas. When his superiors sent him to Alma, they told him he would be ordained with his original class in New Orleans, but when the time came, he didn't hear a word from his home province. He was still keeping in touch with his classmates back at St. Mary's, and most of them had been notified that they were approved for ordination. While they made excited plans, he was out in California wondering what was happening. So he contacted his superiors in New Orleans. Oops! He said later it was obvious from the way they reacted that they had simply forgotten about their one lone seminarian out on the West Coast. Apparently it was too late for the New Orleans ceremony, so they made quick arrangements to get him ordained with his Alma classmates in San Francisco. He would still be a priest, but he felt rejected, and that took some of the luster off the experience.

All the same, he said later, the day of his ordination, June 13, 1958, was the happiest day of his life up to that point. And to his delight, his father was on hand for the ceremony. "The question came up, is he going to come to the ordination or not, in San Francisco. I didn't know whether he would or not. But my sister came out and lived in the area, and she persuaded him that he should come to the ordination, which he did." He was ordained to the priesthood with a large number of Jesuits and Dominicans at St. Mary's Cathedral, San Francisco, a church which has since burned down. Auxiliary Bishop Hugh A. Donohoe officiated.

"Then I had five days at home, after ordination, to visit, and say my first solemn high Mass." His nephew Steve, son of Wayne Jr., made his first Communion at his uncle's first Mass.

Bishop Hugh A. Donohoe with Father Thomas, S.J.

The priests ordained together in San Francisco on June 13, 1958.
Father Thomas is in the top row to the right of the bishop.

FATHER RICHARD THOMAS, S.J.

As a new priest, 1958.

CHAPTER 9

A Brand-New Priest

N ow he was a priest, but he wasn't finished at Alma yet. In those days, seminarians were ordained a year before they finished theology, so he had another year to go. But as new priests, he and his final year classmates were free to leave the seminary grounds, to help out in nearby parishes and perform other priestly duties. "It was the happiest year of our lives," said Father Nigro.

In January 1959 Father Thomas completed "An Interpretation of the Church's Teaching on Sex Education." The 31-page thesis attempts to balance the Church's condemnation of what he called "naturalistic, mass, public, indiscriminate sex education to children on the purely physiological level," and the Catholic commitment to chastity, with the need for better and more useful sex education than Catholic children were actually getting at the time.

"It has been my conviction for years that American Catholic youth is ill-prepared in general to meet the demands of the Sixth and Ninth Commandments" [in Catholic numbering, the commandments forbidding adultery and coveting our neighbor's wife], Father Thomas wrote in the opening paragraph of the thesis.

"Well-intentioned educators and preachers are so shy of this subject that what they say is often too little, too late and too vague to understand," he wrote later on. "Some understanding of sex is needed to understand the Sixth and Ninth commandments. Indeed if all 'sex instruction' were reprobated there could be no place for a talk to a group on the demands of these two commandments or of the virtue of purity. To assert that it is forbidden to explain the Sixth and Ninth commandments or to inculcate purity if this is done publicly is patently against the mind of the Church as expressed by the Council of Trent and common practice. It is against common sense to assert that the Church wants these public talks to be so vague that the hearers will not understand or profit by what is said."

He also noted that "It is impossible to understand the Church's general teaching without some knowledge of sex. Sex occurs in the teaching of the Creation, the Fall, the Incarnation, the Virginity of Mary, the life of celibacy etc."

After examining a long list of statements on the topic by Popes and other Church officials in an attempt to "clarify the mind of the Church," he concludes that Catholic sex education must "avoid the extremes of vagueness on the one hand and positive inducement to sin on the other. The Church and common sense demand that these talks be such as to achieve their purpose: to positively build up the virtue of chastity."

In June 1959 Father Thomas was granted the degree of Bachelor of Sacred Theology. His transcript again shows mostly Bs, with a fair number of Cs and a few As.

Father Thomas spent the summer of 1959 in New Orleans, substituting for vacationing priests in parishes and giving a retreat for black women at Grand Coteau. After that came a year of Jesuit tertianship, a sort of second novitiate, at St. Stanislaus parish in Cleveland. Tertians typically live in community, study, work in a parish during Lent, and volunteer in hospitals.

As a summer substitute and as a tertian, Father Thomas got mixed reviews, from himself and from other people. A report from the New Orleans Jesuit province speaks of him as "well-liked," "pleasant," "generous" and "zealous," "gladly accept[ing] all priestly ministry" and "faithful to his spiritual exercises." But it also said he "gives the impression of not being practical in his thinking" and seeming "somewhat languid in his way of acting; slow in action; not to be rushed," as well as sometimes "brash."

In Cleveland, a report from fellow tertians describes him as "a good community man," "kind, obedient," and an "exemplary religious," but also "lack[ing] circumspection in speech," "much too literal-minded," and "somewhat stubborn." "He should not presume that most differences of view are essential ones...he seems simple in two senses; let him trade one dove for a serpent...his sincerity does not make up for lack of prudence." He also had problems with diction, articulation, and even "overloud exclamations."

He also managed to create "bedlam" – he used the word himself – in a religion class in a Cleveland grammar school; by the time he told the story near the end of his life, he couldn't remember what exactly he did wrong. "I don't know what the heck I did or said. The kids were jumping around and screaming and having a wonderful time, and I lost complete control. I had to run out like a coward, which I was, because I didn't know how to bring them back under control. Fortunately it was the end of the period."

His personal history, somewhere around 1980, says this period ended with "what the tertians facetiously called the 'happiest day of a Jesuit's life' – the last day of tertianship," but apparently that was just a stock Jesuit joke. He doesn't say anything to suggest he's singling out his personal experience as especially bad.

CHAPTER 10

New Orleans: Reaching Beyond the Classroom

I n August 1960, Father Thomas was transferred to New Orleans, and picked up where he left off five years earlier as a Jesuit scholastic in Dallas: teaching at Jesuit High School. His students were freshmen, sophomores and juniors, and he taught them English, religion and speech. Latin, too, just as he had in Dallas; he couldn't seem to get away from it.

As always, he gave his best effort to do the work he was given, but it's obvious classroom teaching wasn't where this new priest's heart was, and neither was Jesuit High School.

"The high school was outstanding in every way except spiritually," Father Thomas recalled years later. "It wasn't a priority." That may or may not be fair, but the 1964 school yearbook, the Blue Jay, really does say "Jesuit excels intellectually, athletically, culturally," with no mention of spirituality.

Teaching high school-aged students is a major priority for Jesuits, but Father Deeves, a teacher for years himself, didn't remember Father Thomas as being very much impressed with that idea. Father Deeves spent several years teaching at Jesuit High in El Paso at a time when Father Thomas had moved on to his life's work at Our Lady's Youth Center there, so the two friends saw a lot of each other until the El Paso school closed in 1972.

"One time he came to me and said 'Jack, you're wasting your time in high school,'" Father Deeves recalled. "He said we were teaching subjects that have nothing to do with God. They do, but he couldn't see that."

Father Deeves responded by quoting Jesuit superior general Father Pedro Arrupe, a man Father Thomas admired, as saying high school was one of Jesuits' most effective and major apostolates. "I didn't mean to rebut him, but at the same time I needed to defend what we were doing," Father Deeves said. The quote was accurate and Father Thomas knew that, so he just stayed silent.

But the New Orleans stories Father Thomas told in the last months of his life weren't about the classroom, nor the Dallas stories either. Instead, he talked about where his heart really was, all the years he was a priest: social justice, the love of the poor, and, in the Dallas and New Orleans days, race relations in particular.

He didn't see many black people at Alma, but he jumped right back into racial controversy in New Orleans. The summer retreat for black women at Grand Coteau was a warm-up; when school started, he organized student field trips to the slums, just as he had in Dallas. He even took the youngsters to see thoroughbred horses in their stables; the lesson was that the horses had better living quarters than the people – including some of the stable employees who lived in those slums. "He didn't teach them social justice, he showed them social justice," said Father Deeves.

Besides his teaching, his job included filling in at parishes on Sundays, and in one parish he read from the pulpit a letter from the U.S. bishops condemning racial segregation. Some of the parishioners complained out loud – "we came to hear Mass, not this" – and tried to convince the rest of the congregation to walk out; a few people did. The pastor wasn't pleased. He told Father Thomas he could say the next Mass but not preach, and he was never invited back to that parish.

That pastor, unfortunately, was not an isolated case among the priests of New Orleans. Their boss, Archbishop Joseph Rummel, had written a letter that said segregation was sinful, but a lot of the priests defied that message openly; "nobody paid any attention to Archbishop Rummel," Father Thomas recalled later. The archbishop was also old and sick, so he couldn't do much to enforce his authority.

But Father Thomas wasn't alone, either. He got together a few allies, especially the parents of one student, and they helped him identify the handful of other people who were ready to speak up for racial justice. Father Thomas and this couple joined together to write a letter to Rome asking for a new archbishop who could bring in some strong leadership on race, and in 1961 John Cody, later a cardinal in Chicago, was moved from his position as bishop of Kansas City-St. Joseph to become coadjutor archbishop of New Orleans.

At a reception for the new archbishop, Father Thomas and his friends planted several people in the reception line-up to tell Archbishop Cody they hoped he would do something about the priests who had been defying Archbishop Rummel, and the new archbishop promised support; if it came to that, he said, he would even excommunicate the racists. In 1962 Archbishop Rummel, still in power along with the new coadjutor, actually did excommunicate three high-profile New Orleans segregationists, including a local judge.

That same year, Jesuit High School in New Orleans, the most prestigious high school in the city, became the first Jesuit high school in the New Orleans province to integrate. Father Thomas was still teaching there, although he didn't have anything in particular to do with the decision to integrate. A special summer school was held for black students to get them up to speed, and they entered in the fall.

On another front, in June 1963 Father Thomas joined eight other Jesuits, including his seminary classmate and friend Father Harold Cohen, to produce a syllabus of high school religious education for the New Orleans province. The resulting 10-page document is aimed at updating and promoting religious education on the same level that education in science and other subjects had been updated and emphasized in recent years.

The syllabus included references to prayer, the liturgy, chastity, academic excellence, and dialogue with non-Catholics. It also stresses Catholic social teaching, vocational guidance, and the need for practical apostolic experience. "Students need practice and instruction in being apostles, in performing the spiritual and corporal works of mercy," the syllabus reads.

The paragraph on vocational guidance will sound especially familiar to those who knew Father Thomas later in his life: "It should be stressed that our aims as Christians in choosing a vocation, career, or occupation should not be pleasure, comfort, money, or prestige. Rather our choice should be based on the principles of the *Spiritual Exercises* [of St. Ignatius Loyola, founder of the Society of Jesus]: How can I best use my talents to serve God? What does God want me to do?"

But even with teaching, subbing in parishes, and fighting racism to keep him on the run, Father Thomas still managed to fit in some time for his original love: horses. Father Louis Lambert was teaching at Jesuit High as a regent at the same time, and he remembered his fellow teacher well.

"He was a horse whisperer," Father Lambert recalled. "When he got there, he went straight to the police department, the mounted police, and went to see every horse. He knew them all by name and could communicate with them extremely well."

The police would turn out to Jesuit High football games with their horses, and Father Thomas, who always loved to watch the sports he was no good at playing, would position himself on the field, near one end zone, and just look at the horses. "They'd notice, and look, and whinny," said Father Lambert. First the horses at the near end, then the horses a football field away. "They were excited. They were happy to communicate with him."

Fr. Harold Rahm (right) showing Fr. Dick Thomas (left) around *Segundo Barrio* in the back of a pickup truck, 1964.

CHAPTER 11

The Call to El Paso

arly in 1964, Father Cecil Lang, acting provincial for the New Orleans province, called Father Thomas into his office and offered him a new job. Would he like to move 1,100 miles west, to El Paso, Texas, and take over from his old high school teacher, Father Harold Rahm, as head of Our Lady's Youth Center?

Father Thomas knew all about OLYC – he had visited Father Rahm there in 1956, on his way to California for his studies at Alma College – and it was a tall order. Despite its name, OLYC was responsible for a lot more than programs for young people.

El Paso, now a city of 650,000, is located at the very western tip of Texas, hundreds of miles from any other major U.S. city, but just across the narrow Rio Grande from the Mexican border city of Ciudad Juárez (1.5 million). OLYC started out with a fairly specific mandate.

Father Rahm, a colorful figure known as the "bicycle priest," had come to town in 1952 as assistant pastor of Sacred Heart Church, the Jesuit parish six blocks from the Rio Grande and the Mexican border. The heavily Hispanic South El Paso neighborhood – *Segundo Barrio* (Second Ward), as its residents call it – was the poorest part of the city. Most of the residents lived in tenements without indoor plumbing. Up until the Chamizal treaty of 1963, a large portion of the parish was in dispute between the U.S. and Mexican governments: the river had changed course and the two countries couldn't agree on whether the land was American or Mexican, so in the meantime no federal funds could be spent there. The whole neighborhood was torn by vicious gang wars. So in 1953, Father Rahm and local basketball hero Buena Ventura "Tula" Irróbali founded OLYC in an abandoned 60-year-old school, mainly to undermine the gang culture by providing wholesome activities for teenagers.

But Father Rahm soon found that he could not get anywhere with youth unless he worked with whole families, so by 1964 the center's work had expanded to an enormous array of programs for all ages, ranging from a massive feeding program and two full-time social workers to a credit union, citizenship classes, youth dances, and even professional wrestling shows, all operated by more than three dozen paid and volunteer staff members

"Big, big, big," Father Thomas remembered four decades later. "There was no other social agency on the south side. We did everything." And he himself had never held authority over anybody other than his students.

Father Rahm, though, thought Father Thomas was just the man for the job. Called by the Society of Jesus to work with the poor in Brazil, Fr. Rahm was allowed to choose any of several hundred Jesuit priests from the New Orleans province to replace him at OLYC. Immediately he thought of his old student from Tampa.

"I may not be a brilliant person," Father Rahm recalled many years later, "but when I see a brilliant person, I know who he is." He also knew the Thomas family well – Father Thomas's brother Bob was by then paying their adopted sister, Marion Cunningham, to work for Father Rahm as a nurse – and "generally, anyone who comes from a good family is a good priest." Finally, "He [Father Thomas] was concerned for the underprivileged, and he lived as an underprivileged person."

Father Rahm traveled to New Orleans to discuss the job, and Father Thomas agreed to come out for a look. Father Rahm remembered driving around town standing in the back of a pickup truck with Father Thomas, taking in the community. "When we finished, he said, 'I will come and take your place.'"

With a school year to finish in New Orleans, Father Thomas made three or four weekend trips to El Paso, flying out on Friday afternoon and returning Sunday evening. He arrived permanently Saturday, May 30, 1964, paid a visit to OLYC, and like Father Rahm before him, moved into the Sacred Heart rectory.

"Thank God who has watched me until this hour," he wrote in his diary the first day. He also noted a few problems: There was no key available to his office, his room at Sacred Heart wasn't ready, and the water was shut off at Camp Juan Diego, the OLYC summer camp at the edge of the city.

He had found his life's work. Along with a mountain of challenges that changed over the years, but never seemed to get any smaller.

CHAPTER 12

Taking on the Task

F ather Thomas held the title of assistant pastor at Sacred Heart, the same title Father Rahm had, but parish work took up only four or five hours of his week. The rest of his time was spent at his real job: running OLYC. Three days after he arrived in town he met with a top staff member. Management experience or no management experience, he was ready to roll.

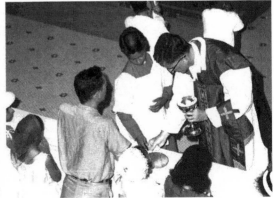

Father Thomas preaching, and distributing Holy Communion at Sacred Heart Church, 1964.

"I outline my thinking at present," he wrote in his diary. "1. We must develop the only resource they [clients] have – the human potential within themselves. 2. Train leaders in the neighborhood. 3. Train staff and recruit more staff. People are more important than buildings. 4. Not a re-habilitation center, ergo shape up or ship out."

The day after that, he issued instructions to the full staff. "Let us thank God for accepting the crosses and difficulties we are taking upon ourselves by accepting our task at Our Lady's Youth Center," he wrote. "Our purpose is to bring life to this neighborhood: Spiritual, mental, physical, material. These conditions are utterly wretched... this task is sacred, holy, enormous, challenging, and thrilling: bringing life to these people. Our purpose is to serve them and not ourselves."

He called on the staff to give 100 percent effort and to be kind to one another ("it would be a traitorous thing to cut down one of our members here"). He also wanted them to be efficient, both on the natural level and on the spiritual level. The center needed reorganizing, he said, so no one would ever be idle. In the meantime, anybody who had nothing to do at a given time should spend that time praying or in spiritual reading.

"He gathered all the staff members and said he wanted to start something different with the staff," recalled Esther Padilla, Tula Irróbali's daughter, who was a young volunteer Girl Scout leader at OLYC at the time. "He wanted to bring God into our lives. He said each individual had to find out what God wanted from each one of us and find out our gifts."

Padilla remembered him as "an odd-looking priest," tall and lanky, with black jeans hung low and high-top tennis shoes; still, "he looked very handsome when he had his priest outfit on." Lorenza Ledesma, another teen volunteer at the time, said Father Thomas came across as very rural, nothing like the street-smart Father Rahm.

Not that the country manners kept Father Thomas off the streets. He was out on the sidewalk from day one. "Met abandoned child on sidewalk," he wrote in his diary the first week. "I went to look for her family in six *presidios* [tenements]. When I returned she was toddling under a railroad freight car close to the other children playing with paper from the boxcar.

"I must learn Spanish. Every morning I walk around the slums during meditation. The water in the canal is a good picture of redemption and redemptive work. From dirty water God can make beauty. Man can make drinking water. So we must redeem these people."

Soon he set out to get started on the Spanish. Hector Bencomo, a neighborhood grocer and city councilman who would go on to become one of Father Thomas's most devoted co-workers, was a merely nominal member of the OLYC board in 1964; "I didn't take it seriously," Bencomo remembered years later. Father Thomas tracked him down at his grocery store, and the two men went out to a drugstore for coffee.

"I'd order coffee and he'd order water," Bencomo said. "I found out he didn't care for coffee or soft drinks—he just wanted to talk." Bencomo was delighted that his new friend was interested in learning about the Mexican people; the Mexican-American shopkeeper knew a lot of Anglo priests who weren't. "He made me feel comfortable. He was like an old friend."

Father Thomas planned on recording radio broadcasts to help him with his Spanish, so Bencomo took him to a friend's store to get a tape recorder. Father Thomas made such a good impression that the store owner gave him the recorder for free. Helen Guajardo, who was hired as secretary at OLYC later the same year, remembered Father Thomas watching Spanish TV, also to learn the language. She said he liked the commercials best.

In his office at Our Lady's Youth Center, 1965.

CHAPTER 13

In a Very Long Shadow

Father Rahm stayed about three weeks before heading off to his new assignment in Brazil. He spent the time trying to get his successor off to a good start. Father Rahm was deeply dedicated to the poor, but he was also cheerfully at home with the big wheels of the community, "full of laughter and joy," recalled Mary Bencomo, Hector's wife. The big wheels threw a fancy banquet to say a fond farewell to him, and hundreds of people turned out for the event. Father Rahm did his best to introduce Father Thomas to the influential people, to make him as well-known as possible. Father Thomas tagged along reluctantly; "I don't think he was too interested in being well-known," Father Rahm chuckled decades later.

Finally, on June 22, Father Rahm left town. He flew out of El Paso airport, a short hop to the Juárez airport before continuing on in the direction of Brazil. Father Thomas turned up too late to catch his departure from El Paso and had to hitch a ride in OLYC board president Art Singer's Piper Cub airplane to say goodbye and get Father Rahm's blessing in Juárez.

In another sense, though, Father Rahm never left town at all. Never in his own lifetime did Father Thomas get out of his predecessor's shadow. A block of what should be Fifth Street in

South El Paso, where it passes Sacred Heart Church, has "Father Rahm Avenue" right there on the standard green municipal street sign. A block to the east, on the side of the parish hall, a colorful mural depicting church history in the El Paso area shows the bicycle priest in his flowing cassock aboard his old two-wheeler. Father Thomas has a place in the mural now, too, trademark black jeans, tennis shoes and all – but painted into leftover space in the background, about half the size of Father Rahm's portrait.

Not all the comparisons were symbolic. Evy Nelson was in fourth grade in about 1968 when she first met Father Thomas; she remembered people shaking their heads over the low-profile newcomer: "He's no Father Rahm." People were still talking that way more than 30 years later: in 2000, Father Rahm marked the 50th anniversary of his ordination – in Brazil, not in El Paso – and the El Paso *Times* published a feature story in honor of the event, complete with a double-column-width head and shoulders photo of Father Rahm in Mass vestments. "Now there is no youth center," one of his old co-workers lamented in a quote in the story. There was no mention at all of Father Thomas or the work still going on at OLYC.

Well, nobody could deny the two men had different ways of doing things. Some of it was just personality, but a lot of it was priorities. Father Thomas had his own set, and much as he admired Father Rahm, he followed his own conscience down a very different path.

Father Sam Rosales, an El Paso-born Jesuit priest, worked closely with both men, starting as far back as 1953 when he was a high school freshman. He joined a Jesuit-inspired lay community at OLYC and worked there as a full-time volunteer until 1964, the year Father Rahm left El Paso; then Father Thomas helped him discern a vocation, so he went off to seminary, but came back to work with Father Thomas in the OLYC ministries from 1980 to 1992.

Father Rahm, said Father Rosales, was a charming, athletic extrovert, front and center all the time, not only at OLYC but in the city at large. Father Thomas was another personality altogether. He kept his head down, even on his own turf at OLYC; "if you came here you would not know where to find him." He would send out assistants to meet anyone who came to see him, and he needed quiet prayer time before he made decisions. "When he held you off, he was praying, and you better not interrupt," said Helen Guajardo.

But retiring or not, he wasn't shy at all, as the Sodality of Our Lady of Guadalupe soon found out. The 1531 apparition of the Blessed Virgin Mary to the Aztec St. Juan Diego at Guadalupe, in what is now Mexico City, plays a huge role in Mexican Catholicism, and the image of the Virgin left miraculously on Juan Diego's cloak can be seen everywhere; it's at the top of OLYC's own stationery to this day. Father Thomas took over from Father Rahm as chaplain for the sodality, and he sat impatiently through one meeting listening to the members discuss what an ophthalmologist had to say about Mary's eyes as shown in the image. Finally he had had enough. "I think Our Lady would be more interested in us helping her poor than in studying her eyeball," he told them. They fired him as chaplain.

Father Thomas's priorities were soon making a different place out of OLYC, too. Both priests were all about serving the poor, but in different ways. To Father Rahm, wholesome activities for the youth were the way to save them from the gangs. There were the sports teams, groups like the Catholic Youth Organization and the Legion of Mary, and dances featuring the popular music of the *day*. There were also food giveaways, for all comers. These programs accomplished a lot, but there were still plenty of unsolved problems at OLYC — for example, a constant parade of alcoholics and other unsavory characters looking for a handout and doing nothing to make the atmosphere wholesome for the young people.

Father Thomas was all for activities, but he always focused on the spiritual side, even when feeding the hungry or doing other corporal works of mercy. "Any time we did anything it was spiritual in a big way," said Father Rosales. Father Thomas kept many of the programs, but he changed a few as well. He disapproved of worldly music – "garbage in, garbage out," he would say – so he cut it off and replaced it with Christian music. He also spent a lot of time praying with people who came in for help and blessing them with holy water and blessed oil. That solved one of the problems in a hurry: the alcoholics and other problem people didn't like the Christian music, and some of them complained that the holy water burned them, so they stopped coming around.

Father Thomas also had his own method for dealing with the beggars who turned up constantly at OLYC. Begging is a profession for many people, he said, and some of them do very well at it. On the other hand, plenty of those people who came to OLYC were in genuine need. Father Deeves once asked him how he could tell the two groups apart. "Make them wait," Father Thomas said. The desperate people would wait for help; the professionals would go look for easier pickings. Also, he suggested, you can tell genuinely poor people by looking at their shoes.

OLYC took up most of his time, but not all. He managed to take time off for some recreation, too. Among his friends, at the time and later, were the family of George Kuper, a Volkswagen dealer who provided him with vehicles. The Kupers had horses. Father Thomas would come to the house, change from his priestly cassock to jeans, and go riding. "He always wanted to be with horses," Susan Kuper Vescovo said. "With him there was no barrier between man and animal. He would talk to them and they understood him. A bad horse was never bad around him. There was a presence about him that was absolutely indescribable."

Indoors, Father Thomas would join the family for games; he was funny and animated, Vescovo said – "an ordinary priest," nothing like the spiritually consumed man she would come to know in her adult life, when she and her husband, Paul, were supplying him with vehicles from their own car dealership.

He also got a new name in El Paso. Instead of "Dick," his new friends among the lay people started calling him "Rick," and he liked it. He was also known as Rick to the many non-Catholic pastors and leaders he worked with over the years. His family and his fellow Jesuits kept calling him Dick, and still do today, but he has been Rick to nearly everybody else ever since 1964.

Father Rick in the parking lot of OLYC,
with one of the demo Volkswagen bugs he drove, 1969.

CHAPTER 14

So Much with So Little

In 1964, Our Lady's Youth Center occupied a battered old brick building a few blocks north of Sacred Heart. Built in 1892, it was at one time a school for black students; later it passed into the hands of Catholic agencies. By the time Father Rahm made a deal to lease the building from its owner, the Knights of Columbus, in 1953, it had been abandoned for 20 years.

By the time Father Thomas arrived in town, Father Rahm had gone a long way toward winning his struggle with the gangs, although gang violence still cropped up from time to time. Meanwhile, though, the work of the center had grown far beyond fighting juvenile delinquency. The building had been fixed up enough to be usable, and was now owned by a non-profit corporation, incorporated as Our Lady's Youth Center. But the premises were still in rough shape, the neighborhood was still desperately poor, and OLYC staff were running like hamsters on an exercise wheel to keep a bewildering variety of programs going.

Money was a constant challenge. OLYC got a substantial United Way grant every year, but that still fell thousands of dollars short of the annual budget. There was little government funding, though the center did get food from Surplus Commodities, a federal program that bought food as part of farm price supports and gave it to the needy. OLYC used the food for its feeding program and summer camp. Donations from a local Christmas appeal, and from the "Anything-a-Month Club" – about 500 supporters across the United States whom Father Thomas kept informed via a monthly newsletter – made up the funding shortage, but usually not until the last minute.

"We wouldn't have any money in the till, but he [Father Thomas] would say 'don't worry, something will come,' and it would," recalled Helen Guajardo. "Something would always come—they just seemed to come in the mail."

"The youth center is able to do so much with so little because our salary scale is low, because we beg things from the businesses on a daily basis, and because we use very poor equipment and are very frugal in our spending," Father Thomas wrote in a 1968 report on OLYC activities.

Programs in Father Thomas's early days, mostly founded by Father Rahm but in some cases by himself, included a social services office; an employment office; Tepeyac credit union; adult classes in English, cooking, sewing, and preparation for U.S. citizenship; awareness programs for social issues; youth programs ranging from after-school lunch for more than 300 children to cubs, scouts, and more than 80 teams in four different sports; first Communion preparation (including a full-time catechist); Camp Juan Diego, a summer camp serving more than 400 children; and even free showers for people with no indoor plumbing at home.

Programs were delivered by full- and part-time paid staff and full- and part-time volunteers. The 1968 report says there were 47 people on staff as of December 1967, with another 15 or 10 to be added to run summer programs in 1968. Pay was low, so OLYC was always on the lookout for new staff to replace workers who found better jobs. Many of the staff were students who lived with their parents and received two meals a day at the center on top of their small salaries.

Key workers included social worker Consuelo Martínez; Helen Guajardo, secretary; and of course Buena Ventura Irróbali – always called Tula, or even "Mr. Tula"; his wife, Romelia, also active in the community, was known as "Mrs. Tula." There were many others.

Guajardo had happy memories of her eight years on the job. Father Thomas gave her a lot of flexibility, even letting her work from home sometimes, and she made sure she took care of business. She also donated to Father Thomas's work rather than her own Protestant church.

"I knew where it went," she said. "I figured it got a better use."

"I had the best understanding with that man that I ever had in my life. He trusted me, and I trusted him."

CHAPTER 15

Changes for the Kingdom

A sk anybody who knew both men, and you'll be told that Father Thomas did not run Our Lady's Youth Center the way Father Rahm had run it.

"Father Thomas came in and he changed everything," said Pochie Heredia, who had met her husband, Neto, at one of Father Rahm's clubs. "No clubs, no nothing." "He used my dance hall for prayer meetings," Father Rahm said years later.

Father Rahm and the Heredias weren't being critical. "What I did was nationally famous, and he made it internationally famous," Father Rahm said. "He couldn't have done better." As for the Heredias, they got with the program and stayed with it for 50 years, an active part of Father Thomas's work and community. But not everybody was so enthusiastic. Esther Padilla stayed too, but she remembered that "a lot of people left. Each time he brought in something new, people left because this was unheard of."

The changes didn't all come overnight, and Father Thomas himself didn't think they were that big a deal, at least in hindsight. "I just stepped into what he'd [Father Rahm] already started," he said years later. "I was just trying to stay on top of what was already going on." The afterschool feeding program, to take one example, was running just fine, and he just stood back and let it run. He focused his attention in other places.

He'd say Mass at Sacred Heart Church each day, and then Tula would set him up for Mass somewhere in the neighborhood. He'd also go into the employment agency each morning to sit and pray. A note in his diary for July 1964 says he went door to door one evening, including a bar, inviting people to come say the rosary. (There were no takers from the bar, but the bartender gave him a $2 donation.)

He also spent time trying to get a handle on the personnel. There was some difference of understanding on the lay staff as to who was supposed to be in charge, and OLYC board was a hands-on operation, with board members coming into the building on a frequent basis and making changes in the programs.

But right from the start, Father Thomas was pushing a spiritual emphasis. OLYC was not just a social agency, Father Rosales remembered hearing him say; "We are here to preach the kingdom." What's more, the spiritual need, as he saw it, was huge. Most of the center's clients were nominal Catholics, but few were practicing – especially among recent arrivals from Juárez, where a population of about 380,000 was served by only about 30 priests.

His notes from his earliest staff meetings make it clear he wasn't afraid to change things around according to his principles. "Each member of the staff, in working with a group, should be alert to the spiritual needs of each person in that group, and endeavor to get this person to lead a full life as a child of God should," he wrote. "Otherwise, this particular activity is purely on a natural level and lacks the results it should have." Even sports should be spiritual, he said; he went so far as to tell the staff that every employee should be prepared to do religious instruction.

Tula was a key figure, totally on board. "Dad and Father had a lot of long meetings," said Ralph Irróbali, Tula's son. "I remember as a child waiting two or three hours for them to come out."

With Tula Irróbali in the OLYC parking lot, 1965.

Paid staff were to perform the most important and productive work and not spend time on what Father Thomas called "less good activity." Lower-priority programs should be left for volunteers, or else dropped.

His top priorities among existing programs were the employment office, the social welfare office, the sports program, catechism, the credit union, night rosary, and neighborhood Mass. Number one on his list of new activities was home visiting, to let the neighborhood residents know about all the services OLYC had to offer.

It wasn't only the center's approach he aimed to change, either; he was hoping to change the outlook of its clients. At an early point, he began to push his flock to give rather than receive. "Jesus says give, the devil says grab" was still one of his mottoes years later, and in 1965 he brought the point up at a staff meeting.

"In the past the center has too often been a 'give-away place,'" he said. "We hurt people's character by giving them too many things and in the wrong way. When kids run up to you on the street and ask for potato chips, for candy, and 'give me a nickel', it's a bad sign. There are many needs in this community, and we have to give things away, but they have to be given in such a way as not to ruin the personality or the character of the person receiving the gift. It is much better for people to earn their own way.

"For example, last year at Camp [Juan Diego], the campers for the first time earned their $2 if they couldn't pay their tuition for the camp. It cost us money to have them earn their own way, but it helped their character." Youngsters did chores around the youth center, collected bottles or washed cars to earn the $2 fee, which covered less than 40 per cent of the cost of camp (despite the tiny $70-a-month salary paid to the camp counselors.)

Visiting kids in the slums of *Segundo Barrio*, 1973.

The "give-don't-grab" principle was applied to adults, too. Under Father Rahm, OLYC had been giving away 1,000 Christmas baskets a year. In 1966, Father Thomas cancelled the program. Instead, anyone coming in for a basket was invited to give a basket to a needy neighbor instead. "They will contribute something toward a basket, say a bag of beans and some rice," he said in the newsletter. "And we will help them to fill up the basket [with additional food] so that they can give a personal present to one of their neighbors in their own name at Christmas time. No matter how needy they themselves are, we would like them to think of sharing with others at this holy season."

Father Thomas often walked around the neighborhood visiting families and with the kids who played in the streets and alleys, 1973.

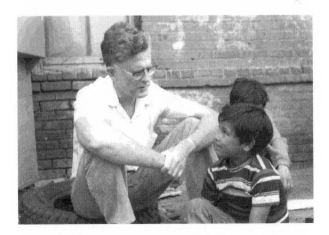

CHAPTER 16

A Heart for a High School

Rick Thomas didn't want to spend his career teaching high school. He was also no good at sports. All the same, he ended up spending a surprising amount of his time hanging around on a high school campus and attending high school sports events. He even "earned" a sports letterman's jacket all his own.

Actually, Father Thomas loved high school students, as long as he didn't have to teach them math and Latin; for that matter he liked sports, as long as somebody else was playing. And for more than 40 years, from his arrival in El Paso until his last illness, he cherished his role as unofficial chaplain and enthusiastic sideline rooter at Bowie High School, the school most of the OLYC youth attended if they made it to high school at all.

In the 60s, Bowie was located in a 40-year-old building deep in South El Paso, about half a mile east of OLYC. Most of the students were Hispanic, most were poor, and many were undersized because they didn't get enough to eat. That didn't keep them from playing football and other sports, though, and in 1966 the football team voted to attend 7:30 a.m. Mass at OLYC on game days.

At the first Friday morning Mass, nearly the whole team turned up, but hardly anybody went to Communion. What's more, they lost that night's game in a landslide. So Father Thomas talked to the team captain, then to the football coach ("a good Methodist"), and arranged to hear the players' confessions the afternoon before Mass. He couldn't get permission to hear confessions on the school grounds, so he parked his green Volkswagen next to the railroad tracks near the school, set up a small plastic crucifix, and heard confessions for more than an hour. Lots of players took Communion the next day, and Bowie lost by only one touchdown that night.

Bowie lost a lot of football games in those days. It wasn't any lack of team spirit or even poor equipment. The simple fact is that most of the players took the field most weeks without a single balanced meal in the day. And when Father Thomas turned up at the games – nearly every football game, as many basketball games he could, and some other sports events – he would walk the sidelines in a prominent position, rooting and praying at the same time. What's more, he was praying for victory. He wasn't satisfied with the standard sports prayer, for the players to do their best and not get hurt. "I pray for my boys to win," he told Helen Guajardo. He said they had enough losses in their lives, and it would be nice if they could at least win on the football field.

Father Thomas spent as much time as he could on campus, and did whatever he could get away with: he would wander around praying the rosary, meeting with students, and keeping a notebook so that he wouldn't forget individual needs. "He was like part of our school," says Grace Hernández, a Bowie graduate and longtime secretary at the school.

In 1969 OLYC opened *La Cueva del Oso* ("the cave of the bear," named for Bowie's mascot) as a prayer, recreation and counseling center in two rented rooms near the school.

In 1973 Bowie moved to a new, modern site a mile farther east, out of the heart of the barrio, and the old Barrie building became Guillen Middle School. OLYC carried on its ministry at

Guillen; meanwhile, Father Thomas started making plans for a new Cueva at the new Bowie location. He thought he had an agreement with the city government to buy land near the school, but the city backed out of the deal and started acquiring the land for another development. "I'd counted on that for years," he said, and he wasn't about to give up. "The Lord let me know as I awakened one morning to contact all the private landowners to buy their land before the city took it by eminent domain." He found one holdout, an older woman who didn't want to sell to the city, and offered her more than the city price. She agreed to sell, and the city decided it couldn't fight the Church and agreed to a land swap. The new Cueva opened in 1976.

On more than one occasion, Father Thomas was barred from the Bowie campus by officials who didn't want a Catholic priest ministering on a public school campus. When that happened, he just carried on his rounds with his rosary and his notebook on the sidewalk; meanwhile, he sent young OLYC staff members on to campus in his place to keep the ministry going. Each time, the ban came to an end and he was allowed back in the school.

Much later, not long before his final illness, he was invited to bless every room on the campus. "He brought gallons and gallons of holy water," said Grace Hernández. Eventually he was given his Bowie letterman jacket and wore it proudly to the games; it's now on view in the school's sports display.

Father Thomas – always a loyal Bowie Bear, 1966.

CHAPTER 17

Camp Juan Diego:
A Break from the Slums

Nobody had to wait until high school to make friends with Father Thomas. Evy Nelson was just in Grade 4 when she first met him, at a children's Mass he was celebrating at Sacred Heart in 1968. "The priest seemed completely geared to making the Mass understandable," she recalled years later. For the Scripture readings, he assigned parts to the children; instead of a homily, he would explain and enact the readings. He also gave the youngsters Bibles and anything else he thought they needed for spiritual nourishment – out of his own pocket if need be.

He was always cheerful around young people, too. "Meet me at the KC," he would tell them; "KC" was local slang for the youth center, from its previous Knights of Columbus days. "He loved to make people laugh."

In the 60s and early 70s, the biggest OLYC event of the year for kids age 9-17 was a week's stay at Camp Juan Diego. Like most other 60s-era OLYC ministries, Camp Juan Diego started out under Father Rahm, in 1958. It was located in the desert near Ysleta, about 14 miles from downtown El Paso, on land donated by a major local landowner, K.B. Ivey. Officially the camp covered less than an acre and a half, but the children were free to roam hundreds of acres of surrounding Ivey land, and the Iveys even helped build a swimming pool and a four-room bunkhouse at the site.

Each summer, the camp drew hundreds of children: 400 in 1967, more than 600 by 1974. The children were recruited by OLYC staff, who pounded the sidewalks of South El Paso, going door to door looking for prospects. Not everybody was interested to start with; sometimes it took two or three visits to the same household to get the kids and their parents to sign up, and no wonder: many of *Segundo Barrio*'s residents had never seen anything more natural than a sidewalk and had no idea of what "camp" was like. "Many have never seen cotton growing, a cornstalk, have never touched a horse, never seen the sunrise or taken a walk in the country," Father Thomas wrote in 1967.

Camp went on for eight weeks every summer, alternating a week for boys and a week for girls. It cost $2 per child, too pricey for many poor families, but those who couldn't pay cash could work for their fee, washing cars, collecting soda bottles, sorting books at OLYC, and doing other odd jobs. The $2 didn't make much of a dent in the cost of the camp, and supervising the youngsters earning their way was one more strain on the OLYC staff, but the actual money wasn't the point: "We try steadily to teach that everything in life is not free and try to promote the concept that we should work to earn our way," Father Thomas said.

Actually, nearly all the children were poor, and a good many were desperately poor. In 1967, one of the campers had his shoe fall apart early in his camp week; "he went through the rest of camp with a rope tied around his foot trying to keep the sole of his shoe to the bottom of his foot." The following year, the records show, OLYC provided shoes to one camper, clothes to another.

Father Rick giving horseback lessons to the boys
at Camp Juan Diego, 1972.

Meanwhile, the camp counselors – some of them from poor homes themselves, some not – weren't getting rich either. They got only $70 a month for recruiting the campers and operating the camp, "so those who want to work at camp must have other motivation than making money as a reason for wanting to work there," Father Thomas said. Apparently he got that one right: in 1968, a competing federal government summer camp tried to hire away Camp Juan Diego counselors for eight times the salary plus shorter working hours, and nobody took the offer.

Camp started each week in the yard at OLYC, where the kids gathered to take the bus to Ysleta. They would spend the week there, sleeping in the bunkhouse, and take the bus back to town on Friday afternoon. At the campsite, they were kept busy morning to evening with activities: swimming, crawfishing, hiking, crafts, lizard- and snake-hunting, picking wolfberries. "The cheapest recreation we have is hunting jackrabbits," Father Thomas said. "At the beginning of camp I offer the boys $5 for anyone who will catch me a full-grown, healthy jackrabbit by running it down. The kids go wild for this offer and so far no one has been able to claim the $5."

In the evening there was Mass, and singing, and teaching by Father Thomas. Al Mills, a Jesuit who worked with Father Thomas as a seminarian and later as a priest, remembered Father Thomas getting the campers to put splints on their arms to teach them the difference between heaven and hell. Heaven was where the splints didn't matter because they were feeding each other; hell was where they only cared about feeding themselves – and they couldn't.

It's no surprise that a summer camp run by Rick Thomas would be big on animals – dogs, rabbits, chickens, ducks, sheep, goats, and especially horses. The youngsters got to bring the animals to Mass (except the horses, which couldn't fit through the door), and Father Thomas would mention them in his sermons. Local TV star Geno Milligan and others lent the camp horses and ponies for the children to touch, feed, brush and ride every day.

"We find it's a wonderful learning experience for a slum child to go to the country and be able to take care of, feed and love various animals," Father Thomas said.

The whole point of Camp Juan Diego was giving children an experience they might never have gotten at home in the slums. "Because the child receives love and appreciation at our camp (and the counselors are trained to create this atmosphere), he or she enjoys it immensely even though the facilities are meager. The child deeply wants to be loved and appreciated, and receiving this, the other circumstances have much less importance."

"Each summer we witness boys and girls [who are] severely disturbed emotionally go through the week of camp without betraying the slightest trace of abnormality...some of these children come to camp with ingrained class hostilities. These children that have been taught to be abrasive, demanding and abusive are completely changed by the friendly, positive atmosphere of camp. This regular draining off of hostile feelings and attitudes has done much to preserve an equilibrium in the El Paso slums not enjoyed in other cities such as ours."

"The children love camp so much that at the end of the week they cry when they have to come home," Father Thomas said.

Obviously, youth activities carried on year-round at OLYC, religious and otherwise. One in-town project was *Las Aguilas del Sol* (the eagles of the sun), the only youth mariachi band in Texas, founded at OLYC in 1972. Father Thomas got them burgundy mariachi outfits with silver buttons down the sides, topped by huge sombreros. He also got them quality sound equipment, which he commandeered for extra duty at prayer meetings. The band won first prize at a high school talent show and played at functions all over town.

"Father was willing to encourage any good gift in any group, in anyone at all, in any way he could help," said Sister Mary Virginia Clark, who worked with him for 17 years. "He believed it was important to cultivate the human spirit."

CHAPTER 18

The War on Poverty

From Day 1, Father Thomas made it clear that Our Lady's Youth Center could never be just a social agency; "we are here to preach the kingdom." But preaching the kingdom didn't *replace* social ministry. It *included* social ministry. And as much as he depended on the power of God to get the work done, Father Thomas never despised what the secular world had to offer to improve life for the poor.

He had barely arrived in El Paso in 1964 when an enormous opportunity arrived courtesy of the secular world. President Lyndon Johnson had announced his War on Poverty in January in the State of the Union message, and Congress formally launched the project in August when it created the Office of Economic Opportunity. The OEO's job was to distribute funds to local anti-poverty projects, and by the fall of 1964 Father Thomas was attending meetings of local officials working to bring the War on Poverty to El Paso.

Unfortunately, those meetings didn't impress Father Thomas very much, and he wasn't shy about saying so. He turned himself into "an unremitting irritant to those formulating the local anti-poverty effort," wrote Robert Glasgow, regional editor of the Arizona *Republic*, in a series of admiring columns about Father

Thomas's work. Father Thomas's main complaint seems to have been that the poor themselves weren't given much of a say in all the high-level decision-making about how to help the poor.

By February 1965 the list of people he had irritated seems to have included his own bishop, Most Rev. Sidney Metzger. Bishop Metzger wasn't an enemy to social justice by any means. That same year he tried to keep local farm workers from going to California to serve as strikebreakers in the Delano grape strike led by César Chávez, and in 1973 he helped organize a national boycott of a clothing manufacturer, to support striking workers. But Father Thomas's outspoken style made him nervous. On Feb. 23 the bishop released a letter to the chair of the local War on Poverty steering committee naming three other priests as the diocese's "sole" representatives to the committee, and the same day Father Thomas got back to OLYC to find a letter from the bishop which he described in his diary as "silencing me and putting me under the three priests." He said the letter left him "low and discouraged."

He met with the bishop on March 5. Afterwards he wrote in his diary that the bishop was "kindly" in the conversation, but "defensive on the poverty issue." The bishop said he felt bad and hadn't intended the letter to be a public reprimand. He said he didn't mean to silence Father Thomas either – he was still free to meet with poverty officials privately and to make suggestions to the steering committee. But Father Thomas said the bishop was afraid "that I was rocking the boat with danger of sinking it."

So Father Thomas stopped "needling" the steering committee (in Glasgow's words). But instead of backing off on his efforts, he stepped them up. He formed his own committee, put together his own project, and took it straight to the OEO, bypassing the official group altogether. Called Community Action of El Paso Inc., Father Thomas's program was an ambitious, multi-pronged plan to raise migrant farm workers out of poverty, mainly by providing them with better skills. Unlike the official project,

Community Action had plenty of poor people involved in the planning: a majority of the board of directors were poor or near-poor; the president was the widow of a warehouseman. Another major difference: the new proposal aimed at federal funds administered by the OEO but granted specifically for agricultural purposes before the OEO was even created. Most War on Poverty projects were required to have some local government funding, but the agricultural funds had different rules, so Father Thomas didn't need local money.

The plan worked. Community Action moved ahead of the official committee's project. In October, Father Thomas got a phone call from Washington asking him to come and bring a poor person with him. "They were anxious to make a good showing, and we jumped in there and proposed this thing, and it looked good, so they were all for it." When he and board member Enrique "Kiki" Rayas arrived Oct. 5, 1965, the OEO announced a $628,104 federal grant for Community Action. Father Thomas and Rayas were on national television, and on the front page of the El Paso *Times* the next day in a photo with El Paso's congressman and an OEO official.

"Everybody in El Paso was mad at me because I upstaged them and got there before they did," Father Thomas remembered with some glee 40 years later. "The rumor was I had influence in Washington because I was a friend of the Kennedy family. There was nothing to that. I didn't know any Kennedys. The truth was I didn't have any friends in Washington."

Well, maybe no personal friends who lived in Washington. But he had a friend who lived in El Paso who knew Lyndon Johnson himself. Frank Galván was an El Paso lawyer who was prominent in GI Forum, a Mexican-American veterans' group working for social justice. He had helped get out the Mexican-American vote for Johnson in the 1964 election. Years later, Father Thomas found out Galván had gone to bat for the project with Johnson, and he was even told that Johnson had gone to the

War on Poverty headquarters in person and taken the paper-
work from desk to desk collecting signatures. "This is how God
works," Father Thomas said. "God's doing all these things, you're
just walking along, you don't know what the heck is going on,
but God is working."

Anyhow, upstaging the official program was the least of
Father Thomas's offenses, from the point of view of the El Paso
power structure. First of all, a local farm official was quoted in
the newspaper the next day saying the whole plan was based on
"a fraud" because there weren't enough farm workers in the area
to justify the program, and local cotton growers couldn't find
enough workers to pick their crop.

It didn't take long to answer that accusation. The fact was, the
program was aimed at farm workers who lived in the El Paso
area but worked somewhere else – as far away as California or
the Midwest – because the pay was better there. The point
wasn't to find them farm jobs, but to give them the skills to sur-
vive and prosper in American society. And there were definitely
enough workers to justify the program; about 500 people signed
up in the first few months.

But even that was nothing compared to the bombshell Father
Thomas dropped while he was in Washington. Too outspoken at
committee meetings? Just watch him in front of a television camera.

"Now gentlemen, I want to talk about something else that
rubs me," he told the media at the announcement ceremony.
"We have a lot of hungry people, little children, babies, old people. Will you tell me how I can get food to these people in El
Paso?"

The reporters present let out a "gasp of astonishment" and
asked more questions, the *Times* story said, and Father Thomas
and Rayas expanded on the subject. They told the press conference about a baby Father Thomas had found starving in a tenement near OLYC, about a dry-cleaning worker who made $18

for 54 hours of work a week, about people who did not know of or could not get to community resources that would have fed them.

The story on these comments, by the *Times'* Washington correspondent, got bigger play on the front page than the funding announcement, and the reaction wasn't friendly. "Poverty stand stirs resentment," read a headline over a follow-up story in the next day's paper, detailing carefully-worded responses from local officials denying that the problem was as bad as Father Thomas said. The comments were fairly diplomatic, but the story suggested that some officials were reluctant to comment and that the anger behind the scenes was a good deal stronger than the official response.

"This is against the chamber of commerce mentality," Father Thomas noted years later. (Not everybody in the power structure was critical, though; the El Paso *Herald-Post* defended his statements in an editorial titled "Why the sniping?," suggesting that he had simply told a well-known truth that most people preferred not to mention.)

Father Thomas refused further comment to local media on his return to El Paso, but he said he was contacted later by a woman he didn't know and told that a group of influential people had gotten together to form a plan to drive him out of town. They appointed two prominent wealthy Catholics to use their influence to get rid of him. One of those two was a man Father Thomas knew reasonably well – in fact, the man was an old friend of Father Rahm. So Father Thomas prayed about it and then went to visit the man at his office. The man received him graciously – "come in, sit down. I'm so happy to see you" – and Father Thomas read him the passage about Herod and the Magi from Matthew Chapter 2, in which King Herod tries to get the wise men to betray the baby Jesus into his power.

"I didn't say a word. I just read that to him, I said goodbye, and I left his office. I don't know whether he got the point – I think he did. He was doing the same thing."

Whatever the group may have planned or attempted, it didn't work. Nothing came of it, and the next time Father Thomas saw the other prominent Catholic involved in the plot, the man handed him a $20 bill.

Meanwhile, the migrant workers' program got off to a good start. Classes began in December 1965, in rented premises. The workers studied English, basic arithmetic, citizenship, home economics and management, health, and if necessary, literacy, in English or even in Spanish. They also got vocational training: auto mechanics, upholstery, sewing, short order and fry cooking, carpentry, building maintenance, TV and radio repair, sewing machine repair, welding, janitorial service, and beauty parlor work, all in actual jobsites scattered around the city. There was a weekly stipend for participants so they could continue to support their families, babysitting for single mothers in the program, and a school bus for participants who lived outside south El Paso, in such locations as Canutillo and Anthony. Father Thomas, even though he was the main author of the program, wasn't involved in management or in charge of the funds; his role was limited to a seat on the board of directors.

In the long run, the program did not fare as well as Father Thomas had hoped, with a series of embarrassing headlines and problems with the OEO. Several leading officials resigned over a period of months, and the group's acting director was quoted in a newspaper story as blaming "sensational and irresponsible publicity" for antagonizing "people who could help the program." The newspaper report interpreted this as a reference to Father Thomas's earlier comments about hungry people in El Paso. But Father Thomas wasn't involved in the management of the program by that time, though he did hear about the problems and helped set up a meeting in a private home for unhappy participants to meet with federal officials.

CHAPTER 19

Other Battlefields

Meanwhile, Rick Thomas had his own war on poverty going, with or without the OEO, and it usually meant butting heads with people in authority. One of his complaints at the Washington press conference was about the federal Surplus Commodities food distribution program, which provided surplus farm production to the needy.

Father Thomas thought the program had some major gaps. For one thing, it was too hard to qualify for food. He said the local income cut off was unrealistically low; a family making 50 cents a month more than the limit "cannot qualify for free food, nor feed itself on that amount." What's more, a lot of people who did qualify didn't even know Surplus Commodities existed, and many of those who did know lived in places like the neighboring communities of Socorro and Canutillo, too far away from the single El Paso distribution point to get there for their food.

At one point Father Thomas managed to convince local beer truckers to deliver the food to outlying areas, but county commissioners turned thumbs down; they said there were too many legal and administrative problems. So Father Thomas wrote the lyrics for a satirical song; a local band wrote the music and recorded it. Some of the lyrics: "I'm hungry in the morning, my belly hurts at night. The beer truck said they'd bring the food, but the commissioners say it's not right... I've heard there's a war on poverty, it must be me they're fighting." The song got played on the radio – once. "It did the job," Father Thomas said. The federal food stamp program came to El Paso soon after, with a higher eligibility limit and no more problems with distribution. "We gave them so much trouble that they rushed to get food stamps to get us off their back," Father Thomas said years later.

In February 1966, Father Thomas and his friends waded into another area of political action when a Texas poll tax that had kept many poor workers off the state voters' list was declared unconstitutional by federal courts. The poll tax had been especially hard on migrant farm workers, because it had to be paid in the winter, when most migrant farm workers are short of money. There was a two-week window of opportunity now to register voters who had been left out. A lot of people in positions of power weren't too eager to see all those new voters, but Father Thomas stood outside factories handing out registration forms, and also went door to door. A lawyer who worked with OLYC hand-delivered, unseen, a box of 2,250 completed forms to the county tax collector's desk. "Mystery in tax office over boxful of forms," read one newspaper headline, but the forms were accepted as valid.

Helping the poor wasn't a surefire way of making friends, Father Thomas discovered. In fact, he found himself facing threats from the establishment power structure and from revolutionaries at the same time. A single newsletter from that time mentions both a 32-page letter from a government official criticizing OLYC's after-school feeding program, and threats of violence from political agitators in the neighborhood.

The government letter complained about the menu, sanitation, cooking standards, and numerous other problems, and according to the newsletter, the writer of the letter "went to various people around town distributing her accusations." All the volunteer cooks and dishwashers left as a result. The newsletter doesn't make the outcome clear or explain the exact status of the complaint, but the feeding program continued. "There is no other feeding program comparable to ours in a radius of many miles," Father Thomas wrote.

As to the threats of violence, he referred cryptically to "my personal efforts to work against this very vicious and dangerous movement. (You can understand why I can't be more explicit in this letter.)" Years later he said the radicals – a communist group – couldn't get any traction in South El Paso because of the work OLYC was able to do for the poor. "The youth center was an obstacle."

One Friday afternoon late in 1969, Father Thomas was called to an alley three blocks from OLYC and found a woman with five children and a meager load of furniture, setting up camp there because she had been evicted for falling four months behind in her rent. OLYC workers had been trying to find her a new place to live, without success. Father Thomas called in a local TV station to film the family's new "home" in the alley, and took some still pictures himself to publish in the newspapers; he also talked the landlady into letting the family back in for the weekend, while he planned to get them into one of 173 federal public housing apartments being kept vacant despite a huge waiting list.

The weekend stretched into a week as the landlady fumed and officials gave Father Thomas the runaround. The following Monday was the deadline for legal eviction; "Mrs. ____ was completely entrapped by the law," Father Thomas wrote in a newsletter. "The law evicting her from her apartment, the law not allowing her to set up furniture and family in the alley, and the law not allowing her into public housing. Nor was there any private housing to which she could go; she couldn't possibly continue to live on Monday morning without violating some law."

By Thursday he had decided to build the family a shack next to the vacant public housing. That threat got the attention of the mayor (not to mention the chief of police), and the mayor made a few phone calls. Father Thomas was told the woman could move into the public housing, but there were further hassles and the threat of a phone call to George Romney, secretary of housing and urban development in Washington, before the family was finally moved into public housing at 4 p.m. Friday, a week after her original eviction. "Thank God she got a home and I didn't have to go to jail for building her a shack on public property," Father Thomas wrote in the newsletter. "They probably put her ahead of somebody," he said years later.

Woman evicted with her five children and all their furniture, in the alley near OLYC, 1969.

Yet another battle over housing came in early 1970. Living quarters in South El Paso were still atrocious; in a newsletter Father Thomas described a tenement three blocks from OLYC in which about 600 people lived in half a square block. In the meantime, the federal government planned to spend $15 million on what is now the Border Highway along the Rio Grande. In protest, Father Thomas had 6,000 lapel pins made. Half were in Spanish and said "*Casa sí, camino no*" (houses yes, highway no), and the other half in English, saying "Damn red tape, housing now." He wrote another song, too; lyrics included "We need houses more than a highway." He lost that battle.

There was a happier story in December 1970, but even that incident had its share of trouble and controversy. Gisella O'Neil of Hyannis Port, Mass., a fashion designer and supporter of Jesuit missionary work, read an article by Father Thomas in *The Jesuit* magazine about the work of OLYC, and organized a drive for food, clothing and medical supplies, entitled Operation We Care. She started with 10 Catholic parishes, but the news media picked up the story, and Protestant and Jewish groups on Cape Cod joined in. When the drive was done, the New Hampshire National Guard flew the 20-ton shipment to El Paso, where it was unloaded by soldiers from Fort Bliss and welcomed by El Paso Mayor Peter de Wetter, who made Mrs. O'Neil an honorary citizen of El Paso. The supplies were distributed to the needy in El Paso and Juárez, half on each side of the border.

To Father Thomas's astonishment, this obvious feel-good story brought in as much criticism as it did praise, in the media and on radio talk shows. Pickets turned up at OLYC the afternoon of Jan. 4 and returned daily for a week. Some of the complaints were from poverty activists who believed they should have been allowed to handle the distribution; others were from people who didn't think any of the goods should have gone to Juárez, although Mrs. O'Neil had intended them for use at Father Thomas's discretion on both sides of the border.

"We're glad of the opposition because it proves we're doing God's work," Father Thomas wrote in one newsletter. In another, he wrote, "a lot of people are concerned about how I am taking all this. I tell them I am full of peace and joy, feeding the very hungry, clothing the ragged poor, educating the illiterate, finding jobs for the unemployed, getting medical help for the sick and the aged. So you know I am happy." One good outcome of the Operation We Care controversy, he noted, was that one local citizen started a successful drive for blankets and warm clothing after several people in South El Paso died during a cold spell at the beginning of January.

Father Thomas worked within the power structure, too, whenever he could. At various times in the 1960s he served on the board of directors of the El Paso chapter of the National Conference of Christians and Jews; as a member of the El Paso Citizens Committee for Decent Literature, working to get obscene magazines out of the hands of young people and restricted to under-the-counter sales to adults; as a member of the Optimists service club; on the board of the General Assistance Agency, which supervised El Paso County's welfare program; and as chair of the South Central Area Council. At one point he had his own radio slot on local station KROD.

Meanwhile, all the time the War on Poverty was going on, the United States was fighting a real shooting war, in Vietnam. It was one of the hottest political issues of the 60s, and huge numbers of draft-age Americans believed it was an unjust war. One of them was Rubén García. Today García is director of Annunciation House, an El Paso shelter for undocumented immigrants; in 1969 he was a brand-new graduate of the Jesuit-run Rockhurst University in Kansas City, and had just returned to his native city to work at OLYC.

It was at OLYC that García put in his claim as a conscientious objector under the draft law, and Father Thomas helped him with his application, on more than one level. "We had many conversations about that," said García: whether it's possible to oppose war, how a Christian can live in the world when confronted with violence, what Catholic teaching has to say on the subject. Father Thomas didn't explicitly support García's position, but he did support his right to take it, and wrote the draft board a letter on his behalf. He also warned him to be ready for plenty of trouble: El Paso had three military bases at the time plus a strong military tradition, so conscientious objection wasn't necessarily a popular or easy position to take. "You're a voice in the wilderness, Rubén, and there aren't going to be a lot of people speaking out for you."

García believes most wars are unjust, including the First World War and the Korean War; he said the Second World War would come closest to the status of a just war. That wasn't good enough for the local draft board, which turned down his application. But Father Thomas knew one of the board members personally and arranged for García to meet the man. García asked him why he had been turned down and the man replied, "I don't believe there is such a thing as a Catholic conscientious objector." What would it take to convince him? "A letter from the Pope prohibiting you from serving in the military if your conscience opposes it."

That isn't the law – members of any denomination can qualify as conscientious objectors on the basis of their individual religious consciences – and García's lawyer asked him for a memo on the meeting, then took it to the state director of Selective Service, who sent it to Washington for a ruling. García won his case and did alternative service rather than going into the army. The draft board member wasn't too happy with that outcome; he had thought the one-on-one meeting was confidential, although nobody had actually promised that.

"I never asked him [Father Thomas] if he got any flak for setting up that meeting," García said.

CHAPTER 20

A Ministry in Crisis

"**S**o you know I am happy." Happy to be helping the poor. That's what Father Thomas told his supporters, and it was the truth – as far as it went. He certainly wouldn't have been happy doing anything else.

But in a lot of ways, he was frustrated and unhappy. Unhappy about the results of his work. Unhappy over the constant uphill battle to get a little cooperation from his outside associates, his co-workers, the Church, even his own religious community. Unhappy, above all, at the sheer human misery he saw every day.

Most months, the Anything-a-Month Club newsletter was crammed to narrow margins with typing, plus maybe a photo or two. But March 1969, was different. The 8½ -by-11 newsletter was mostly white space. There was nothing much to write about. Here's the complete text:

> Dear friend, the special letter by a guest writer that I planned to send you this month did not materialize.
>
> I might have told you about the progress we made at summer camp planting trees and grass, but we have gotten neither pump nor electricity to our new well. Hence no planting.
>
> I had hoped to find some religious men and/or women to work with the poor here. That has failed, too.

> It would be nice to tell you about our volunteer leaders working with the Girl Scouts, Cadettes and Brownies, but they have all quit months ago.
>
> Please pray for us during Lent. We still plan to win.

Rick Thomas took poverty personally. He was never satisfied that anybody was doing enough about it – including himself. And there was never any shortage of reminders that everybody's efforts were falling short.

Just a few weeks after he got to El Paso, he paid a visit to a tenement where he met a mother with four children. Two of the children were naked, there was no food in the household, and the baby was drinking sugar water because the mother had no milk. He invited them all to OLYC for food and other services.

It wouldn't be the last story like that, and nowhere near the worst. His diary, the newsletter, OLYC's newspaper clipping scrapbooks, and his own end-of-life reminiscences are loaded with references to the desperation he saw on the streets every day.

In January 1967, three children, aged 4 to 7, died in a tenement fire two blocks from Sacred Heart. OLYC coordinated relief efforts for the surviving members of the family. Investigators found seven building code violations in the building, though none of the violations actually caused the fire; it started when a gas heater ignited nearby bedding.

In February of the same year, under the headline "South E.P. Slums Likely to Blow Up," the El Paso Herald-Post reported on a UTEP seminar on housing. The picture was grim: everything from broken stairways and toilets without lights ("at night you light matches to see your way around") to high rates of unemployment, infant death and tuberculosis. The city had a choice, one speaker warned: peaceful improvements today or violence tomorrow.

One night later that year Father Thomas and Father Edmundo Rodríguez, a new Jesuit priest assigned to OLYC for his tertianship, discovered some boys trying to sleep in the center's dumpster. Another time Father Rodríguez found about a dozen youngsters sleeping on the Sacred Heart rectory roof; they had climbed up on the drainpipes. The two priests offered them food and showers at OLYC, and soon they were attracting about 80 street kids, mostly illegal immigrants from Juárez.

Father Thomas told one heart-wrenching story about a wedding at Sacred Heart in 1971. Those were the days when wedding guests threw rice at the couple as they left the church, and after the wedding party was gone, two young boys and an elderly woman squatted down and gathered the rice up off the sidewalk with their hands. "It was pitiful and yet wonderful to watch the smile of gladness on the lady's face as she scraped together the precious food mixed with sand," he wrote. "A prospector finding gold nuggets in his pan could not have been more thrilled."

Then there was the death of a homeless man named Carlos in 1969. Carlos died of cold and exposure in a tenement a block from Sacred Heart rectory, in a bathroom stall "not much bigger than a coffin." Father Thomas found out about it three days later. He told the story in a blistering, shame-filled newsletter, and sent a copy to every Jesuit in the New Orleans province, along with an additional letter addressed just to the Jesuits.

Carlos died, Father Thomas wrote in the newsletter, because "his 'neighbors' were too busy to do what Jesus said we must do to save ourselves from eternal fire." In the letter to the Jesuits, he said "the poor and the middle class or rich have a mutual need for each other. The poor need the rich: their money, their initiative, their education. The rich need the poor because there is no other way for them to go to heaven."

The problem, he said, was that the Jesuits of the province had the arrangement all wrong: they were mainly working with the middle class and the wealthy, but Jesus was more interested in the poor.

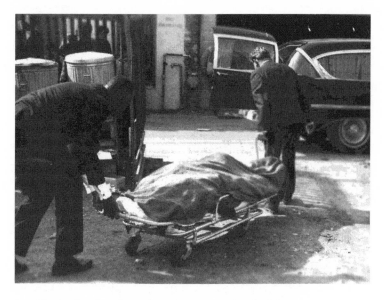

The body of Carlos, a homeless man who died from exposure
to the cold near Sacred Heart rectory, 1969.

"May I recommend multiple, prolonged visits to your city's
slums," he said to his brother priests. "I say multiple and prolonged because until one gets on a first-name basis with more
than one family, he won't begin to absorb their attitudes and
comprehend their true needs."

From the time of his arrival in El Paso, Father Thomas strug-
gled to find ways to fix the desperate poverty of the 25,000 people wedged into the filthy tenements of *Segundo Barrio*. His
work was a series of triumphs and frustrations for himself. It also
did a lot to annoy some people, in the community and even in
the Church.

His war on poverty started with himself. Helen Guajardo remembered that any personal gifts he might get, like money for
new shoes or a coat, got passed on to the Anything-a-Month Club
to help the poor.

Rickie Feuille, who served for years as president of the OLYC
board of directors, recalled that his wife, Louann, once saw

Father Thomas walking in a rare El Paso snowfall in shoes so worn, his socks showed through. She bought him a new pair, but when she ran into him again two weeks later, there he was wearing the old ones. He had given the new shoes to a barefoot man. "He needed them a lot worse than I did," he told her.

For a while, his housing was a lot more comfortable than his shoes. For his first six years in El Paso, he lived in the rectory at Sacred Heart, where he had the title of assistant pastor and lived with other Jesuits. It was not a happy fit, and eventually he decided living in a rectory was part of the problem – not just for himself but for the poor.

"Dick did not get along well with other Jesuits," recalled Father Rodríguez, who also lived at Sacred Heart during the year he spent in El Paso, 1967-68. "I think up to then, I was the only Jesuit who was able to work with him, because I had many ideas which he liked and also because I was willing to take on almost any task he wanted done. He was very committed to the poor and seemed to feel that the other Jesuits were not."

In fairness, Father Rodríguez noted, the Sacred Heart pastor at the time, Father Bob Gafford, was a man who worked tirelessly himself to help the poor, and as the local Jesuit superior, he did nothing to interfere with Father Thomas's projects. But Father Dick McGowan, another Jesuit who worked with Father Thomas (1971-72), said Father Thomas and Father Gafford still didn't get along very well. Other Jesuits at the parish could be an even bigger problem, Father Rodríguez said – especially priests from Spain and Italy who also lived at Sacred Heart.

"Dick [Thomas] and I were priests of the streets," Father Rodríguez said. "I would often say Mass in one of the *presidios* [tenements]. And Dick and I would walk around and talk to construction workers and other street people." But the house minister (second in command), an Italian priest, "told me that I should not be going out into the *barrios* but that I should wait in the rectory for people to come to me."

At the end of his life, Father Thomas remembered the dumpster incident as a turning point. As he recalled it, the boys weren't willing to go to an orphanage that Father Rodríguez contacted in Juárez, so the two priests allowed them to sleep in the Jesuit car they were using.

The boys spent several nights in the car and went about their own adventures during the day. Then another Jesuit noticed the smell, and that was the end of the arrangement.

"We had to call the whole thing off because they stunk the car up, and we [Jesuits] weren't going to get involved," Father Thomas recalled.

Father Thomas got frustrated by the restrictions on how he could use his living space. He was still frustrated in 1969 when he was trying to help the woman in the alley (see chapter 19), and he wrote about it in the newsletter at the time: "I did some real soul searching and wished that our order's rules would permit me to let the family have my own room."

Eventually, he said years later, "it became clear you can't do what you're supposed to do and live in one of these [Jesuit] houses. It became clear to me that the Society [of Jesus] wasn't going to do anything, and so I began to find lay individuals who would do something, and that's what I've been trying to do it ever since – get lay people to do what we [Jesuits] won't do."

Father Thomas in his simple bedroom at Sacred Heart rectory, 1969.

CHAPTER 21

Always a Jesuit

Father Thomas's relationship with the Society of Jesus was a complicated one throughout his time in the priesthood. He had only become a Jesuit in the first place because it was the first option he was offered at a time when he didn't want to be a priest at all. And from at least the time he arrived in El Paso, he was what Jesuits call a "lone ranger" – a Jesuit who operates his ministry on his own, with little connection to the Jesuit community.

That's not necessarily bad, said Father Mark Lewis, a former New Orleans provincial superior of the society. "The first lone ranger was St. Francis Xavier. It's not particularly frowned upon. It's just a different way of being a Jesuit." Nonetheless, it can lead to misunderstandings. Father Thomas eventually became convinced, rightly or wrongly, that he was not welcome at certain Jesuit gatherings, and some of his fellow Jesuits believed he wasn't obedient enough to attend if asked.

The "not obedient" part was certainly wrong; if he was ordered to attend a meeting, he went, even if some of his fellow Jesuits seemed surprised to see him. The OLYC ministry was not closely supervised by the Society, and both sides seemed to like it that way, said Father McGowan; "Dick was not really under anybody." But he was upright, scandal-free, and doing good work, and the provincials who visited knew that and let him be, without inspecting the operation too closely. Father Thomas always obeyed actual orders; he later attributed a major development in his ministry, the acquisition of the Lord's Ranch, to his willingness to obey an order that went directly against his own convictions (see chapter 35). He even told Father McGowan he would leave OLYC instantly if ordered by his provincial.

But more significantly, Father Thomas was immersed to his core in the spiritual teachings of the founder of the Society of Jesus, St. Ignatius Loyola. Many decades later, Nathan O'Halloran, who grew up in the OLYC community in daily contact with Father Thomas, joined the Jesuits himself; he said he was constantly astonished, as he studied for the priesthood, to find out how much of what Father Thomas had taught him – his love of poverty, his method of prayer, his love of Scripture, his focus on children – was taken from the teachings of St. Ignatius.

"He lived out Ignatian spirituality perfectly," Father O'Halloran said. And while Father Thomas never said a word to push his young protégé either toward or away from the Society, Father O'Halloran said, "all my desire to be a Jesuit came from watching him. I just couldn't imagine being anything other than what Father Thomas was."

With Nathan O'Halloran on the day Nathan took his first vows
in the Society of Jesus, Grand Coteau, Louisiana, 2005.

CHAPTER 22

Moving Out of the Rectory

In the late 60s, Father Thomas made up his mind to get out of "these houses" as soon as he was allowed, and eventually he got the chance. His own memory was a bit hazy on the exact date, but according to his office calendar, the big move came on Jan. 19, 1970. Nino Aguilera, a prominent volunteer at OLYC, asked him to live with some youngsters who didn't have a home, and his Jesuit provincial gave the approval, so he moved into a two-bedroom apartment on South Ochoa, half a dozen blocks from Sacred Heart.

It was a first try, and it didn't work out particularly well, because Father Thomas left for work early in the morning and usually came home late at night, so there wasn't a lot of interaction with the youngsters. "It gave them a house, but it didn't give them a home, because I wasn't there."

So that arrangement collapsed, but he still had permission to live away from the rectory. Within a few months he moved on, to an old house on St. Vrain Street, on the northern edge of *Segundo Barrio*. The tiny backyard caught a lot of sun, and for the first time in a while, Father Thomas got a chance to be a country boy again. He dug up the yard for irrigation and planted it in vegetables for the poor.

Soon Bert Hernández, a ministry volunteer from a nearby parish who was also a political activist, joined Father Thomas in the house. The two jogged through the streets half an hour every morning for exercise, as the neighbors watched. "They kind of kept their schedule by Father," Hernández said.

Indoors, the house was as simple as Father Thomas could make it. The two men slept on army cots. "He just had it set up very humbly," said Hernández. "Our heads were in trying to do something. We didn't really care about anything, other than having a roof over our heads."

One day Hernández came home to find the door locked. He'd forgotten his key, so he knocked on the door. And kept on knocking. He tried the back door – nothing. Finally, worried that Father Thomas might be ill, he called the police, but they found Father Thomas sound asleep and perfectly fine.

"You called the *police* on me, Bert?" Father Thomas teased the young activist.

Eventually Hernández and Father Thomas went off in different directions but stayed on good terms. "He really loved the Lord and the Lord's people," Hernández said. "In the Church, you see a lot of nonsense, and then you see a guy like him. It's really refreshing."

Next stop, in 1971, was a former private Catholic school on South Oregon, near today's El Paso-Los Angeles bus terminal. Father Dick McGowan arrived in town to work with Father Thomas and got the job of fixing the building up to house two dozen volunteers for a Jesuit summer project in the neighborhood. They called it *Casa Grande* (big house). Father McGowan installed a swamp cooler (a low-tech, low-cost substitute for air conditioning that uses evaporation) so that the volunteers could cool off a little when they finished a day's work, but he said Father Thomas thought that was an unnecessary indulgence. When the volunteer project ended, Father Thomas, Father McGowan, Father Al Mills and a couple of other Jesuits continued to live at *Casa Grande* until the diocese kicked them out to use the building as a drug rehabilitation center.

Now where? The men asked themselves. There was a housing shortage at the time, and they didn't want to rent a place in the neighborhood and take it away from somebody with more need and less money. So instead they moved into the OLYC building. It suited Father Thomas perfectly, but Father McGowan and Mills (later laicized) were still shaking their heads about the experience more than four decades later.

The priests set up cots in the hall. Father Thomas offered Father McGowan the cot in his office and said he himself would sleep on the floor under the cot; the office was too small for side-by-side cots. No thanks, said Father McGowan, and took a spot in the hall. Father Mills was in the storeroom; "this is what Jesus would want," Father Thomas told him. The men were to take turns cooking. "I had never cooked in my life," Mills said.

Father McGowan had to put up with the Boy Scouts trooping through the hall near his cot, but he wouldn't put up with the broken glass and rats in the basement where they were supposed to shower. He showered at the YMCA. Father Thomas, who took sponge baths in a basin, didn't approve. "He thought it was a luxurious indulgence. I thought it was basic health care."

After a few months, the other Jesuits gave up on the experiment and rented a house north of the freeway, some distance from the neighborhood. It was a pretty simple place, said Father McGowan, but again Father Thomas didn't approve. "He thought we were living high on the hog." "You deserted the poor," he told his fellow Jesuits after his one and only trip to the new house for a dinner invitation. "I told him the poor don't know where we sleep and they don't care."

Living at OLYC was no failed experiment from Father Thomas's point of view, though. He had found a long-term home. He stayed there full time into the mid-70s and part time into the late 80s, sleeping on the army cot in his office and refusing all offers to make his living quarters more comfortable. In the winter, he even heated his long johns or his blankets in the oven to keep warm and turned down anybody who wanted to give him an electric blanket. One of the people who offered, later on, was Frank Alarcón, who led the ministry to the people who lived at the Juárez municipal dump (see chapter 34). "Do the people at the dump have electric blankets?" Father Thomas demanded.

Father McGowan said Jesuits tend to adopt the lifestyle of the people they work with, but Father Thomas took that policy to extremes. "He always compared anything we proposed to do to what the people in the neighborhood were able to do." He even disapproved of Father McGowan's Karmann-Ghia, a sporty but not particularly expensive Volkswagen model.

"I don't think it was just religious asceticism," said Father McGowan. "Some of it was just his personality. He wasn't interested in those things."

Whatever the reason, Father Thomas never thought he had gone far enough. Years later an interviewer asked him how he could live so simply. His answer: "I don't know that I'm living simply yet."

One benefit of the move to OLYC, Helen Guajardo recalled, is that it cut down on break-ins. But it also led to a few unexpected adventures for Father Thomas.

Once, coming in late on a Saturday night, he was headed upstairs in the dark, looking for a light switch that was some distance from the door. "I took one step and stepped on something and it moved. Man, I screamed. Then I was jumping up and down to get away from this thing I was stepping on. I couldn't see anything. I was screaming bloody murder."

He managed to reach the switch, and the light revealed a drunk man on the floor, just as scared as he was. He had been sleeping; Father Thomas guessed he had been visiting the Tepeyac credit union, passed out in the bathroom, and gotten locked in when nobody noticed him there. Father Thomas let him out.

"It was the most scared I ever was in my life," he said laughing.

Another time at OLYC, Father Thomas had to sleep across the entrance door because the lock was broken. He tied up his dog Mar, a fierce-looking German shepherd, on the porch on a short rope. A passerby noticed the door was ajar and called the police, who turned up, two in a cruiser, and asked him his business. "I said 'I live here. This is my home.' He said 'come out.' I said 'you come in here.' We went around and around a bit." Eventually the police left.

Reading Scripture in his office, 1969.

CHAPTER 23

Baptized in the Holy Spirit

For Rick Thomas, the job at OLYC was never just about alleviating poverty. It was about bringing life to the people he served. And "life" meant God, even more than it meant food or shelter. So, as unhappy as he was about the physical poverty of South El Paso, he was even more upset about the spiritual poverty. The "God" part wasn't happening, for the most part, and he was desperate to find a way to make his priesthood meaningful. By 1969, his co-worker Jean Soto remembered him testifying, he was just barely clinging to his priesthood. The men in his family lived a long time, and he didn't know how he could carry on into old age.

"Can I hang on till death? That was my thought," he said years later. "Can I hang on until I die?"

But late that year, he found the answer: a new spirituality known today as the Catholic charismatic renewal. It didn't come a moment too soon.

"People would say 'you're doing a good job at the Youth Center,'" he said years later. "That might be, but I knew deep down that there was nobody being touched in any significant way. I'd be asked to say a prayer for this group or say Mass for that group or help children make their first Communion, but there wasn't the lasting fruit that I would have hoped to have been associated

133

with as a priest." He wondered, he said, "why there was so little vitality in the teaching or practice of Christianity."

He had been trying for a long time to find ways to fill the gap. Aida Frietze-Lewis, an OLYC volunteer, remembered some of his training programs from around this time. The sessions, some of them lasting all day, were based on a popularized version of the *Spiritual Exercises* of Jesuit founder St. Ignatius of Loyola, and staff members and volunteers would kneel before the image of Our Lady of Guadalupe and commit themselves to her. "He was searching for a way to add a spiritual mission to the social emphasis without losing the social outreach," she said. He also explored other programs in the Church; Father Rodríguez remembered him looking into the Movement for a Better World, a pastoral program for Church and society founded in 1952 by the Jesuit Father Riccardo Lombardi at the request of Pope Pius XII. But as of 1969 he hadn't found anything that met his needs, and it was beginning to wear him down.

"I thought Dick was very intent on finding a silver bullet which would convert the poor and draw them out of poverty," said Father Rodríguez. "Dick seemed to think that if he could learn something which would engage people body and soul, emotions, will, intellect, and imagination, they could be turned into holier, more industrious, more balanced persons. He was searching. I guess he eventually landed on the charismatic renewal as the closest he came to such a 'silver bullet.'"

In a nutshell, the charismatic renewal is based on the belief that speaking in tongues and other visible manifestations of the Holy Spirit, as seen in chapter 2 of the New Testament book of Acts and chapter 14 of First Corinthians, did not die in the early decades of Christianity, but continue to be valid and available down to our own time. The rediscovery of this belief in modern times is usually traced to the founding of the Pentecostal churches around 1900; it hit more mainstream Protestant denominations in the early 1960s and came into the Catholic

Church in 1967, and as Father Thomas found, speaking in tongues is the least of it. The Holy Spirit can revolutionize an entire ministry by running it on God's power instead of human power.

Not many Catholics knew about the charismatic renewal yet in 1969. One of the few was Father Thomas's old seminary friend and hiking buddy, Father Harold ("Abie") Cohen. Father Cohen was teaching at Loyola University in New Orleans when he heard about the renewal and experienced what Catholics call "baptism in the Holy Spirit." He started holding charismatic prayer meetings at Loyola and other locations; he was a leading figure in the renewal until his death in 2001. He wrote Father Thomas several letters talking up this new movement of the Holy Spirit.

Coming up on Christmas 1969, Father Thomas got called to New Orleans on Jesuit business. He ran into Father Cohen at Loyola and asked if he could attend one of those prayer meetings. Sure enough, there was one scheduled, but it conflicted with a committee meeting Father Thomas had to attend; Father Cohen told him to feel free to come late to the prayer meeting, and he did – so late the prayer meeting was over and only four or five people, all nuns except for Father Cohen, were still on hand.

One of the nuns was Sister Mary Virginia Clark, a 43-year-old Daughter of Charity from St. Louis, stationed for a year in New Orleans. Sister Mary Virginia would later spend 17 years as Father Thomas's chief co-worker in El Paso (see chapter 27), but at the time what she was mainly thinking about was getting home by her curfew. "I had no idea I would ever be working with him at all."

She was on her way out the door, but Father Cohen asked her to stay long enough to help pray over Father Thomas for baptism in the Holy Spirit. "He told me, 'This guy loves the poor,'" she recalled years later. "I remember thinking, 'Gee, this guy is skinny. But he loves the poor, and won't the poor be happy to get this."

Father Thomas showed up at the meeting with a severe headache; he was ready for prayer, but not for anything else, and when Father Cohen tried to read him the passage about reviving the dry bones in Ezekiel 37, Father Thomas cut him off. "My head was pounding, pom, pom, pom, pom. I said, 'Abie, I don't want to hear all that. Just shoot it to me.' Whatever it was, I wanted it, and [then I wanted] to go to bed.

"So they prayed. Nothing happened. I went outside hoping that Abie would hurry up and take me where I was going to spend the night." The headache wasn't healed, either. Father Cohen drove him back to his quarters and he went to bed right away.

"I went to sleep. But in the middle of the night I woke up and I found myself in deep prayer, and it startled me, because I hadn't prayed like that in years. And there were no preliminaries – I just woke up in the middle of profound prayer. I noticed it when I got back to El Paso, that it was very easy for me to pray, and it had not been easy before."

It was a gift he never lost. He also got another gift he needed just as much: an energy boost. That, too, was lasting. "I can do more in a day now than I could have done in a year before," he said 30 years later. "I was never a lazy person, but now there's a power and effectiveness that wasn't there before."

Other gifts took longer. He didn't pray in tongues, the best-known trademark of the charismatic renewal, for years, and other things came to him in God's good time.

"It wasn't like being in the dark and having the stadium lights go on," he said. "It was a gradual experience."

CHAPTER 24

Trying It at Home

He was due to fly back to El Paso the morning after the prayer meeting. Father Cohen drove him to the airport and handed him four pamphlets on the charismatic renewal. One of the pamphlets was about prayer meetings. When Father Thomas got home, he showed it to Tula Irróbali, and the two of them decided to use it as a format for the usual OLYC Christmastime staff retreat, which was coming up soon.

The pamphlets didn't give much direction. There was no instruction on standard charismatic subjects like speaking in tongues, or even baptism in the Spirit. The pamphlets just said to read Scripture, sing songs and serve coffee afterward. "We thought the coffee was an essential part of it."

Only four or five people attended the retreat, at a cloistered convent where they drove each day, and none of them had ever been present for a prayer meeting or knew anything about the charismatic gifts. Father Thomas and Tula didn't tell them the event was a charismatic prayer meeting.

"All we'd do was sit in a circle and somebody would read a Scripture," Father Thomas said. "We knew four songs." The songs included "*De Colores*," a not-especially-charismatic song associated with the *Cursillo* movement – "nothing to do with anything," he said later – and "*Bendito*," a lyrical Spanish-language praise song still popular in the OLYC community. "Nothing unusual happened, but everybody was happy with the experience."

Then, as Lent approached in 1970, Father Thomas got word that Father Cohen was coming to town, and he scheduled a prayer meeting at Our Lady's Youth Center. The date, to judge from not particularly clear notes in Father Thomas's calendar for the year, was probably Feb. 10, the day before Ash Wednesday.

Father Cohen arrived with two friends from Arizona and led the meeting. One of the visitors from Arizona gave a prophecy, which charismatics believe is a word from God directed to the meeting. Father Thomas didn't know what a prophecy was. "It took me a while to catch on," he said. "I didn't know anything about anything. Nothing, nothing, nothing, nothing."

But he was about to learn the one thing he needed to know most about the Holy Spirit.

Father Thomas promised parents he would always take their children home after OLYC events, and at the end of the meeting, there were two high school boys who needed to get home and do their homework. As he headed out the door with the boys, he saw a teenage girl sitting on a bench outside the meeting room. "What are you doing here?" he asked. "I'm waiting for my sister," she answered. "Why not go inside and get her?" he responded, and went off to drive the boys home.

The girl on the bench was 17-year-old Isabel Beltrán; her sister Josefina, 14, was inside the meeting. Isabel took Father Thomas at his word and went into the meeting room. The meeting was finished, but Mrs. Tula greeted her and said "come on, Isabel, let us pray for you. Something wonderful is happening." What was happening was that one of the visitors from Arizona had already prayed over Josefina, and now a group – Isabel didn't see how many, but it included both the Tulas – began to pray for Isabel.

"I just got the gift of tongues," she said. "It was an outburst. I couldn't stop it. Everybody was very happy. I was filled with the Holy Spirit. I felt the difference. It was a beautiful feeling. I knew something good had happened.

"I knew that I was a Catholic, and I went through all the rituals of the Catholic Church. I attended regularly, but I didn't experience anything out of the ordinary. I just went to church because my parents went to church. It wasn't until I was baptized in the Holy Spirit that Jesus became real to me."

Somebody gave her a Bible, since she didn't have one at home, and from that moment she had an urge to read it. She had no problem understanding it, and she had a photographic memory so she could remember many passages.

Meanwhile, Father Thomas had a shock waiting for him.

"When I came back into the room after taking these boys home, about 10 minutes lapse in time, both these girls had got the gift of tongues and were speaking in tongues, but I didn't know what was going on."

"The next day some of the staff said, 'do you know what happened to the two sisters?' I said 'no, what happened?' 'Well, we don't know, but something happened to them.' All week long I heard these rumors about the two sisters, and what had happened to the two sisters."

Come Saturday, Father Thomas finally had time to visit the sisters at home, a few blocks from OLYC. Isabel greeted him at the door. He asked her what she was doing. "Reading the Bible," she answered. He asked about Josefina; she was somewhere else in the apartment, also reading the Bible. He invited them back to his office at OLYC. "I said, now you tell me everything that's happened to you since the other night."

When they got home from the prayer meeting, she told him, "a strange noise kept coming out of our mouth all night." It happened at school, too, whenever their classes got boring. They had also started going to Mass daily.

Then the sisters had some questions for him. "When I got through all the questions I had, they said, 'now Fr. Thomas, explain to us what happened.' I said, 'I don't know what happened.' They said, 'didn't they teach you that in the seminary?' I said 'no, they didn't.'

"I didn't know what had happened, but I knew God had acted. The Lord used this to get my attention to be respectful of whatever He wanted to do. From that moment I got very respectful. I told God, I don't know what You're doing, but that doesn't make any difference," Father Thomas said years later. "You do what You want and I'll cooperate. I still have that attitude."

"Once we give God permission, God begins to do all kinds of things. We let Him do whatever He wants, and He does incredible things."

Father Thomas had found his answers: the answer to the problem of spiritual fruit in the OLYC ministries, the answer to the problem of personal survival in the priesthood.

"It was God that was going to take him to whatever age God wished," said Jean Soto.

Inviting the Holy Spirit would change the OLYC ministries in far-reaching ways over the coming years. Some of the changes were visible immediately. Aida Frietze-Lewis said OLYC workers continued to make social outreach visits, "but we weren't just visiting, we were praying.

"I could tell whatever Father had been looking for in the other meetings, he had found."

CHAPTER 25

Learning on the Job

Now that Father Thomas had his answer, he ran with it. Charismatic prayer meetings got going right away at OLYC. Soon there were two prayer meetings a week at OLYC: Tuesday for youth, Wednesday for adults. Then the two nights switched. Then the Tuesday meeting was cancelled altogether, and the adults were invited to join the young people on Wednesday – still the OLYC prayer meeting night more than four decades later.

"The adults were dead," Father Thomas said, "and so we said we're going to forget Tuesday and have it all Wednesday and hope the youth will crank up the adults. It's been on Wednesday ever since." Some prayer meetings were also held in tenement backyards, and later on Sundays at Camp Juan Diego.

When he retold the story years later, Father Thomas said he and his friends learned how to conduct meetings mainly from Bible study, and put what they learned into practice, but very slowly. "It's like introducing anything new. You don't start off at full speed. You do what you can, little by little, until you can do what you're supposed to do."

Father Thomas apparently saw himself as alone in El Paso as a Catholic charismatic leader, at least at first. "There wasn't anybody around to talk to," he recalled near the end of his life. "No

Catholics, and a few non-Catholics, but the non-Catholics I didn't trust because they wanted me to leave the Church. I just had to learn from my observations."

Eventually he discovered Catholic charismatic meetings at Loretto Academy, a Catholic school in what was then a middle-class Anglo neighborhood about three miles from OLYC and began attending them. The meeting was organized by local residents Paul and Laurie Bross. The Brosses had been baptized in the Spirit in a prayer group in Albuquerque, at the invitation of friends there. They couldn't find a Catholic charismatic prayer group in El Paso, so they began holding meetings in their home. Soon the meetings outgrew the house, but the Sisters of Loretto heard about the renewal and offered free use of their library for the meetings, apparently around the same time the OLYC meetings were getting started.

Father Thomas began attending the Loretto meetings about a month after they started and was one of a number of priests who celebrated Mass, but Paul Bross said he otherwise played a low-key role, so low that Paul was unaware at the time that Father Thomas had any charismatic background apart from Loretto. "He never showed any of the characteristics of someone who was in the Spirit," Paul said. "He was more of a curious observer. My impression is that he was trying to figure out what was causing all this. He was a part of it, wanted to be a part of it, but he couldn't give himself over entirely to it." He hardly ever asked questions; even when the Brosses invited him to their home and became good personal friends, the only thing he asked was how Paul had first gotten involved in the renewal.

Early on, Father Thomas began taking youth from OLYC to the meetings. The Tulas attended too. Frank Alarcón, later to be one of Father Thomas's chief co-workers in Juárez, first met him at Loretto, as did Joanne Ivey, who would later help found a separate Catholic charismatic ministry, Open Arms, still flourishing today.

As time went on, it was clear to the Brosses that Father Thomas had come to regard the meetings as genuine. He invited the Brosses to lead a prayer meeting at OLYC, which they did, and eventually began to urge them to help out at OLYC and concentrate more on South El Paso. They did a certain amount of this – for one thing, they turned up to offer moral support at a public meeting when Father Thomas was under criticism for his handling of the shipment of food and supplies from Massachusetts (see chapter 19) – but soon it got to be more than they could handle.

"He was inundating us," said Paul, who had a full-time job with irregular hours, doing often-urgent phone maintenance work which included nearby Fort Bliss. "I told him, I can't do all this. I can only do what I can do."

The Loretto meetings ended about two years later, for a variety of reasons.

Prayer meeting at OLYC – Fr. Thomas giving a teaching while Fr. Sam Rosales translates into Spanish, 1980.

CHAPTER 26

Prayer Meetings at OLYC

A ida Frietze-Lewis remembered her first time at the weekly prayer meeting at OLYC. She didn't really come for the meeting; she came to make an announcement. She was planning a pilgrimage to make the Stations of the Cross in the desert and was getting the word out to Catholic groups she had known. When she came to OLYC, she was invited to speak about the pilgrimage at the prayer meeting.

When she got there, she found herself in the midst of 2½ hours of Scripture, praise and singing: "so much singing – more than we had ever done – and all different ages. Wall to wall people." If there was speaking in tongues, she didn't notice. At the end of the meeting, Mrs. Tula invited people into another room for ministry. Frietze-Lewis forgot her own announcement. Mr. Tula was giving a presentation on baptism in the Spirit and the joy it had brought into his own life. Frietze-Lewis was ready to believe it when she saw the Tulas, Father Thomas, and other people she was familiar with in the room, eager expressions on their faces. "They just looked different."

Then she was invited to sit for prayer for baptism in the Spirit, had an overwhelming experience of the Holy Spirit, and began attending prayer meetings, until she left for Europe a few months later.

Jean Soto remembered 50 to 75 people attending the early prayer meetings, about 90 per cent of them Hispanic. There was singing, spontaneous prayer, and exercise of the gifts of the Holy Spirit: tongues, prophecy, word of knowledge. Sometimes there was prayer for the sick, or other intentions as requested. Deliverance ministry was offered, too, in private if necessary; Soto said Father Thomas was "the soul of discretion. There were never any slips about someone's personal condition or affairs. It just never happened." Always there was a Mass, and Father Thomas would preach. The meetings would last about three hours, sometimes more.

At one meeting, Father Thomas was asked the purpose of the charismatic renewal. He said that "the purpose of the charismatic renewal is to build up the body of Christ." The emphasis was on mission, not on having the gifts of the Spirit for their own sake. They were to be used for the good of the community.

"We were a very happy group," Soto said. "We had a lot of joy in the Lord."

Rachel Solis turned up at the prayer meeting in early 1972, taken by a friend. She had been in an accident, gotten a concussion, suffered from vertigo, and also had heart problems. "A lot of that was healed with the laying on of hands," she said. Her husband, Ralph, later ordained a deacon, was suffering from gout and could hardly walk, so she talked him into coming to a meeting, too. It wasn't an easy sell, because Ralph was reluctant to go where people prayed in tongues. "I'm Catholic but I don't do that," he said.

It didn't get any easier the night he finally attended the meeting. Normally there was plenty of parking at OLYC, but not that night, so they had to walk two blocks in the cold, gout and all. "He was using me as a crutch," Rachel remembered. Once they got to the center, Ralph saw the stairs and was ready to turn back; no way could he make that climb. But Tula and another man carried him up the stairs and on into the noisy meeting.

"That building just shook with praise," said Rachel. "Father Thomas would say 'leave your problems outside; you're here to praise the Lord and nothing else.'" Ralph was healed at that meeting. "The gout never returned," said Rachel. "We saw a lot of miracles."

In July 1971, a meeting was started at Camp Juan Diego, Sunday afternoons. It would attract 50 people of all ages and sizes. They would stay from early afternoon until after supper, with a large-group prayer meeting, and also broken down into smaller groups by age. There were teachings in Spanish and English, Mass in Spanish, and a community meal, with the teens washing the dishes.

"You feel like it's a little piece of heaven," said Pochie Heredia, who started attending with her husband, Neto, after her sister was healed of rheumatoid arthritis at one of the meetings.

Sister Mary Virginia Clark at Camp Juan Diego , introducing one of the kids to the camp's dog; and below, overseeing the afterschool feeding program at OLYC, 1973.

CHAPTER 27

Mother Superior

A round New Years of 1971, Father Thomas went to a Catholic charismatic leadership conference in Ann Arbor, Michigan, and found himself at the same event as three of the most influential people in his life – though with two of the three, he didn't know it yet.

One was his old friend Father Cohen, who had introduced him to baptism in the Holy Spirit in the first place. The second was Sister Mary Virginia Clark, the Daughter of Charity who had been part of the group praying over him in New Orleans. The third was Bobbie Cavnar, a Dallas businessman and war hero who had founded the charismatic prayer community Sister Mary Virginia was attending at the time; Cavnar and Father Thomas didn't actually meet face to face at Ann Arbor, but they'd make up for lost time later.

Father Thomas had decided he needed somebody with "spiritual horsepower," so when he saw Father Cohen at the conference, he asked if he could recommend anybody. Father Cohen pointed out Sister Mary Virginia. Father Thomas asked her for permission to write her. She remembered him well, from the 1969 prayer meeting; they exchanged letters, and he invited her to El Paso, to work at OLYC – the start of a 17-year collaboration with one of his most important co-workers.

Sister Mary Virginia had joined the Daughters of Charity in her native St. Louis in 1947, hoping to work with the poor. In the late 60s, she had heard of the charismatic renewal and was baptized in the Spirit at a meeting at a Lutheran seminary. "My life has never been the same," she said. "My heart has never been the same." The Catholic charismatic renewal was brand new at the time, and controversial; while she was in New Orleans, she got permission from her superior to attend Father Cohen's prayer group, but on the condition that she keep a curfew and avoid notoriety. That was why she was so anxious to go home from Father Cohen's meeting when he called her back to pray with Father Thomas.

By the time Father Thomas invited her to El Paso in 1971, she was principal of St. Anne's School in Dallas, and attending a prayer meeting led by Bobbie Cavnar. Cavnar, a Dallas businessman and heavily-decorated Air Force veteran, was highly skeptical of the charismatic renewal when he first heard about it – he even had it investigated by the FBI when his son Jim got involved – but he was baptized in the Spirit himself in May 1970. He went on to become a major leader of the renewal and founder of the Christian Community of God's Delight, as well as a close friend of Father Thomas until Bobbie's death in 2002.

Cavnar encouraged Sister Mary Virginia to pay a visit to El Paso at Easter. Father Thomas would later describe the visit as a turning point, and it didn't take him long to notice. She flew in on Holy Saturday. Right away he bustled her into his car and drove her around town to meet some of his friends. At once he knew he had made the right choice. He was stunned by her gift of prophecy – what charismatics believe are specific messages from God, for groups or individuals – and her insight into strangers that he himself knew well, people he had heard in the confessional.

"Every place we went, she had a personal prophecy for every person," he said years later. "I saw her lay out their life before them, in a way that I knew only God could know. I could see that God was working through her, and I was so happy. I just cried and cried all day long, it was so beautiful."

For her part, Sister Mary Virginia became convinced that God was calling her to stay.

From the point of view of the Daughters of Charity, Sister Mary Virginia's request was a long way out of the ordinary: leaving her work in the order to serve in an unconnected ministry. "You go where you're sent," she said later. Her local superior asked her to call her provincial superior. There was no one to replace her as principal, her provincial told her, but she could go for the summer to test the call from God. Already she felt called to a more permanent stay, but she felt God telling her "just go. By the end of the summer she'll [her provincial] understand." She said she knew in her heart that she would be staying much longer than one summer, but "I had the wisdom to keep my mouth shut." As the time got close, she asked Father Thomas how to prepare for the ministry. He told her to eat simply and not to use the air conditioning in her car.

On arrival in El Paso, Sister Mary Virginia moved in with the Daughters of Charity at their convent but spent her time working at OLYC ministries. At the end of the summer came the good news from Dallas that she had been expecting all along: she was free to stay in El Paso.

It was the start of a long partnership between Father Thomas and the nun he called "mother superior;" she called him "father inferior." "He enjoyed that," she recalled years later. She would remain in the OLYC community until her superiors sent her to other work in Amarillo in 1988.

CHAPTER 28

Taking the Battle Seriously

It didn't take long for Sister Mary Virginia to decide that Father Thomas needed to meet her friend Bobbie Cavnar, to learn what Cavnar knew about spiritual warfare: the constant battle of the kingdom of God against the kingdom of darkness, evil spirits and other manifestations. "I wasn't any good in that area," she said, and without that knowledge, "he [Father Thomas] would not be able to continue in maturity in the prayer group."

For sure, he had a lot to learn about the kingdom of darkness. As a young priest, he didn't take the subject seriously at all. "I had heard of witch hunts in Salem, Massachusetts," he said. "I had seen drawings at Halloween of an elderly hag wearing a black hat astride a broom flying through the sky. That was about the sum of my knowledge of witches."

So when a middle-aged woman from south El Paso turned up at OLYC asking for advice because she had a witch living next door, he didn't take her seriously either. "It was like saying her neighbor had the tooth fairy in a box." "Do you see her go in and out of her house on a broom?" he asked her. The woman didn't find the smart-aleck answer very helpful, and the conversation didn't last long.

Then Bobbie Cavnar came into his life, followed shortly by a woman Father Thomas calls "Mrs. V" and an incident that would lead to a whole new ministry. He'd be blending spiritual warfare with everything he did for the rest of his life.

Immediately after Sister Mary Virginia's visit – the very next day, Cavnar recalled in a 1983 testimony – Father Thomas turned up in Dallas, waiting in the breakfast room when Cavnar got home from his day at the office. The conversation, Cavnar recalled, lasted seven hours, and it didn't go smoothly.

"We were at his house having supper," Father Thomas recalled later, "and Bobbie began talking to me about evil spirits. I didn't understand what he was talking about. I said, 'Bobbie, I'm going to go outside and walk around a little bit and see if I can grasp what you've been telling me.' I went outside and I walked up and down the street, trying to fit in my head what Bobbie was telling me, which I'd never heard before."

In Cavnar's recollection, Father Thomas was more than puzzled – he was angry. "He was saying, 'you're absolutely crazy. You're the kind of guy in the charismatic renewal that gives it a bad name," Cavnar said. Part of Cavnar's message was that Church blessings and sacramentals are extremely powerful when the blessing prayers are said in a thorough way, using wording such as in the old Roman Ritual, but pretty much useless if the priest's blessing is just "the old one-two-three" that most priests give. Anyhow, Father Thomas went home to El Paso; "I never thought I'd see him again," Cavnar said.

But just a few weeks later, at a non-Catholic charismatic event, Father Thomas was approached by a woman from the Foursquare Gospel church pastored by a minister he knew, Paul McEachern. "This lady said, 'I want you to come and bless my house.'" It isn't clear why the woman wanted a blessing from a Catholic priest, but he was happy to oblige. "I said 'I'll bless it tomorrow.' I figured I'm going to go horseback riding, but I'll go by and bless her house on the way. Little did I know that this Saturday would change the whole course of my life."

He dropped by the house, expecting he would only be there a few minutes. He met the woman's husband. The husband went to the garage to do some work. The phone rang, and the woman answered it. Father Thomas wandered around the house, saying prayers from the house blessing ritual and sprinkling holy water from a shaving lotion bottle. When he passed by Mrs. V, who was still on the phone, he sprinkled her playfully with holy water, and then went on to the next room. But when he got back to the living room, there was a shock waiting for him.

"She's sitting across the room in a chair. Her eyes are real big looking at me. At that moment I got a gift. I said, 'You didn't like that holy water, did you?' She fell on the floor and started clawing the rug and screaming. I said 'oh my God, what am I going to do now?' Her husband's going to come in here in a minute, and he's going to wonder, what did I do to his wife?" All he could think to do was throw more holy water. "She screamed even louder, as if I had hit her with fire." So he stopped throwing water and she calmed down a little bit. Her husband came back in about then, but he didn't seem surprised about any of it.

Meanwhile, Father Thomas thought of a solution: Bobbie Cavnar. He phoned Sister Mary Virginia for Cavnar's number. "I got in touch with Bobbie, and I told him, 'this is what happened, what do I do now?' and he said 'bind the spirit.' I didn't know what the heck he was talking about." Cavnar asked him to put Mrs. V on the phone, but by the time Father Thomas made it to an extension phone in the bedroom to listen to the conversation, Mrs. V had thrown the phone down. So Cavnar told Father Thomas to make a tape of prayers from his Roman Ritual book to play to the woman, while Cavnar phoned the prophets in his own prayer group for discernment.

Meanwhile, Father Thomas had some interesting experiences with reading the ritual prayers. "I noticed when I got on certain parts, she got real active. I learned some parts of this thing make that devil squirm. I learned that from watching her reaction when I read all this stuff." It took the rest of the day. "A hundred and forty-five dollars later – and I paid the phone bill – we got that woman settled down," Cavnar said. There was no horseback ride for Father Thomas that day.

Cavnar said he told Father Thomas not to visit Mrs. V again alone; he should take a woman with him, at least, or better yet a married couple. He should also put on New Testament tapes for her to listen to. Soon, Mrs. V asked Father Thomas to help Pastor McEachern pray for deliverance for her, another totally new concept for Father Thomas. The two clergymen agreed that the difference between their churches wouldn't cause any division in their work. They took Pastor McEachern's wife along and spent two days praying, singing, reading the Bible to the woman, and using holy water, which was a totally new concept to Pastor McEachern. At one point Father Thomas was back on the phone to Cavnar, calling him out of a weekday business meeting. The results weren't perfect; Pastor McEachern blamed that on an unknown satanic object in the household.

Father Thomas never saw Mrs. V again. But he never made jokes about broomsticks again, either. "Little by little, God opened my eyes in His mercy."

Another lesson on spiritual warfare came at the original Cueva across the street from the old Bowie High School location. Father Thomas, Sister Mary Virginia, and Mrs. Tula decided to pray there during the school's lunch hours, from 11:30 to 1:30 every day; they didn't do any ministry or invite any of the students in – they just wanted to see what God would do. But some of the students came in anyhow, out of curiosity, and some of those who came had apparently been dabbling in occult activities. What happened to those students showed the three people what God was doing.

"We prayed everything we could think of," Father Thomas said. "We were trying to fill up two hours." That included reading Psalms and other passages from the Bible, and that's when the action started. "Some kid would come in. It would be like he was hit with a baseball bat or something. He'd jerk and his eyes would cross, and he might go out in the yard and vomit. Of course, that got my attention. What's going on here?" That was the start of one of the OLYC community's most powerful prayers; it later came to be called "executing the sentence" (based on Psalm 149:9) a form of prayer Father Nathan O'Halloran said also has a basis in the practice of "Ignatian repetition" learned by Jesuits from the *Spiritual Exercises* of St. Ignatius. The prayer consists of reading appropriate Scripture passages over and over (for an example, see chapter 45, on the first day of the jail ministry in 1979.) "I gradually learned that the Scripture has power," Father Thomas said. "It was just that experience of watching the kids and their reaction to hearing the Scripture that I learned to execute the sentence. It was that simple. It took a while for it to soak in.

"That was a growing, learning process, as everything has been. I didn't know doodly when I started, and whatever I have learned has just been from watching and observing."

The key point in all this, Father Thomas said, is obedience to the most neglected of the 10 commandments, the commandment that's listed as number 1 for a good reason: "You shall have no other gods before Me." Occult activities like joining a Satanic cult, playing with a Ouija board, going to a fortune teller, or seeking healing from a *curandera* (folk healer) violate that commandment by placing another god – ultimately Satan – above the real God, and open the individual to bondage that can be very difficult to break.

Father Thomas went to enormous lengths to drive home the importance of the First Commandment, teaching everyone who would listen to stay away from even the most harmless-looking words and practices that detract from the sovereignty of God. It was impossible for even a casual visitor to the community to miss the point. Everybody who has spent any length of time on the Lord's Ranch, or in OLYC ministries, knows two words you don't say: "Good luck." Father Thomas gave that warning himself in a tape about the occult, made in 1976 and still in use in the community. He said, "If God is the Father Almighty there is no place for luck, good or bad, because God is in control of everything...It is very much a part of our vocabulary, and it is a sign that part of our speech has not come under the Lordship of Jesus Christ. If Jesus is the Lord, then there is no room for good or bad luck."

In the OLYC community, you don't say "good luck," you don't read your horoscope in the newspaper, you don't throw rice at a wedding (if a couple insisted, Father Thomas would refuse to officiate), you don't make a wish on your birthday candles. By themselves, those things won't put you in Mrs. V's condition, but all of them imply reliance – sometimes explicitly, sometimes just implicitly – on a spiritual power other than God.

As surprising as the move into spiritual warfare may have been to Father Thomas at the time, it was probably just a natural outgrowth of his lifelong willingness to take the unseen world seriously. Remember, this is a man who was ready to change his entire life in a direction he had never thought about and had no desire for, simply because he believed he heard God talking to him; a man who saw his duty to care for the poor as a question of getting to heaven. His former co-worker Jean Soto, who later became a professor of religious studies at Santa Clara University in California, described him as a transitional figure between the pre-Vatican II Catholic Church, with its emphasis on the unseen world, and the post-Vatican II Church, with its focus on the world we can see. Father Thomas wouldn't likely disagree; his whole career was based on the unseen world, and after his encounter with Mrs. V, even his work with the things he could see, like poverty and abortion, took on an element of spiritual warfare.

"There's the kingdom of God, and the kingdom of Satan," Father Thomas said. "And most people are experiencing the kingdom of Satan most of the time." The key to ministry was to expand the kingdom of God into every area of activity and defeat the other place.

Blessing holy water after a Mass at the Lord's Ranch, 2001.
Father Thomas often blessed sacramentals for people to use in their homes.

CHAPTER 29

The Renewal Crosses the River

Early in 1971, a year or so after charismatic prayer meetings had begun at OLYC, meetings also started up in Juárez, hosted in private homes. But they didn't exactly take off, due mostly to the cautious attitude of Bishop Manuel Talamás Camandari. Father Thomas kept the bishop informed about what was going on, and the bishop wasn't hostile, but he was definitely wary. "For example," Father Thomas said, "he wanted two diocesan priests to be present at each of the prayer meetings to be sure that nothing harmful or dangerous would occur." That was asking a lot in a city where just 40 priests had to minister to half a million Catholics. "Because of these and similar restrictions, the meetings limped along with very poor attendance and relatively poor results." Half a dozen to a dozen people attended, most from Juárez, but some, including the Tulas and Sister Mary Virginia, from El Paso.

In September 1972, the OLYC Bible study discerned that Father Thomas should ask the bishop for clear direction for the Juárez meeting. "Bishop, we want you to bless us or curse us, but don't ignore us," he phrased it later. He spoke to the bishop and the bishop promised a letter in reply; Father Thomas picked it up the next day on his way to the prayer meeting. Taking it for granted that the letter would be favorable, he stuck it in his pocket and didn't open it until he parked his vehicle outside the house where the meeting was being held. To his shock, the letter said there were to be no more prayer meetings of this type in the diocese of Juárez.

"I thought he'd bless us," Father Thomas said.

He had to read the letter at least twice at the meeting, as newcomers arrived late. Some people began to sob. "Everybody's broken-hearted. I said don't worry about it. We're going to obey the bishop, and God's going to work." Then everybody headed home.

But as they left, an elderly woman, new to the meeting, asked for prayer. She had been walking on crutches since she was hit by a car eight years earlier. They laid hands on her, prayed a quick prayer, and then the people from El Paso drove back over the river.

Now that the meetings were cancelled, the group began riding around Juárez in a van praying instead, to avoid violating the bishop's directions. But two weeks later, a relative of the woman on crutches came from Juárez to OLYC asking if Father Thomas knew what had happened to her. She had been completely healed the night of the meeting. The next day she had gone to church without crutches – a point not lost on her pastor, who knew her well. At home in her tenement "she was running up and down the stairs telling everybody 'I've been healed, I've been healed, I've been healed.'" Father Thomas tracked her down and asked her to tell Bishop Talamás the story; it took her two trips to get see the bishop, but it turned out he already knew about it.

That wasn't the only healing, either. At one point Father Thomas had prayed briefly over a woman with a heart condition, a woman well known to the bishop because she and her husband ran the Christian Family Movement in Juárez. Nothing apparent had happened at the time. But since the prayer, she had been in a terrible car accident near Chihuahua and needed surgery. Her husband said no, her heart condition wouldn't stand anesthetic – but tests showed her heart was OK, and she had the surgery successfully. She told the bishop.

Finally, Guillermina Villalva, a political activist and former atheist who later became a key co-worker with Father Thomas, was deathly sick with a massive bladder infection and blood clots; her husband, Antonio, and her father were both doctors and they expected her to die. A visiting charismatic priest prayed for her, and she too was healed; the priest asked her to go see the bishop and ask for prayer meetings to resume.

"God had talked to the bishop three times," said Father Thomas. "Three miracles where there was no question of fraud or anything, and they were outstanding, they were incurable. So the bishop said, 'you can have the prayer meetings, but not in the Catholic church. I don't want you in a Catholic institution.'"

The meetings started up again in November 1972 in the dingy basement of Antonio Villalva's medical office on Lerdo Street, a few blocks from the Stanton Street bridge, with similar attendance to the earlier meetings. Over time the bishop changed his attitude, so much so that eventually he wanted a charismatic Mass in every parish every Sunday, though that never happened.

Praying over people after Mass, 1972.

CHAPTER 30

A Book to Be Obeyed

Early in Sister Mary Virginia's time in El Paso, Father Thomas set off in another direction, and she ended up playing a key role in it. Still looking for the "silver bullet," he was determined to fit the charismatic experience into his work for the poor. In 1971 or 1972, he heard from Father Cohen about the Church of the Redeemer, an Episcopal congregation in Houston that was combining spiritual work with social work, so he did what he usually did when he heard about something promising: he went to see for himself. "If they were firmly entrenched in the Spirit, in a wholesome manner, Father went to visit them," said Sister Mary Virginia. "He wanted to glean, to take the good fruit. Wherever he went, he picked up what was good, to help others with. He came back very happy with what he had learned. You could see him maturing and learning and clasping to his heart what God was doing."

What he found in Houston, he recalled years later, was a highly-developed Christian community, deeply devoted to social work in the surrounding poor neighborhood, with disadvantaged people of all sorts – "it was tremendous work they did. It was a big, strong community." He stayed several days and noted several major points. "The first thing I learned was the power of the body of Christ. They'd have a household with 35 people in it, and a couple in charge, and they'd take in dope addicts, they had single men, single women, they'd do all kinds of stuff. This amazed me. I'd never seen the body of Christ so alive and active. So I said, what do they do? Then I said, well, they study the Bible all the time." The church offered constant Bible study, on a busy schedule at various days, times and levels, to include as many people as it could. "From that day on, never a day passed that Father didn't read God's Word," said Mike Halloran, a longtime co-worker.

Father Thomas brought that lesson back to El Paso with him, and it wasn't just a personal one. He wanted to recreate the Houston experience in El Paso, and as usual, he didn't do anything by halves. He set up a Bible study at OLYC that met five mornings a week, 9 to 11:30, in Sister Mary Virginia's office. Initially there were six or eight people, including Jean Soto and Frank Alarcón. At the beginning of each meeting, Sister Mary Virginia would deliver a long prophecy, which would be recorded. Usually the prophecy would make no sense to the listeners at the time and have no obvious theme. Setting it aside for the moment, group members would share insights from their own Bible reading during the meeting, and at the end the prophecy would be replayed. At that point it would make sense, tying all the Bible passages together.

"We had no plan, no theme, nothing," Father Thomas said. "People would say, 'I've read this verse, I read that verse.' None of this tied together except at the end, when we were all finished. I'd be able to see that all these things formed a unity and God was teaching us something new. So He taught us all kinds of wonderful things in this disorganized way. 'Oh, God's teaching us about holy water, what do you know?'"

One time, a woman none of them had ever seen before walked in in the middle of the Bible study, after the prophecy. She asked to speak to Father Thomas, but she didn't know him by sight, so she didn't recognize him sitting there. The participants just motioned her to sit down. So down she sat, the Bible study continued, and at the end the group replayed the prophecy, which, as usual, hadn't appeared to relate to anything at the time it was given. When she heard it replayed, though, the woman got up with a smile on her face. "That's wonderful," she said. "That answers all my questions." Away she went, never to be seen again. She never knew Father Thomas had been there.

Father Thomas's approach to the Bible combined sophisticated biblical knowledge with an almost childlike literalness of interpretation. Not literal in the usual fundamentalist sense; he wasn't too concerned about whether the book of Jonah, the prophet swallowed by a great fish, is intended to be an actual historical account, and he couldn't be bothered to get into scholarly debates about whether St. Paul is really the human author of Ephesians. "That doesn't affect the contents," he said. Rather, he took the Bible as "a book to be obeyed rather than dissected." He said, "The Bible is meant to change your life. Don't bother to read Scripture if it's not going to change your life."

Rachel Solis attended the Bible study in the early 70s. She remembered Father Thomas saying that some things in the Bible are intended just for the time they were written, and don't apply in the same way to our own times. All the same, he said, those things still carry a command for us. For example, most widows are no longer homeless as they were in biblical times, but we are still commanded not to forget the poor and the widow, even in our times. "It will apply to you, because Jesus doesn't change," he said. "The Ten Commandments are still there. They won't change to accommodate anyone."

But Father Thomas's idea of obeying the Bible was a lot more detailed than simply following the Ten Commandments and remembering the poor. "We'd read something, and say 'we don't do that,' so we'd start doing it.'" An example: early on, the group read Psalm 149 ("let them praise his name with dancing") and Psalm 150 ("praise him with tambourine and dance") and decided that directive was more than a poetical decoration; "it is very clear in Sacred Scripture that God wants us to dance in his honor," Father Thomas said, and dance they did; over the years OLYC community members would dance boisterously in astonishing circumstances: in front of the taco vendors and bystanders outside the Juárez municipal jail; *inside* the jail, and also inside the Juárez mental hospital; at outdoor Mass on bitterly cold February days at the food bank in a Juárez shantytown; at Father Thomas's own wake; and always at the weekly prayer meeting, where Father Thomas was still leading the dancing in his mid-70s.

It was Bible study, and the idea of literal obedience, that led the community to the best-known event in its history. Christmas 1972 was coming on, and one day's readings included Luke 14:12-14: "When you give a luncheon or a dinner, do not invite your friends or your brothers or your relatives or rich neighbors, in case they may invite you in return, and you would be repaid. But when you give a banquet, invite the poor, the crippled, the lame, and the blind. And you will be blessed, because they cannot repay you, for you will be repaid at the resurrection of the righteous."

"We had to ask ourselves if we had ever done this," Father Thomas wrote later. "When do Christians carry out this simple thing that Jesus told us to do when we have a little party?" Giving food to the poor was nothing new at OLYC, but this passage wasn't about giving food. It was about *sharing* food, hosts and guests eating together. "He said all our lives we've gone to parties and returned favors," said Sister Mary Virginia. So the question was, "How can we spend Christmas instead of sitting around a tree getting presents and adulation for ourselves?"

Father Thomas had a pretty good idea where the poor, the crippled, the lame and the blind could be found: at the Juárez dump, where desperately poor people lived, not near, but *in*, the garbage, scavenging whatever they could find – everything from tin cans to discarded hospital gowns, loaded with disease. They financed – if that's the word – their unimaginably subhuman standard of living with the least amount of money the local scrap dealer, safe with a government monopoly, could get away with paying them; they ate discarded food, melon rind, rats, anything they could get their hands on.

"I had been to the dump a number of times, just to observe," Father Thomas said. "I never did anything – I didn't know what to do."

Well, now he knew. Here's where Bible study was taking the community. "The room that we were sitting in, you could look out the window and see the *colonias* (squatter slums of Juárez)," said Jean Soto. "The words [of Luke 14] were like a branding iron, in Father's heart and in all our hearts."

"So we decided to do it," Father Thomas said. "Not approximate it, but do it." He said he was going to the dump for Christmas dinner, and anybody who wanted to come with him was welcome.

One of the many "homes" at the garbage dump in Juárez, 1972.

CHAPTER 31

Christmas 1972:
The Great Multiplication

C hristmas Day, 1972. Easily the most famous day in the history of the OLYC community. If you know enough about Father Thomas to be interested in his biography, there's a good chance you've already heard about it. For sure, nobody who went to the Juárez dump that day will ever forget it.

Said Frank Alarcón: "That day we met Jesus face to face."

Eleven a.m. was the appointed hour. The Juárez prayer group was invited, too. On the El Paso side, the people gathered at OLYC. They had been told to bring something for themselves and something to share. Alarcón brought his favorite meal: 25 baloney sandwiches – two loaves of bread worth. Jean Soto brought hams and cakes. There were burritos, tamales, chocolate, fruit, candy for the children.

Finally, six carloads left the youth center. They headed across the border, then stopped and waited for two more carloads from the Juárez side. Nobody knew what to expect at the dump, but the day didn't get off to a promising start. The weather was dark, cloudy and damp. Nobody was cheering the group on. As they waited, a man came out of a dental shop to check them out.

"What are you looking for?" he shouted. "Jesus the Lord!" Father Thomas shouted back. "We don't need Jesus," the man yelled. "We need money!" Finally the Juárez cars arrived, and the group drove off to the dump, about six miles from the border crossing. The scene there wasn't any more promising than the weather.

For one thing, nobody at the dump had any idea it was Christmas. The visitors didn't grasp the point yet, but the fact is that life at the dump was so far out of touch with what most of us think is normal that nobody even knew the day of the week. Worse yet, they weren't exactly into peace and good will. They were split into two hostile camps, not even on speaking terms. They had divided up the dump, and nobody from one side was allowed in the territory of the other side, the long-standing scavengers trying to shut out newer arrivals. "Everyone was desperate for their money," said Sister Mary Virginia. "They didn't want the opportunity for their money to be taken from them." The visitors explained what they had in mind, but it didn't soften anybody's heart. "Feed us," each group said. "Then feed them."

There was no way Father Thomas was going to build that sort of hostility into a Christmas dinner. "We prayed to God that this rift might be healed," he wrote later. "After negotiating with both groups, walking back and forth over the garbage between the two encampments, we decided to have dinner in neutral territory at one side of the dump." The two groups lined up on opposite sides of a large table, still hostile, still not mixing.

Then Father Thomas asked Guillermina Villalva to explain to the people what was happening and to sing something. "The people did not know if we were Protestants or Catholics," she wrote later. "I could not think of anything to sing except 'O Maria, Madre Mia'; this hymn would give us away as being Catholics."

"We told them we had come to be with them on Christmas day," Father Thomas wrote. "This was the day Jesus was born in love. We were going to sing his praises for a while. Then if anyone was sick we would pray with them for healing because Jesus liked to heal. We began with '*Bendito*,' a hymn very familiar to Catholics in Mexico. As we sang, the Lord began to work, and the people softened. When it came time to pray for the sick, the people crowded around, forgetting their barriers. We prayed for a large number of them."

God sent a little help, too, Sister Mary Virginia said. A large truck came barreling in, and the two groups had to mingle as they scrambled to get out of the way.

Finally, the people got to line up for the food. "We told them that we had not come to give them anything, we had come to share our dinner with them," Father Thomas wrote. "This is the difference between taking a Christmas basket to a poor family and sharing Christmas dinner with them or inviting them to your dinner. We all began to experience a friendliness and an at-homeness."

But now came the biggest crisis of all. The OLYC people simply didn't understand the depths of poverty the dump people lived in. They assumed there wouldn't be many people rag-picking at a garbage dump on Christmas Day; it hadn't sunk in that these people had no place else to go, even if they had known it was Christmas. So, bottom line, the visitors hadn't brought enough food. Exact numbers differ a bit depending on who tells the story, but in two written accounts, Father Thomas said there was food for 120 people; "we thought that was a lot," said Alarcón. But when the OLYC people arrived with the food, word got out fast, and it was close to 300 people who actually showed up.

"I prayed aloud that God would bless the people and the food," Father Thomas said. "Then I invited the people to come share dinner with us, warning them that we didn't have enough food for everyone, but that they were welcome to share what we had." The dump people said to feed the children first, and the meal began.

They shared. And they shared. And they shared. "Father came to me and he said 'you pray,'" said Sister Mary Virginia. "'You pray over here while we see what we can do.' He said 'we don't know if we have enough food.' I didn't want to tell him then [but] I knew we were going to have enough food. God would not do that to His people, when we came out here with our hearts obeying His word. He would not go back on His word. I knew this in my heart. I knew we would have enough food." And sure enough, as she watched, gallon jugs of *atole* (a hot drink made with corn flour) multiplied before her eyes. "I saw bags of tamales put down and I saw them burst open into many more. I said, 'oh man, God, this is so exciting.' Then God said, 'mind your business. Your business is to pray. I'll take care of this. I'll take care of the feast.'"

With no end in sight to the meal, Alarcón got suspicious and got up on top of his pickup camper to see what was happening. He saw children coming again and again for more candy. He saw the OLYC people handing out burritos and endlessly slicing ham. "We had a little ham and that ham fed over 100 people," said Rachel Solís. "We just kept cutting and cutting and cutting. The kids were stuffing their shirts with candy." The adults were not only eating but taking food back home with them. The eight car-loads of prayer group members ate their fill, too.

In the middle of all this, Father Thomas himself was slow to get the picture. At one point somebody offered him a plate of food, but he turned it down. He said there wasn't enough for everyone, and he wanted to make sure the poor were fed. "There's plenty!" the volunteer told him. "There can't be," he answered. Then he saw food in back of a station wagon. "Where did that come from?" he asked. "I'm thick-headed – it slowly began to dawn on me what had happened there."

By the end of the day, though, there wasn't much question. After everyone had had their meal – and gone back to picking garbage – there was still enough food left to drop off at three orphanages on the way back to El Paso. It was just like the story of Jesus multiplying the loaves and fishes in the Bible – but "when you see it with your own eyes, it has a different meaning," Rachel Solís said.

Children at the garbage dump in Juárez, Mexico, waiting for the meal to begin on Christmas Day, 1972.

CHAPTER 32

"We've Got to Do Something"

A lot of people call it a miracle. "It seemed like every week had its account of some manifestation of God's Spirit moving," Evy Nelson said. "This was the one people talked about." It has been featured in books, magazine articles, and videos, and for myself, it's usually the first story I tell to people who want to know about this community I sometimes visit in El Paso.

So it's a surprise to read the main sources for this biography and see how little stress Father Thomas and his friends placed on the miracle of multiplication of the food. Not that they didn't believe in it – they certainly did. Father Thomas got a good chuckle out of the theory you might sometimes hear in trendy sermons, that the real miracle of Jesus' multiplication of loaves and fishes was that his preaching had led people to share the fish and bread they had been hoarding in their pockets. He knew first-hand that Jesus multiplies food, literally.

But as far as he was concerned it wasn't the point of the story, and the documents reflect that. The date isn't even circled in his office calendar; for that matter there's no entry even for plans to visit the dump. He wrote at least three accounts of Christmas 1972 – an Anything-a-Month newsletter in February 1973, an article for *New Covenant* magazine in May 1973, and a couple of paragraphs in what appears to be a personal testimony covering his life from birth to the late 70s. In each case, the multiplication is just part of the story, with no special emphasis. The point of the story, as it always was for Father Thomas, was the encounter with the poor.

"This was the most beautiful Christmas any of us ever spent *because we shared our Christmas dinner with God's poor*," [emphasis added] he wrote in the newsletter. In the testimony, he describes the miracle in what is almost a throwaway line: "This first Christmas at the dump was the first time the community experienced the multiplication of food." In the *New Covenant* article, he said experiencing the humanity and nobility of the dump residents, the physical healings, and overcoming the hostility of the two groups had permanently changed the lives of the visitors; once again, the multiplication takes up only a single sentence in a four-page article, a rather vague one this time: "Somehow, there was enough for everybody."

The *New Covenant* article does include a brief separate account of the multiplication by Frank Alarcón, but also a longer reflection on the day by Jean Soto which doesn't mention the multiplication at all. In a separate document on the group's work at the dump, Guillermina Villalva said there was plenty of food left over, but she doesn't specifically refer to the multiplication.

Anyway, there were lots of other things besides leftover ham and burritos to attract the visitors' attention at the dump. Somebody brought them a severely retarded boy of about 11, caked in dirt and unable to speak. Sister Mary Virginia and others prayed with him, and when the OLYC people came back for a visit at a later date, he had started talking. After dinner, the visitors wandered around the dump, talking to the people and taking note of their "housing." Most of them had found some sort of cover to make a roof, balanced on piles of tin cans, that they could crawl under for shelter, but Father Thomas met one woman who had only a piece of plastic garbage bag to lie on or under in the middle of the cans. Another woman was nursing a five-month-old baby, named Anita. The group saw or discerned that the child was near death. Father Thomas prayed with her and baptized her; there was no water supply, so he sent someone away with a handkerchief, trying to find enough water to at least moisten it, and performed the baptism with a few drops wrung out of the cloth. Anita survived and was still alive when Father Thomas retold the story more than 30 years later.

Some of the dump residents took the U.S. visitors
to see their homes, Christmas Day 1972.

Back at OLYC after dropping the food off at the orphanages, the group prayed together for a while before everyone headed home. Again, they were focused on the poor, not on the miracle. A 16-year-old girl prayed, "Lord, I thank you for letting me go to the dump today. Now I know the real meaning of Christmas. I know that if Jesus were born today, he would have been born in the dump."

All the same, nobody was ignoring the multiplication. In John's gospel, the nearest word to "miracle" is "sign," and in the community, the multiplication was definitely interpreted as a sign. It got their attention; it demonstrated the power of obedience to God's Word; and it pinpointed where God wanted the community working: *el basurero*, the Juárez dump. So gradually, clumsily – or at least, Father Thomas saw it that way – the group began looking for ways to minister there. "We were real slow," he said. "We didn't know what to do. We thought we've got to do something, we can't abandon them."

About two weeks after the Christmas visit, about 30 people met together and made an agreement to commit their lives to God's service. They began visiting the dump every Saturday, no matter the weather, which was especially bad that winter, with heavy rain and even snow. As time went on they began to put together a ministry among the dump residents (see chapter 34).

They also began functioning more formally as a community. Eventually they formed a sort of council, not exactly a governing council, but a group to consult one another and the Lord. The original four were Father Thomas, Sister Mary Virginia, and two married lay people: Jean Soto, who would later go on to earn a Ph.D., and Manny Basurto, an auto mechanic who had had a major life conversion. They were called the Juniors. "He [Father Thomas] didn't want us to be called elders, because we didn't know enough," said Soto. The word was taken from the first edition (1970) of the New American Bible, "let the greater among you be as the junior, the leader as the servant" (Luke 22:26b). They met weekly to discuss and discern whatever business came forward. "We were all completely free to bring up anything whatsoever that we felt needed the attention of the Juniors," said Soto. They worked by consensus: they gave their opinions, then discussed disagreements and clarified positions until they reached agreement; Soto said it probably didn't work every time, but she can't remember an exception. Father Thomas was "first among equals."

CHAPTER 33

Juárez Man

In later years, nothing looked more natural to people who knew Father Thomas than watching the skinny priest in his sweatshirt and black jeans, chatting away comfortably in his Florida-accented Spanish to people outside the Juárez jail or in the meeting room at the food bank OLYC set up in the middle of the *colonias*. Anglo or not, he just seemed to belong in that setting. Frank Alarcón remembered that it was Father Thomas who suggested the Christmas 1972 trip to the dump – a destination Alarcón, an El Paso-born Hispanic, never would have thought of himself.

"He'd been there before," Alarcón said. "I didn't know anything about the dump. He was a Juárez man. I wasn't."

Father Thomas didn't grow up with Hispanics, and he didn't meet many early in his time in seminary. The first he could recall meeting were in a Spanish-speaking church in Dallas when he was teaching high school there during his regency year. Serious exposure didn't come until early in his time in California, but when it came, it made a lasting impression.

During his seminary years at Alma, he met a priest who worked with *braceros*, migrant farm workers from Mexico. He went with the priest to the barracks where the workers would sleep, all together in the same room. The visits would be unexpected, and at around 8 or 9 p.m. the workers, exhausted from their day in the fields, would already be asleep.

"The priest would go in there and he'd say '*la Misa*' [Mass]. All those guys would get up. No complaints. They'd all get up and they'd come to Mass. Boy, was it moving – their faith, their devotion, their love. There wasn't a one that didn't go. They all got up right away and stumbled into where we were going to have Mass."

The priest would preach about the suffering of Jesus – "they could identify with that" – and carry on with Mass. Nobody would go to Communion, which is typical for Mexico, and Father Thomas figured most of the men weren't married in the Church, but "they all got on their knees. They prayed fervently."

He also noticed their footgear: strips of tires. "It wasn't made into a shoe. They just took eight inches of automobile tire and added straps over the top, and that was their shoes. I'd never seen that."

That priest was one of the few he knew at the time who bothered ministering to the Mexican population, and he got in some trouble for it, especially when he complained – "rightfully," Father Thomas said – about the way the *braceros* were treated.

When Father Thomas came to El Paso in 1964, one of his first priorities was learning Spanish. He noted the need in his diary his first week in town, and when he went to meet Hector Bencomo, the two men went to get Father Thomas a tape recorder, so he could record Spanish-language radio commercials for practice. He did a lot better with Spanish than he did with Latin. An article in the Spanish-language newspaper *Paso del Norte* in 2004 said he spoke Spanish "perfectly, although with an obvious American accent."

There's no question that he was comfortable in Spanish, but he would have laughed at the "perfectly" part. At the end of his life he recalled a prayer meeting many years earlier, where the bishop of Juárez had come to hear him teach, and he was more than a little nervous about it but pushed on ahead anyhow. "Guillermina [Villalva] told me later, 'that's the first time in my life I ever heard you speak without making any mistakes in Spanish.' I make mistakes all the time now [2006], and more then. God protected me."

When he got to El Paso Father Rahm had told him that if he wanted to understand Mexican spirituality and culture, he needed to see the basilica of Our Lady of Guadalupe in Mexico City. Our Lady of Guadalupe is patroness not only of Mexico but of all the Americas, and a major focus of Hispanic Catholicism, especially among the indigenous peoples; the basilica is the most heavily visited Catholic shrine in the world. So off Father Thomas went for a visit, early in his time at OLYC. Walking to the shrine, still several blocks away, he felt the presence of the Blessed Virgin and began sobbing; later he rated the visit as one of the best days of his life.

Around 1967 Father Thomas met Antonio Aguilar, the superstar actor and singer known as *el Charro* [cowboy] *de Mexico;* Father Thomas called him the John Wayne of Mexico. Aguilar brought his musical rodeo show to El Paso many times, and they met when Aguilar saw Father Thomas leaning over a fence watching the performers practice with the horses. On each visit, Father Thomas would say Mass for the traveling troupe, and hear confessions. Aguilar himself would always go to confession first to encourage his employees. Father Thomas also coached Aguilar to speak unaccented English in the 1969 movie *The Undefeated*, in which he appeared with the real John Wayne.

Father Thomas's sense of kinship with the people of Mexico was a matter of action as well as feelings. He saw the poor of Juárez as part of his ministry. Even before the Christmas at the dump, he and other OLYC volunteers had been trying to help out south of the river. To cite a few examples, in July 1970 OLYC opened a school in an unused building behind the church of *San Pedro y San Pablo* in the Colonia of the Fallen Ones. A hundred students turned up for the first day. In December of the same year, a substantial portion of the 20-ton Operation We Care shipment of food, clothing and medical care from Massachusetts (see chapter 19) went to the needy in Juárez. And in April 1971, OLYC began distributing nutrient-fortified tortillas in Juárez.

Not everybody thought Father Thomas's concern for Mexicans or Mexico was something to admire. His work in Juárez was one of the reasons some people both inside and outside the Church called him a radical and a communist. Not all the critics were Anglos, either; many of El Paso's Mexican-Americans would have liked him to forget about the other side of the river. They had left it behind and they wished he would. Meanwhile, in Mexico, his work was up against a long-standing tradition of government anti-clericalism, and he had to get special government permission to say Mass at the dump and the food bank.

None of this seemed to slow him down at all.

"In Juárez, somebody asked him once, 'are you Mexican?'" Hector Bencomo recalled.

"'No,'" he said, "'but my heart is.'"

Father Thomas visiting with two of the elderly women receiving
their weekly groceries from the Lord's Food Bank in Juárez, Mexico, 1999.

CHAPTER 34

A New Life Built on Garbage

etween 700 and 1,000 families lived at the Juárez dump.
They lived, or at least they managed to exist, by collecting and sorting bottles, cans and cardboard to sell to a
concession holder who had a monopoly on the salvage trade.
The price they got for their pickings was pitiful. "An adult who
works hard and has no bad breaks during the week can make $5
in seven days," Father Thomas said. On that kind of money, they
could buy groceries for three days; they lived on whatever they
could find in the garbage the other four days. "The people ate
garbage, wore garbage, and lived in garbage houses," Father
Thomas said. "The children were so black and sooty they appeared never to have had a bath in their lives." Worse still, every
man, woman and child there had tuberculosis. It wasn't a
friendly place, either. "Those people from the dump were
mean," said Frank Alarcón. "Even the police were afraid to come
out here."

It was hard to know where to start. Father Thomas remembered one early attempt – he wasn't sure whether it was before
or after the Christmas dinner. An El Paso merchant collected
clothes for the dump people, and four or five cars loaded up and
crossed the border to deliver them. But the volunteers didn't really know what they were getting into; they had no authority,

and nobody at the dump had any idea who they were, so the distribution degenerated into chaos as more than 100 people swarmed the scene grabbing for the clothes. One of the volunteers, terrified of the crowd, climbed on top of his car, on his knees, and started throwing clothes to the people "like you'd feed the fish."

Eventually the OLYC workers got better organized. "We asked the people what they wanted, what they were interested in, and what they wanted of us," Guillermina Villalva wrote later. "The people said they wanted a church, a school, a park, and a baseball team. Shortly thereafter the people themselves built a cardboard church with old bed springs to sit on. Bishop Talamás of Juárez visited the dump and he began to ask for donations from within the diocese, and a chapel was built." Father Thomas remembered the church part a bit differently: diocesan officials heard about the dump ministry and told the OLYC volunteers they needed to build a church and pay for it themselves. Anyhow, it was quite a while before Mass was celebrated in the church, and in the meantime the small brick chapel was used to give the children baths, running each child through a series of three tubs. Eventually Father Thomas and Father Alfonso Madrid began celebrating Mass. A prayer meeting started at the dump in December 1973.

In February 1973, the group began building houses, making adobe bricks on site and replacing the cardboard shacks and piles of tin cans. In March, a food co-operative was formed. The result was the Lord's Store. It had modest beginnings, Alarcón said – a woman at the weekly OLYC prayer meeting donated 50 cents. Other donations followed, and soon the group had $5, then $50, then $500. At the $500 mark, the group prayed about what to do with the money – should it be spent on clothes? Medicine? Housing? – and felt led to set up a grocery store. Antonio Villalva, Guillermina's husband, took a leading role.

The idea was to buy food with the $500, sell it at cost, and use the same money over and over. "The store idea saved the dignity of the ragpickers," Father Thomas said. "They could buy the food they wanted and stretch their little earnings because they were paying much less than they otherwise would. The trash pickers purchase what they want rather than accepting what is handed them. In this way, they save their dignity, which is necessary to maintain in underprivileged persons."

"While some are running the store, those who don't speak Spanish pray. Others visit the sick. The teenagers teach young children about Jesus. Everyone has a contribution to make."

The day it opened, the store ran into a wall of suspicion from the residents, who weren't used to getting anything good from outsiders with something to sell. Only five or 10 people bought groceries. Trust improved with time, more customers came forward, and the store moved deeper into the heart of the dump. But the bigger problem was that wholesale cost wasn't cheap enough. The desperately poor residents still couldn't afford it. So prices were cut in half, and soon the volunteers were spending $1,000 a week and getting back just $500 from sales. Remembering the biblical command to sell what you have and give to the poor, the volunteers – none too well off themselves – began selling their jewelry, silver, televisions and stereos to make up the shortfall. One woman sold her wedding ring.

"To some this type of generosity might seem extravagant," Father Thomas wrote in a newsletter, "and indeed it is extravagant. But the people who do these things see that God's love for man in Jesus Christ is extravagant also. They take seriously the words of Jesus, 'I tell you solemnly, insofar as you did this to one of the least of these brothers of mine you did it to me.' A wife selling her wedding rings to help feed a poor stranger may seem extreme, but what mother would not give her jewelry in ransom for her own child?"

It was an encounter with the Lord's Store in 1974 that brought into the ministry Sergio and Lucía Conde, who would become two of Father Thomas's biggest supporters. Nobody was more surprised about that than Sergio, who was the chief tax collector for Juárez and had planned on shutting the store down because it didn't have a business permit or pay taxes.

But when he called the store's organizers into his office for a chat, and maybe a short jail sentence, who should he find in front of him but Guillermina Villalva, a former schoolmate of his wife. Villalva explained how the store worked. To his own astonishment, Sergio let the workers go. Then the Condes, Christmas-and-Easter Catholics up until then, started attending the OLYC prayer meeting and visiting the dump. They sold off their own belongings, starting with an antique bracelet Sergio had given Lucía as an anniversary present; they emptied their bank account; and Sergio quit his secular job to run the Lord's Store.

Meanwhile, in March 1973, Irma Padilla of Juárez started a school for the dump children. At first it was a total failure. Brain-damaged by malnutrition, the children couldn't learn a single letter of the alphabet. Food from the volunteers helped cure the malnutrition but couldn't reverse the brain damage. With nothing being accomplished, the school shut down. Then a group of women from El Paso who led a Bible study for the adults at the dump offered to pray for the children. They prayed; then they went home and forgot about it. But Padilla got a call two weeks later to come see what had happened to the children, and she found them writing words from her lessons in the dust of a parked car. She reopened the school.

In 1975 life at the dump took a major leap forward when government officials pulled the salvage concession from the monopoly holder, allowing the dump workers to form their own co-operative to sell the salvaged garbage. While community members, notably Guillermina Villalva, had been lobbying all levels of government for better arrangements for the dump residents,

Father Thomas saw the actual announcement by the Juárez mayor as "out of the blue sky" when it came. "All of us recognize this breakthrough was a direct act of God and nothing we can take credit for. The breaking of the chains of exploitation came after months of praying that something might be done. We know that this is a special act of God because the people profiting from the exploitation were making a gigantic profit from the toil of these modern-day slaves." Once the co-op got up and running, the workers were paid 10 times what they had been getting for their salvage, and soon they could pay for their food without a subsidy.

Improved nutrition also helped bring an end to tuberculosis. By the end of 1977, only four dump residents still had TB, Father Thomas wrote in a newsletter.

One ongoing problem was water. Until the late 70s, the community had to have water trucked in. Sometimes the trucks broke down. Once, Alarcón recalled, that happened when Bishop Patricio Flores of El Paso, Bishop Metzger's successor, was visiting the dump ministry. The bishop pitched in to help push the truck to the brow of a hill so it could get a rolling start.

"Father started laughing and laughing," said Alarcón. "He said, 'I read about Jesus walking on water, but this is the first time I heard of a bishop pushing a water truck.'"

Then opportunity struck. Irma Padilla's husband, Paco, noticed city crews digging for water mains near the dump. Paco worked in a government office and knew how things worked: everybody has power, and everybody responds to greater power.

So, as Sister Mary Virginia told the story, Paco went into the city office and said he had a message from an important person who wanted the water pipe extended to the dump. Who is this person? "I am not at liberty to tell you who this is," he said; "However, I will say this to you: he has power over everyone. ("This of course was Jesus Christ," Sister Mary Virginia said.) He would be highly pleased with your decision to sign that paper and get water out to the *basurero*." And sure enough, the water line went in.

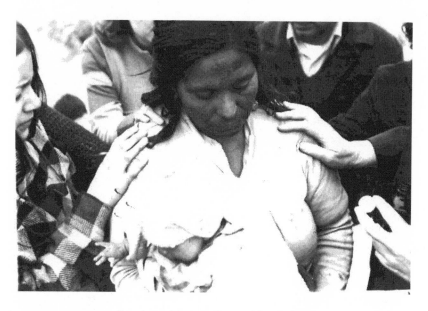

Praying with a mother and her baby,
who lived on the garbage dump in Juárez, 1972.

CHAPTER 35

The Lord's Ranch

Meanwhile, back on the El Paso side of the river, Camp Juan Diego (see chapter 17) continued to be one of the most important programs at OLYC, as it had been since the days of Father Rahm. But its days were coming to an end, and the drive to replace it led to one of the OLYC community's biggest and best-known ministries.

The land for the camp had belonged to K. B. Ivey, a major local landowner, who had donated the 1.4-acre parcel to Father Rahm in 1958. The deal was a generous one, in that Ivey also gave the children free run of his adjoining landholdings, including a swimming pool, and helped build the camp's bunkhouse. "We have had free use of his swimming pool and hundreds of acres of his land for many years," Father Thomas noted. But in 1974, with suburban development marching toward the site and property taxes going up, the Ivey family decided to reassemble its holdings for development and approached Father Thomas for the return of the land.

Father Thomas negotiated a sale price; that raised a few eyebrows, including Father Rahm's, because the land had been a gift to OLYC in the first place. "I would never have charged them money," Father Rahm said years later, although he added that Father Thomas might not have felt he had a choice, given the need to protect the ministries. Then Father Thomas went look-ing for property for a new summer camp. The result of a long and difficult search was the Lord's Ranch, a name which today is almost synonymous with the OLYC community in many peo-ple's minds.

At first, the solution seemed to be a square mile of land owned by the Jesuits at Horizon City, east of El Paso, about 15 miles by road from OLYC. The land had originally been donated to the Jesuit high school; Fr. Deeves described it as "just a piece of sand." The Jesuit provincial superior, Father Thomas Clancy, offered this land as a replacement camp, and Sister Mary Virginia received a prophecy that water would be found there.

A test well was drilled, and it found water, all right, but not much of it, and very salty. Father Clancy was more impressed with the test results than he was with the prophecy and told Father Thomas to keep looking. Father Thomas wanted to argue about it; he told Father Clancy "that's God telling us there's water there." "As far as that well goes, I am God," the provincial shot back. One evening not long afterward, Father Thomas, pre-occupied with his worries, mentioned the trouble to a 10-year-old child in front of the youth center, and the youngster told him "you have to obey your provincial." Father Thomas took that message as coming from God and stopped trying to change Father Clancy's mind.

The next promising candidate was railroad land in the north-east of the city near Zaragoza and Montana, about the same dis-tance away from OLYC as Horizon City. The railroad was prepared to sell as much land as the camp needed. But water was a question again, and although the predictions were optimistic, a series of obstacles kept putting off the drilling of a test well.

Again Father Clancy said keep going, and this time Father Thomas started looking to the west and north, with the help of a realtor. He saw several sites that weren't suitable, and then he ran across a promising parcel in the desert in Fillmore Pass near

Vado, NM, about 33 miles north of OLYC. The land was vacant at the time, with just one farm nearby, and most of it was in the hands of a single owner, a land developer. The soil was good, the water was good, the view was good. The price wasn't so good, though: half a million 1974 dollars, non-negotiable. "There was no question of buying it – it was out of sight!" Father Thomas recalled later. Back in town, he went for a walk on the railroad land and prayed. "I was walking back and forth, and I was saying, 'God, what are you trying to tell me?' The Lord let me know real clear, 'use your common sense day by day.'" He decided that apart from price and distance from the city, all the pluses were with the Vado land. "Common sense told you that this [Vado] was far superior to that [railroad land], but there wasn't any money to buy this thing."

So on a Saturday evening in early September, Father Thomas and OLYC board member Dr. Alejandro Durán and his wife rode around the Vado land on horseback, then knelt in the desert at sundown and said "Lord, we claim this land for You."

The community prayed for a solution, and soon Father Thomas found out there were two adjoining 80-acre parcels at the site that the landowner with the half-million price tag didn't actually own. The owner of one parcel, a widow living in San Jose, Calif., had refused to sell to the developer; the owner of the other parcel lived in Los Angeles, and she couldn't be found, either by the developer or by the OLYC realtor.

"We were praying every day at the center, and it came clear, write this lady in San Jose and tell her 'we'd like to buy the land, it's going to be used for poor kids, can we buy it?' She writes back and says 'yes, if it's going to be used for poor kids, you can buy it.'" Her price was a lot lower than what the developer was asking. "That was only 80 acres and we could handle that financially." The deed to the land, the northwest corner of the present ranch at the entrance gate, came through Dec. 23, 1974.

The community started developing the land in February (see chapter 35), but in the meantime Father Thomas still wanted the other 80 acres. "In prayer at the youth center, the word was I should go to California and look for the lady that nobody can find." Sister Mary Virginia had a vision of an airplane in God's hands, so off Father Thomas flew to Los Angeles, armed only with the owner's name, Bertha Williams; an address that was obviously no longer correct; and the name of a charismatic contact who was a total stranger. The contact met him at the airport, the two men had lunch, and they started searching for what amounted to a needle in an entire barn full of hay.

"Williams is the most common name in the United States," Father Thomas said. "It's not Smith, it's not Jones, it's Williams. We spent all afternoon going from door to door in Los Angeles, 'do you know Bertha Williams?'"

They got one lead, but it was thin. Somewhere in an unspecified grammar school in Los Angeles, there was a girl named Williams, first name and grade level also not specified, who was a relative of Bertha. "When we went to bed that night, our goal for the next day was to go to every public school in Los Angeles and check every girl in every public school named Williams and see if we could find this girl who was the daughter or granddaughter of Bertha Williams. Imagine how many schools there are in Los Angeles! We would have to go to every school and get them to tell us – whether they would or not, I don't know about that – if you have any girl in your school by the name of Williams. It wasn't an encouraging prospect."

But shortly after Father Thomas went to bed in his helper's home, the phone rang. It was a relative of Bertha Williams who had got wind of the search and wanted to know what was going on. He agreed to meet the next day, and when Father Thomas explained what he wanted, the man told him Bertha Williams had died several years earlier, leaving no will, and the land was now owned by 35 or 40 relatives, some in California and some in Texas. Nobody had reported the death, but the taxes were paid up to date. All the owners would have to consent to a sale, but the man said they'd all probably be willing, and he gave Father Thomas the list of names.

"Less than 30 hours after I arrived in Los Angeles, we had the whole thing solved. God was taking care of us, that's all." With the help of OLYC board member Rickie Feuille, a prominent El Paso lawyer, Father Thomas contacted the owners, and they all agreed to sell. It took a while, but OLYC got title in July 1975. Together the two parcels formed a half-mile-square quarter section, the original Lord's Ranch and still the site of nearly all the buildings.

Where did the money for the purchase come from? There's no simple answer except "God." Father Thomas approached at least one major funding agency: OLYC archives contain a 40-page binder labeled "History of Our Lady's Youth Center" which begins with a cover letter to the Dallas Community Chest Trust Fund, dated Oct. 29, 1974. The letter says OLYC is "seeking to ultimately raise One Million Dollars for the purpose of relocating and expanding our long-existing camp." The document contains an extensive account of OLYC's history and programs and a detailed proposal for development of the eventual Lord's Ranch land, at that point not yet purchased, near Vado. But clearly the Community Chest appeal didn't get anywhere.

"Money came from donations," Father Thomas told a newspaper reporter in 1976. "When the word got around, lots of people liked the idea and we got small gifts and we got large ones." Jean Soto was one of the individual donors, but she said Father Thomas never asked her, or the group, to donate. "He had no knowledge of it until I put it [the donation] in his hand." Rickie Feuille said funds came in from all over, including South America, Europe and Mexico.

Around the beginning of 1976, OLYC signed a lease with the Bureau of Land Management for 320 additional acres, to the south of the original property, to make an L-shaped 480-acre parcel. Cost was $720 a year for the BLM-leased land, and the lease gave OLYC an option to buy the land at a later date.

Entrance to the newly acquired property for the Lord's Ranch, 1975.

CHAPTER 36

Building for the Lord

W ork on the Lord's Ranch began Feb. 9, 1975. Sunday after Sunday, community members, as many as 200 of them according to the March 1975 newsletter, would drive half an hour or more out to the property, dig out mesquite bushes, plant trees and gardens, celebrate Mass out of the back of a van, and then go home. It wasn't exactly a standard Sunday outing. It was freezing cold in February; later in the year it got brutally hot. There was no coffee or soda, and the food was nothing special – often donations of food thrown away from supermarkets; Pochie Heredia remembered eating beans, tortillas and onions cooked in a pot in a hole in the ground. Sister Mary Virginia said Father Thomas assigned the cooking to people who couldn't cook, so they wouldn't notice how bad the food and the facilities were.

"It was hard, but God would give us the strength to work in the sun," said Heredia. "We were always praising Him." Sister Mary Virginia said, "We were happy – people didn't complain. Every time we needed something, God would provide. Every single time."

Other agencies joined in the work, including army engineers, Seabees, Job Corps, the gas and telephone companies, and many others. Numerous goods and services were donated, along with the loan of equipment. A fence was built, a well was drilled, trees were planted. Buildings went up using adobe made on site from earth, water and grass.

The first two structures were a swimming pool and a latrine. The swimming pool was a priority because the main point of the ranch was to replace Camp Juan Diego, and there was nowhere in South El Paso for the children to swim in the summer heat. Somebody told Father Thomas to contact George Thomas (no relation), a prominent El Paso home builder he had never met. George Thomas said he hired Juan Molina to build pools, and if OLYC would pay Molina his usual wages, George would lend his truck and equipment. Father Thomas spent the night before Molina's arrival at the site, and in the morning prayed about the size and location. "I said, 'God, where do you want this swimming pool? How big do you want it?'" Molina did "a super job," and the pool was ready for the first swim June 18.

The community originally intended to open a full-fledged summer camp at the ranch in June, just like the one at Camp Juan Diego. That didn't happen, because there was no place yet for them to eat or sleep or bathe, and there was no way to provide for the large numbers of children – more than 600 in 1974 – that had turned out in previous years. But there were some day campers. "None of them spent the night – there were no buildings out here," Father Thomas said. "We brought them out every morning from El Paso, whoever wanted to come out, we'd bring them out here, bring their lunch, go swimming and whatever. There was nothing to do out here except swim and chase lizards." The youngsters were happy to help with the work, too, watering trees and plants and gathering rocks to build animal pens.

The first major structure to be completed was the machine shop, in 1976. In addition to its main function, it had enough sheltered space to serve as primitive living quarters, for volunteers willing to sleep on cots on a concrete floor. "Everything was there," said Father Thomas. "We ate, slept, we had one *baño* [the usual Spanish expression for latrine]. We all lived in there, whoever lived at the ranch. Everything was in the shop. That was a big improvement, of course. That's the first house we could live in."

Mass was celebrated at the shop, too. Prayer and worship had been part of the ranch from the beginning: while the Sunday work was going on, a group of volunteers was assigned to sit in a Dodge van and pray all day. "It's very exhausting to work all day in the sun, and equally exhausting to pray continually for the same period of time," Father Thomas wrote, "but we have found that the Lord blesses us in an outstanding way if six or so people dedicate themselves to praying during the entire day." Mass was celebrated from the back of the van at first, then in a straw shelter. When the machine shop was built, Mass moved there, and when the first real dormitory was built in 1978, that became the ranch "church." It became a tradition over the years to have Mass and other community activities in whatever the newest building happened to be. "People learned they could pray at any time or in any circumstances," Sister Mary Virginia said. "People were in prayer all the time, ministry all the time. It made the ranch strong."

Right from the beginning, workers reported healings. One woman was healed of a bad back as she made bricks for the latrine. A man was healed of asthma during a sandstorm – he forgot to take his medicine, and he didn't notice until he got back home that he was no longer suffering from the symptoms.

From day one, the ranch was intended to be more than a summer camp. Father Thomas wanted to grow food for the poor, too, so half a dozen kinds of fruit trees were planted within the first three months, along with grapevines and a variety of vegetables; the first squash was picked July 11. Eventually there were more than 2,000 trees. Beehives were also in place within a couple of years. None of the volunteers ate the food grown on the ranch. From the beginning the ranch's produce was donated to the poor: at first to known needy people, then via a food bank at OLYC, and by the end of 1975 to the first of several food bank sites in Juárez (see chapter 37).

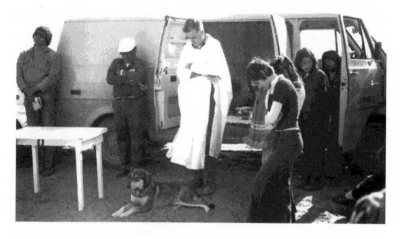

Celebrating Mass from the van before there were any buildings at the Lord's Ranch, 1975.

That first squash crop consisted of four tiny squashes, "as big as my fingers," Father Thomas remembered years later. Dutifully, the community gave the squash away to a poor elderly woman they knew. Over time the crop grew, to maybe a pound a week. Then, a couple of months into the growing season, something astonishing happened. Three people were picking squash, including Lorenza Ledesma, who had been going to OLYC since her early teens. They were putting the squash into garbage bags as they picked. "I realized the bag was heavier than it should be," Ledesma said. "I was mentally blaming the other people for putting their squash in my bag." But when she looked up for her co-workers, she saw they were both too far away for that to happen – and when she talked to them, she found out they had been thinking the same thing about her. They could barely carry the bags of squash they ended up with.

In 1978, Father Thomas decided the ranch needed to raise chickens, so he put Mary Ann Raths, now Halloran (see chapter 39), in charge. She didn't know anything about chickens, so he got her a book. An old farmer offered to donate some chicks, so the two of them went off to his house to collect the chickens, who were running loose on the floor. It gave her a long-lasting job – she has kept chickens at the ranch off and on right down to the present day, long after the ranch had given up active farming – and a permanent nickname. "Mother Hen," Father Thomas called her until the day he died, and although it made a perfect name for a woman who was completely devoted to the eight children she eventually raised on the ranch, it actually started with the chickens, before she was even married. "First he started calling me Mary Hen, but pretty soon it was Mother Hen, and that's been my nickname ever since," she said. "He called me Mother Hen more than he called me my name."

Next he asked if they should expand to cows and goats – a big jump from chickens, since chickens don't have to be milked. "Are you sure?" he asked. "Think about it more. No days off." Mary Ann was willing, so they went out and got one goat, named Curly, who had never been milked by humans – and small wonder. "She was the meanest goat we ever had," Mary Ann recalled. She had one teat, and it took five people to milk her – two to hold her front legs, two on the back, and one to do the milking. She gave very little milk.

One day Father rode by on horseback and Mary Ann proudly held up a container with about half a cup of milk in it: "Look, Father! We got milk from her." "I should hope so," he responded. "There's five of you working on it."

Later they got more goats, sweeter-tempered and more productive, and eventually a buck named Sam who turned out to be a pedigreed French Alpine milk sire. "Since the Lord had sent us a super male milk goat, we took this to mean He wanted us to produce goat milk for the poor," Father Thomas recalled later. Most of the milk was made into cheese by Sister Mary Virginia, for pregnant food bank clients who often suffered from calcium deficiency and didn't have either the money or the refrigeration to drink milk very often. The first batch was made on Easter weekend 1979 and distributed at the food bank the same week. Soon after the ranch added cows, which the ranchers raised for the next 10 years.

Taking a break from Ranch work to play with one of the dogs, 1976.

CHAPTER 37

The Lord's Food Bank

From the time the ranch began to grow food, the community was able to find poor people to give it to. But it was food grown somewhere else that provided the push to start a food bank.

In the fall of 1975 a farmer in Mesquite, near Vado, had a field full of onions he didn't want – thousands of pounds of them. He called the ranch. "He said 'you can have all the onions in my field,'" Father Thomas said. "'As many as you can get out by Monday, you can have. Then I'm going to start plowing the field.' We spent all weekend getting onions out of his field, because the price had dropped down and he couldn't afford to get them out." It was no easy job, because the onions were already in sacks and the farmer wanted to keep the sacks, so the workers had to dump the onions out of the sacks into a truck, take them to the ranch, and return for the next load. "We just threw them on the ground. We just kept going and going," Father Thomas said.

With so many onions to give away, the community covered the usual recipients and looked for something to do with the rest. The answer was a food bank at OLYC. The bank had only onions to give at first, but that didn't stop it from becoming an immediate success. In fact, it was a little too successful: within a few weeks the word had spread across the border, and so many people were crossing the river illegally to get at the food, that the community decided to open a branch on the Juárez side.

Father Thomas checked out three parishes in the Juárez hills, and the pastor of one agreed to let the food bank have a room in the church. "Hundreds of people came," said Martha Medrano, the food bank manager at the time. After a year, the food bank became the victim of its own success when the pastor decided the crowds were too big, and one day the workers found the door locked. So the operation moved to a nearby private home for the next year, but Medrano said the house, with electricity and running water, was too nice for the purpose, so the food bank moved again, to what the workers called the "burlap cathedral" because Mass was celebrated in an open area under the shade of burlap bags. Meanwhile, the food bank operation continued for a while on the El Paso side, but was allowed to peter out when other food banks were started there and the OLYC community was concentrating its energies in Juárez.

The food bank operation wasn't very secure in any of its early homes, and finding a replacement was never easy because the bank needed a lot of storage space. Finally the Lord sent a solution by an unexpected means.

One night, at the prayer meeting at OLYC, a man from Juárez walked up to Father Thomas and handed him a letter. "The letter says 'your request for land has been granted. You are to come up with a master plan within 48 hours, how you're going to develop this land,'" Father Thomas said. "I didn't know anything about a letter, I never wrote a request, I never signed a letter, I didn't know there was any land, didn't know anything about anything until this guy brings a letter one night." The letter also contained a survey drawing of a 14-acre mesa (flat-topped hill), the vacant land the food bank was being offered in *Colonia Plutarco Elías Calles* – a neighborhood named, paradoxically, for the ex-president who was probably Mexico's worst persecutor of the Catholic Church. There were no roads there, no water, nothing.

It wasn't even suitable for squatters, because the water trucks couldn't get up the hill.

So Father Thomas turned to El Paso architect George Du Sang, a friend of the community. "God bless him, he comes up with a beautiful master plan." The site was granted in 1981 and is still the location of the main food bank today. "I don't know til today who wrote the letter and signed my name saying we want that land," Father Thomas said shortly before his death. "I suspect I know but I'm not sure. Nobody has said anything. I suspect that one guy wrote it. I've never asked him. That's how God works."

"The Lord's Food Bank is based on two ideas from the Bible: the community storehouse for the widow and orphan to eat from, and St. Paul's admonition 'if they don't work, don't let them eat,'" Father Thomas explained at the time. "God blessed the project, supplying more and more food until as many as a thousand families were being fed per week in three different locations in Ciudad Juárez."

There was more to be had at the food bank than food. Each week Father Thomas would hear confessions, then say Mass. Many of those attending didn't normally go to church, Sister Mary Virginia said; "This Mass was for them. They didn't have to dress up for it." Medrano brought people to the prayer meetings by the vanload; "there were many conversions, many miracles," she said. Father Thomas taught simple lessons from Scripture.

In keeping with the "if they don't work, don't let them eat" rule, everybody who wanted food was given a job. Those who couldn't do anything physical went into the prayer room and prayed for the others; the physically fit dug ditches, built and repaired houses, cleaned homes and churches, and did other work. At food distribution time, the volunteers would hand out tickets to everybody who had worked, without worrying about the huge numbers of people who often turned up, and count on

God to multiply the food if necessary; "Jesus is the underwriter of our bank," Father Thomas once explained. "We never ran out," recalled Carmen Molina, a later manager. "I don't remember running out of anything."

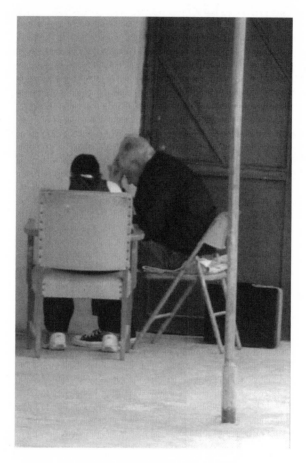

Hearing confessions outside at
the Lord's Food Bank in Juárez, 2002.

Besides handing out food on site, volunteers delivered it to shut-ins. Women went out in teams, walking through the neighborhood looking for people who needed food. The food bank also distributed clothing. A medical clinic was set up in 1980, and continues today, along with a dental clinic and a Montessori school.

At the clinics, volunteer doctors and dentists from both sides of the border cared for the patients, but "prayer first" was the rule, because Father Thomas followed the teaching of Sirach 38:9-14, in the Catholic Old Testament, which says the doctor should be called in only after prayer, repentance, and liturgical means. Volunteers say many were healed before they even got to see the doctor.

Pregnant women and new mothers got special attention. While pregnant, the women would sew layettes, and be given a layette in turn when they gave birth. After the birth, the new mothers would be given vitamins and special food.

Mass in the "burlap cathedral" (above) and below,
Father Thomas (back row, third from left) with some of the men
and children from the Food Bank, Juárez, Mexico, 1977.

CHAPTER 38

Making It Work in Juárez

eanwhile, charismatic prayer meetings continued on the Juárez side of the river. Challenges continued, too. While Father Thomas was always on friendly terms with Bishop Talamás – "he was a good guy," Father Thomas said years later – the bishop was still wary when it came to dealing with charismatic prayer meetings. He had been rector of a seminary, and he was particular about theological language. Somebody was reporting the contents of Father Thomas's prayer meeting sermons to him, and he had his own comments to make. "He told me early on, 'do not use the words "baptism in the Holy Spirit,"'" Father Thomas recalled. "I said 'what are we supposed to use?' [He said] *'renovación de confirmación.'* When he told me that, I opened the Bible to Acts, chapter 1. It says, 'in a few days you'll be baptized in the Holy Spirit.' I said 'OK, Bishop, when I read this, am I supposed to say "in a few days you'll have *reno-vación* of the sacrament of confirmation?"'" He didn't know that was in the New Testament. That kind of shocked him. 'Am I supposed to say that every time I read this passage?' I don't know how he dealt with that."

"Every few weeks he'd call me in and say 'instead of saying it this way, you should have said it that way.' I wasn't preaching error or anything, I just wasn't using the exact vocabulary he wanted me to use. After a while I got tired and I quit preaching at the prayer meeting. I said Mass and no sermon." But somebody complained about *that*, so after a few weeks the bishop called Father Thomas in and asked why he wasn't preaching. "I said, 'Bishop, I've got enough sin on me already, and I don't want to say things that are wrong. I don't want to sin any more, and that's why I'm not preaching.' He said 'you start preaching again.' That's the last I heard from him on that deal. I started preaching the next week."

At one prayer meeting, the bishop turned up in person near the beginning and sat down to listen. "I was wrestling in my mind, 'shall I give my teaching or not?' I was real nervous." Father Thomas decided to go ahead, and it turned out well; that was the time he said God protected him from making mistakes in Spanish (see chapter 33). "The bishop didn't hear any mistakes at all."

One thing Bishop Talamás never had to worry about from Father Thomas was disobedience. In fact, he had the opposite problem. "The bishop knew from years of dealing with me that I was going to do whatever he said. This frightened him. I don't know that [there was] anybody else that he could be assured they were going to do everything he said. I'd ask him 'should we do this, or that, or nothing, or what?' As soon as I'd ask him that question he'd start working his fingers. I said, 'I'm going to obey you absolutely. Whatever you say I'm going to do absolutely and you're going to be responsible before God, not me.'"

Eventually, the bishop found an unexpected way of dealing with the problem. When the Juárez food bank began at Holy Spirit Church, there was no teaching going on in the parish, and the pastor didn't want Father Thomas to teach either. So Father Thomas asked the bishop for direction. "This puts the bishop in a delicate situation because the pastor has his own authority, and he makes decisions, and the bishop doesn't want to get him mad and he doesn't want to meddle in something that's going to become messy. He says to me, 'I want you to go see Guillermina [Villalva] and ask her what she thinks.'" That wasn't the answer Father Thomas was expecting, and he asked the bishop not once but twice to repeat himself. "I said again, 'Bishop, I want to be sure I hear you. You're telling me that I'm to go to Guillermina and tell her, and then whatever she says, I'm to do and you're going to back it up?' He said, 'yes, I'll back up whatever she tells you.' I go drive right away and find Guillermina, and I say, 'guess what, Guillermina – you're my bishop.'

"So ever after that, Guillermina was my bishop, in that I asked her everything. It was a big joke with me, that I had a lady bishop. I had a lot of fun, introducing her as my bishop in the U.S. This went on for years, I guess until she died" [in a 1991 plane crash].

With Bishop Talamás and Guillermina Villalva, 1979.

Over time, the bishop stopped worrying about prayer meetings in church buildings, and meetings were held in many Juárez churches and even in the diocesan education building across from the chancery office. One of the locations was the huge *Natividad* Church, which had very poor attendance. Lucía and Sergio Conde said the priest there invited the prayer group, and the group began prayer meetings that filled a couple of pews. "In six months the church was filled to the very end, with people who were praising the Lord," said Lucía. "The people came by the thousands." Another was the Mission of Our Lady of Guadalupe next door to the Juárez cathedral. Soon the meeting had to move into the main cathedral building. "It was full, all the way from the altar to the outside door."

The Condes say Father Thomas and the prayer meetings brought a whole new understanding of Catholicism to the people of Juárez. Before, said Lucía, "it was very empty. People were praying many rosaries but not connecting with God." Instead of focusing on saints – devout Mexicans sometimes wear holes in the saints' statues as they venerate them – Father Thomas urged the people simply to come to God and be in His presence. "This was very strange," said Lucía. "It was new to say, 'I love God, I come to church because I want to meet God.' God for us is a father, a friend, one you can talk to and get a response, a real person."

Father Thomas challenged people on other fronts, too. He told them to give up witches and tarot readings and other occult activities (see chapter 28) – in short, "not to try to find power outside of God," Lucía said. That's no small matter in Mexico, where the occult is even mixed in with Catholic practices. He also told them to forget about being a success in a worldly sense; that message didn't go over in Mexico any better than it would anywhere else. Sergio remembered one meeting when Father told the congregation they should give up their possessions. "A rich man yelled out 'Father, don't say that!' Father smiled and kept on talking."

All the same, Father Thomas got through to a lot of people, said Sergio – "the first time I met him, I saw Father's eyes penetrate to here" [slapping the back of his head]. There were many conversions, of businessmen, professionals, and ordinary people.

Even after the renewal was accepted, Father Thomas had occasional problems with Church politics. One day he was called in to chancery to see the bishop. He found two priests there, with a long list of wild allegations and complaints. Supposedly Father Thomas had been kidnapped; supposedly he was allowing Protestant ministers to teach at food bank; supposedly he had gotten married.

"It was all wild stuff but related to me and my ministry. None of it had a scrap of truth to it. It went on for about an hour. We went on and on and on and on about all these accusations. I just said, 'well, that just never happened.' And there was no question that the bishop believed what I said.

"[The bishop] turned to the two priests and said 'is there anything else?' They said 'holy water.'" Father Thomas did use sacramentals a lot in his ministry, even going so far as to give people holy water to drink, and the two priests didn't approve. "The bishop turned to me and said 'use your common sense,' and he dismissed us. We all left."

CHAPTER 39

A Community in the Desert

"*El que no quiera trabajar, que tampoco coma* – if anyone will not work, let him not eat." (2 Thess 3:10). That biblical motto, on a sign at the Lord's Ranch to this day, has been the operating principle from the beginning, on the ranch just as much as at the food bank. And from the beginning, people of all types were welcome to come to the ranch to work, eat and play, year-round—young and old, parents and children, Anglo and Hispanic. Not all of them were stereotyped church people, either.

At first, all the workers at the ranch were local residents. But to Father Thomas's surprise, word got out, and soon people from across North America began arriving to join the community. Nineteen-year-old Mary Ann Raths was the first. In 1976 she read about the Christmas multiplication and wrote Father Thomas, asking for permission to come spend a year in the OLYC community. "He wrote back and said 'why don't you come and see?' He didn't quite know what to think about me wanting to come." When they met face to face, "the first thing he said was 'I hear you play guitar. Do you play by ear?' When I said 'yes,' he quipped, 'You must have a tough ear.' I thought, 'this guy's a character.'"

By 1978, more people from out of the area started arriving. One of them was Mike Halloran, Mary Ann's future husband, who eventually became the ranch manager. Other newcomers from the same period included Mike's parents, Bill and Marion, who retired to El Paso from Rhode Island to work with the poor through the OLYC community. Enough people began to arrive that a system developed to screen people for their intentions. Sister Mary Virginia said Father Thomas required anyone who wanted to come to the ranch to write a letter of request, to help him get to know them.

When larger numbers started arriving, the only buildings on the ranch were the pool, the latrine, the machine shop, and a barn with some corrals. Even Father Thomas and Sister Mary Virginia mostly lived in town except on weekends, when they stayed in the makeshift dormitories in the machine shop. Mary Ann lived in town when she first arrived. But in the summer of 1977 she asked to live on the ranch full-time. Father Thomas was surprised. "I didn't think anyone would ever ask me to live on the ranch," he said. Mary Ann remembered those days fondly. Sometimes she and Father Thomas would plant trees together, talking about things as they worked. "I loved the way Father taught," she said. "Early on we had a good relationship, real respectful. All this time I was growing spiritually because he was a constant teacher. He just put God in everything."

In late 1978, to make space for the increase of newcomers, Father Thomas made plans for the first real residence: Ezekiel House, the building nearest the front gate today. Residents slept on cots upstairs. "Everyone there really admired Father and wanted to live a holy life," said Mary Ann. "We'd often praise the Lord at night."

At first there were few if any rules, so it was no special problem when Mike and Mary Ann fell in love while milking cows that December. They married in June 1979. Eventually, though, the growing number of volunteers made more rules necessary.

With a couple of dozen single people of both sexes on the premises, each courting couple was required to choose a "romance director" as a guide; not everybody felt this system worked well.

Concerning romance, Father Thomas taught the principle "Master, mission, mate." "First you have to establish who your Master is – in other words, who you are going to follow," Ellen Hogarty explains. "Then you need to discern your calling or mission in life – what is your personal vocation that God is inviting you to. Only after getting those clear is when you should consider a mate. If your vocation is marriage, hopefully you would want to look for a spouse that has the same Master, the same mission or goals, and then you can both support one another and be more effective in serving the Lord. You can't find a suitable marriage partner if you don't know who your Master is and what your calling is. So you have to discover the three Ms in that order."

Work went on seven days a week, since Father Thomas taught that works of charity are exempt from the Sabbath rest. Individuals got either Wednesday or Friday, staggered to keep the milking going, to make sure they got the rest they needed, but Father Thomas sometimes groused about the "day off" mentality, which he said meant three days wasted, including a day of anticipation and a day of recovery.

Out of solidarity with the poor, Father Thomas expected the ranchers to live frugally. Showers were limited to two a week, navy style: turn the shower on, get wet, turn it off, lather up, turn it on again to rinse. Shampoo just once and watch the toilet paper use.

But there were plenty of good times, too, like talent shows and music nights. And Father Thomas's lighter side was on view frequently, for example when he brought a donkey into the machine shop dorm to wake people up in the morning. "He loved doing things like that," said Mary Ann.

Father Thomas even worked a donkey into at least one of the several weddings that took place at the ranch. The bride and groom knew Father Thomas's old friend and seminary classmate Father Jack Deeves, then working in Dallas, and asked him to help officiate; he never forgot the experience. He showed up in his full clerical suit, but Father Thomas, the main celebrant, was in his usual casual attire, and it was obvious he hadn't done a lot of weddings, because he asked his friend for advice repeatedly. "He kept referring to me as the apostolic delegate," Father Deeves recalled. "He'd say, 'I have to consult the apostolic delegate.'"

The wedding took place in a tent pavilion with hay bales and planks for an altar. Sister Mary Virginia had decorated a dog with a bonnet and flower basket to serve as a flower girl, and there was a parade of animals, including Old Abe the burro. "Jack, are you going to participate in this wedding or not?" Father Thomas demanded. "If you are, get up here and ride Old Abe." Father Deeves rode the donkey for a few minutes, and Father Thomas appeared satisfied.

Celebrating the wedding of Mike and Mary Ann Halloran
at the Lord's Ranch, 1979.

CHAPTER 40

Reaching Out to the Poor

O ver in Juárez, the dump and food bank ministries always had a large spiritual element along with the physical food, with plenty of prayer and teaching for everybody who attended. Even so, Father Thomas and his friends didn't think they were doing enough to reach out and evangelize more of the poor. In 1977 they decided to step up their efforts.

The previous year, Father Thomas had phoned Sister Briege McKenna, a charismatic Irish nun with a healing ministry who was touring North America at the time and asked her to come to the dump and pray with the people there. She had only a brief time available, but she came to town and prayed for a crowd of more than 700 at the dump, as well as about 200 people who gathered at the Lord's Ranch on the other side of the border. In an incident which has been retold many times in recent years, a woman at the dump brought a child she had found on her way to the meeting. He had been severely burned and she found him smoldering in the dump, with gangrenous legs; Father Thomas placed him under the altar during Mass, and at the end he crawled out with his burns healed.

So in the summer of 1977, Father Thomas invited Sister Briege back, and Bishop Talamás gave approval for a five-day evangelistic campaign in August. A team of about three dozen people prepared for the campaign by prayer, for a ministry of preaching, prayer, teaching and healing. It was an all-out effort. The El Paso residents commuted across the river each day, and they took naps at Sergio and Lucía Conde's home at midday before rushing back to preach and pray. "Father kept a very strong pace," said Lucía. Some team members began to flag with the effort, and the team began to dwindle. "Sister and he talked about it, and the next day he was easier," Lucía said.

Sister Briege was known for "bilocation" (incidents where she was reported to be in two different places at the same time), and this was one of several times where the same thing happened with Father Thomas. "People from the dump saw him at the time he was with us," said Sergio. "Now I am in a class with Sister McKenna," Father Thomas chuckled.

Father Thomas started the campaign daily at 9 a.m. with no advance advertising. "We would just start singing and praying, and people would start streaming into the church," said Jean Soto, who was part of the campaign. "It's not like there was a notice in the bulletin. All of these people coming into the church at an hour when there would [normally] be nothing going on." The campaign would go all morning, and then resume from late afternoon to a late dinner time. The meetings were rowdy: "When we evangelize it's a lot of fun," Father Thomas said. "There's no tavern or dance hall anywhere in the city that's having the fun we're having in church. Everybody's laughing and dancing and being healed of their diseases and throwing off all their sorrows. It's just a fun experience."

"We dance in church. We're trying to bring dancing back where it belongs. Dancing should be for the glory of God, not for the glory of Satan."

On day 3 they found the church door locked, apparently because the local pastor didn't want anybody dancing in his church. Father Thomas was unfazed – "we just start praising in the streets," he said. In the course of the day, a member of the team received a prophetic word: *"cuide a los hombres"* (take care of the men)." That came as a surprise. "Up to then there had been scarcely any men at all involved in the prayer movement," Father Thomas said. "So the message raised the question, 'What men? There aren't any.'"

As usual, God had His own ideas about that, and those ideas led to a major step forward for the community. About a dozen men (one source gives the number as 16) stopped by to watch the "crazy people" dancing and praising. "These were the men the Lord Himself had chosen," Father Thomas exulted later; he said some of them had been drunkards, thieves and wife-beaters, but God had something different in mind for them. The team invited them into a parked van, where Sergio Conde invited them to accept Jesus. They did; they also went to confession, received the gift of tongues, and in the evening, when the church was finally unlocked and full of people, they gave their testimony. As Father Thomas later told the story, there was a brief interruption when everybody heard a loud thump: an older woman had fainted with shock and delight when her son stepped up to testify. She had been trying for seven years just to get him to attend church. One of the men was healed of alcoholism, arthritis, diabetes and tuberculosis, witnessed by medical tests the following year.

This group of men came to be known as the "apostles," and Father Thomas took the command to take care of them seriously. He met with them weekly for years in a discipleship program that ranged from learning to read, write and do simple math, to Bible study and prayer, to labor skills including building houses for the poor. He brought them to the Lord's Ranch for retreats and used his beloved horses as examples to explain topics like prayer; the apostles were mostly from the countryside, and horses were something they could understand. He also took a group of them to the 1978 national Catholic charismatic conference at Notre Dame, and while they were there he bought some of them their first new shoes. Father Thomas later said it was the story of the apostles that began to attract visitors to the community, and they certainly attracted other men to the ministries—when another Jesuit, Fr. James McCown, visited the food bank the following year, he found 50 men jammed into a small room praising God from 5 a.m. onward.

Some of the men had only been able to feed their families two or three times a week before their conversion, Father McCown wrote. Afterwards they were still poor, but now they got groceries from the food bank, along with moral support and friendship from one another.

CHAPTER 41

"Spirit of death, I cast you out"

That 1978 trip to Notre Dame brought a huge encounter with the power of God, before the group had even left El Paso.

It was Aug. 16. The group from Juárez crossed the river in the morning. The border crossing didn't go smoothly, and the travelers were tired when they arrived at OLYC in time for a community prayer meeting. After lunch Father Thomas declared a *siesta*, around 2 p.m. About the same time, a 47-year-old Juárez woman, the wife of one of the apostles, fainted. There didn't seem to be any serious concern, so Father Thomas told everyone to calm down and take their *siesta*; he lay down on the floor himself and fell fast asleep.

A nun of the Daughters of Charity, who was also a registered nurse and resuscitation expert, had just finished washing dishes and returned to the meeting area when she was called to help. The woman was now unresponsive and breathing much too fast; her pulse was OK at that moment, but after the nurse worked with her for a few minutes her pulse and breathing stopped altogether. There were no vital signs.

The nurse woke Father Thomas up to call a doctor and an ambulance and began resuscitation efforts. But Father Thomas, who said in an interview years later that he would normally have called the ambulance, was too groggy to focus on the job, and instead woke up other people and asked them to pray.

Meanwhile, the nurse and a student nurse tried mouth-to-mouth resuscitation and the Heimlich maneuver, but the airway was blocked, and they couldn't find or clear the obstruction. When they breathed air into the woman's mouth, it bulged out her cheeks instead of going to her lungs. The nurse said later she had had the same problem with another patient in the past and the patient died even though a doctor had been present to help with the resuscitation.

"It became clear that I should cast out the spirit of death," Father Thomas said later, "and I laid my hand on [the woman] and said in a whisper, 'Spirit of death, I cast you out in Jesus' name.'"

The woman took a sudden breath and started to regurgitate. Her pulse and breathing went back to normal. "I took her by the hand and she slowly got to her feet. She rested for several minutes and then began dancing with the community to praise the Lord. People estimated that she was without any vital signs for 10 minutes."

She said she hadn't been in pain at any point. She had seen a vision of a priest dressed for Mass; the priest told her not to believe the lies of the enemy. She said she was filled with joy.

The woman went on to Notre Dame with the rest of the party. Father Thomas told the story at the Notre Dame conference, but with shockingly little emphasis for such a spectacular event. *New Covenant* magazine published the account in its coverage of the conference, along with the stories of two of the apostles and one other woman from Juárez, but the headline didn't even mention the resuscitation, and the woman's story is placed fourth of the four accounts.

Father Thomas's almost offhand attitude toward an actual revival from the dead says a lot about the way he looked at signs and wonders. He believed they're just a normal part of the Christian life, to be accepted as part of what the Lord is doing rather than singled out for their own sake. The woman's healing is documented in OLYC archives along with other healings and apparently miraculous events, with first-person testimony from the nurse and from Father Thomas but was never presented to Church authorities for authentication as a miracle. It also isn't mentioned in *Miracles in El Paso?*, a 1982 book on the OLYC ministries by Father Rene Laurentin, a specialist on the miracles of Lourdes, even though the issue of modern-day miracles is the main point of the book, and the book does include the Christmas multiplication, the healing of Irma Padilla's students, and several other apparent miracles.

CHAPTER 42

Letting God Pay the Bills

To Father Thomas, the foundational event in the development of the community wasn't his baptism in the Spirit, or the first prayer meeting, or the Christmas miracle, or the construction of the Lord's Ranch. In a 1985 interview with *New Covenant* magazine, he told editor Fred Lilly that the community got its real start with something that sounds a lot less spectacular: the decision to get out of the United Way fundraising drive. That happened Feb. 22, 1978.

From the day he arrived in El Paso, Father Thomas always believed in trusting in God for funding. All the same, OLYC was a United Way member agency, the way Father Rahm had set it up, with conventional fundraising and about 20 salaried employees. By 1977 the center was getting $60,000 a year from the United Way, and never for a minute was Father Thomas allowed to forget that fact.

All member agencies were required to go out of their way to promote the United Way in all their activities. Father Rahm had taken that seriously, and Father Thomas did too. "His [Father Rahm's] thing, and rightly so, was 'do everything they say. If they ask you to go give a speech, give a speech. Do everything United Way says, because that's where you get your money.'" In 1967 OLYC won an award as "the agency best identified with the

[United] Fund," and a 1976 newsletter shows Marie Heredia, one of the young people at OLYC, in full *sombrero* and *serape*, riding a donkey named Sarah as part of the United Way kickoff day at El Paso Civic Center.

But there was a lot more to the arrangement than wearing sombreros and pocketing $60,000 a year, and neither side was really all that happy. For one thing, there were restrictions: no United Way money was supposed to be spent on the Lord's Ranch, because the ranch was in New Mexico; spending it in Juárez was out of the question. That might have been all right, except that United Way agencies weren't allowed to do any separate fundraising on their own. It was an accounting nightmare, too: "How do you divide a gallon of gas?" asked Sister Mary Virginia.

Father Thomas was also convinced that United Way politics had more to do with who got money than merit or need did. What's more, he told Fred Lilly in the *New Covenant* interview, "we were vigorously proclaiming the word of God. United Way started getting nervous about that."

The last straw came when 1978 funding allocations were announced. OLYC's share was cut to $37,000, and the United Way demanded an audit that would have cost $10,000. "We had a meeting to protest the cut to $37,000," Father Thomas said. "We put on a show, I think in the bank building. They sent some officials down to see our show and in the show, we told them all the things we were doing. Well, that didn't do any good. $37,000 is it."

But Father Thomas could be stubborn, too. He said OLYC needed $60,000 and would leave the United Way if it didn't get that total; "you can go back and tell them that," he told Rickie Feuille, a prominent El Paso lawyer who was a United Way board member (and former president) at the time. The United Way reacted with disbelief, said Feuille. "They said, 'You can't drop out. Nobody has ever dropped out. That would be a terrible disgrace.'"

"So we decided, I decided, against the board's better judgment, forget the United Way," said Father Thomas. "We'll do it ourselves. They were all pretty much against getting out of the United Way, because what are you going to do? It's better to have $37,000 than nothing at all." Father Thomas, though, got his way at the board table. He said the center couldn't live with the funding cut, the politics, the spending restrictions, and the audit. And he trusted God to take care of it.

"The day we got out of the United Way officially was one of the happiest days I've had in El Paso," he said.

For his part, Feuille, an Anglican, quit the United Way board and joined the board of OLYC, becoming chairman a year later. "I never regretted it," he said. "I was just impressed with the work Fr. Rick was doing in serving the poor and underprivileged."

Meanwhile, Father Thomas held a retreat for employees at the machine shop on the Lord's Ranch; Carmen Molina, who worked at the youth center, remembered a similar meeting there. He told the employees OLYC was now a totally volunteer agency. "I said we quit the United Way. We don't have any funds coming in. If you want a job you've got it. If you want a salary you don't. Most of them left." As Mary Ann Halloran remembered it, day workers at the Lord's Ranch quit, and while most of the staff at the center itself stayed on for the time being, about two-thirds left in the long run.

Father Thomas had been preaching for a long time that Christians should work free for the Lord, and now it was official OLYC policy. Nobody who stayed actually went hungry or homeless. Some received groceries, some were housed in a couple of buildings OLYC had acquired, some lived at home with their parents or other family members. But nobody on staff drew a salary.

The "no funds coming in" part didn't stay true for long. "I asked somebody at the youth center how we were doing financially, and it just blew me away," Father Thomas said. "I couldn't get my head around it. They said we've collected $125,000. Forget the United Way! We started the food bank, and God blessed us. We already had $125,000 before I knew anything. It just blew me away, because we had been trying to scrape by with $60,000. And this was in less than a year. All this money was coming in. Well, that's God."

According to Feuille, OLYC's total donations the first year out of the fund came to several times the figure Father Thomas had asked the United Way for. Feuille called the United Way with the news, "with quite a bit of glee...they were just astonished." Feuille said OLYC donations never dropped below that new level in later years.

But money or no money, Father Thomas never went back to paying salaries. Working free for the Lord became a permanent rule, for its own sake and its spiritual value. And that seems to be why he told Fred Lilly the break with the United Way was the real beginning of the community. "Those who remained began living like the community described in the Acts of the Apostles," he told Lilly.

"It's been that way ever since," Father Thomas said at the end of his life. "We give everything away and try to help everybody we can. We've never had any money problems since, except every once in a while, [if] we've been doing something we shouldn't, and the money is cut off. [When that happens] you better check and see what you're doing."

Sister Mary Virginia remembered the community that developed in this atmosphere as a wonderful place to be. "Every day was fun and exciting," she said. "Good things were always happening. If you couldn't pay attention to that, you just weren't paying attention."

CHAPTER 43

New Times in Town

E ven before the break from the United Way, the work of OLYC in El Paso had been slowly changing. Sports programs, once a huge part of the center's work, had come to an end when Tula died of cancer in 1976 at the age of 53. Also in 1976, OLYC lost federal funding for a feeding program that served 200 children a day, due to new regulations. The program continued, but with no milk or fruit. "The meals are not as completely nutritious or appetizing as before but the children are still coming anyway," Father Thomas wrote in a newsletter at the time.

But there wasn't much immediate change when the center left the United Way in 1978. "All the ministries kept going. I can't think of anything we cut out," said Mary Ann Halloran. Two-thirds of the OLYC staff left eventually, she said, but they left one by one over time, and "when somebody moved on, the Lord brought somebody else. He still does that."

The new Cueva ministry to students opened in March 1976 across from the three-year-old Bowie High School campus, serving mainly Bowie students but open to people of all ages from anywhere in the city. It was attracting 10 to 30 visits a day within a couple of weeks of opening. It featured live-in house parents, OLYC workers Ernest and Esther Padilla. Also living at La Cueva was Fe, a black Labrador retriever Father Thomas had picked out specifically for guard work. Originally Esther wouldn't let Fe into the house – "I did not like dogs in the house. Dogs are outside." But when rowdies began threatening the operation and one even took a punch at Ernest, the Padillas wanted to hire a guard. Father Thomas suggested they let Fe inside instead.

"Within a week she had the whole thing in order," Father Thomas said. "Anybody who came in that was disruptive, she'd go and growl at them. Otherwise she was real nice. She knew who belonged and who didn't, and she'd take care of it."

Soon after Fe came indoors, a boy came in with a knife concealed in his pocket. Sister Mary Virginia recalled how Fe barked at the boy, then followed him as he ran out of the building and treed him on the hood of a car. "How did she know I had a knife in my pocket?" the teen demanded.

"That's a gift of God, that she would know this guy had a knife," Father Thomas said. "She chased him right on out. This all within a week after she was inside. They had no more problem." Esther had no more objection to dogs in the house, either. "I learned to love that dog," she said. Fe even babysat the Padilla children while Esther counseled students in another room.

Father Thomas said Mass for the Bowie football team at the Cueva; everybody else was welcome too. He heard the players' confessions, and let the team use the building for meetings. Victor Montes, a former gang member who later became an active member of the OLYC community, was a defensive back on the Bowie team when he met Father Thomas at Mass in the Cueva in the fall of 1977, his senior year. "His sermons were only 5-10 minutes long, but they would challenge you." He taught the players what it took to be a man, said Montes: love God with all your heart, and everything else will follow. He also listened. "Father always had time for the kids from Bowie. If we asked him for time he would give us time."

In 1980 the community got a second priest to help Father Thomas: Father Sam Rosales, the Jesuit Father Thomas had helped discern his vocation (see chapter 13). Father Rosales was assigned to Sacred Heart in 1980, officially working half time with the OLYC community, but in practice nearly full time.

Celebrating Mass for Bowie high school students
at La Cueva Counseling Center, 1982.

CHAPTER 44

God's Power in the Jailhouse

I n 1979, Father Thomas got an invitation to minister in an unexpected place: the Juárez city jail. The administrator, whose wife had been going to prayer meetings, had decided there was no hope for many of the prisoners except in the power of God. That sounded good to Father Thomas and his friends, but there were some reservations too. The group didn't really have the capacity to do any follow-up when the men got out of jail; all it could offer was what Father Thomas later called a "seed planting." But Manny Basurto, one of the "Juniors," felt a strong leading from God to go ahead with the project, and on a weekend in August Father Thomas gathered the community at the Lord's Ranch for a retreat to prepare for the new ministry.

As usual, God had the decisive word. The meeting was held in a building next to the swimming pool. A builder had asked to buy some water he needed for a project he was working on near the ranch; Father Thomas let him have the water for free, and he drained most of the pool. There was no time to refill the pool over the weekend, and if there had been time, it would have meant running a diesel engine that could be heard half a mile away. What's more, everybody who knew how to operate the pump was in the retreat. So it's safe to say the pump did not run.

But when the group came out of the building at the end of the retreat, the pool was not only full, it was overflowing. "That was a clear sign from God," said Mike Halloran, who was in the retreat. The group decided the jail ministry would be blessed, and on Wednesday, Aug. 22, 1979, a team of about three dozen turned up at the jail.

"What we thought we would do is have some people outside praying while two or three people went around and talked to the prisoners," Father Thomas said later. "God had a different plan. We went all around outside the jail looking to see if there was a house or a patio or a yard we could borrow to get a group together to praise the Lord. We couldn't find a spot."

Hoping to get some advice from a friend, Father Thomas went into the jail to use the administrator's phone. "I said, 'We're looking for a place outside where we can pray while others go inside to talk to the prisoners.' He said, 'No – you bring them all in here.'"

In they went, singing *"Cristo rompe las cadenas del pecado"* – Christ breaks the chains of sin. "We were all singing that together, scared to death, not knowing what was going to happen. The prisoners didn't want us, the guards didn't want us, the police didn't want us. They were screaming and mocking and cursing us."

The noise was so loud it drowned out the loudspeaker system the group had brought. The prisoners – 75 to 100 in a cell – were peering out into the courtyard where the volunteers were, screaming and throwing things. So Father Thomas drew his sword, the word of God, and told everybody to sing or recite Phil. 2:10-11, "so that at the name of Jesus every knee should bend, in heaven and on earth and under the earth, and every tongue should confess that Jesus Christ is Lord, to the glory of God the Father," some in English and some in Spanish. The music ministry worked in 20-minute shifts, and the music went on for an hour and a half. Then everything changed.

"There was total silence when we stopped singing," Father Thomas said. "The men were on their knees in the cells, crying.

We asked the administrator to open the cells and let them out. Every single man came out for prayer – every single one. The administrator couldn't believe it. He said, 'These are the most incorrigible prisoners we have.'"

The Wednesday jail ministry carried on and carries on to this day. A second jail was added in 1982, and the dreaded *Judicial*, where even the prisoners' families don't know where their relatives are, was added later that same year. Father Thomas had known about the *Judicial* for a while and had been praying to get a chance for ministry there, and one day when the volunteers were visiting the municipal jail across the street, the warden asked them to take some food to the prisoners at the *Judicial*. "To be allowed to visit those prisoners is unheard of," said Sergio Conde. "No one is ever permitted to see them, neither relatives nor even their lawyers." The *Judicial* visit turned into a regular part of the weekly ministry.

The jail ministry changed in various ways over time; jails were added or dropped as circumstances dictated, and volunteers have not always been allowed into the cells. The basics have continued: preaching, praise music, use of sacramentals (holy water and blessed salt) and bringing the prisoners food and drink. While some volunteers minister to the prisoners, others are always providing prayer support, and when the visit is over, the volunteers meet on a nearby street corner to share what happened with various prisoners.

The visitors usually dance, too. Quoting Psalm 149, Father Thomas was convinced God wants His people to dance in praise, even in prison.

"We have found that men dancing to praise the Lord in a jail setting has a great impact on the prisoners," he said. "This cracks the hardness of their hearts and brings on a conversion."

The attitude of the prisoners has improved spectacularly since that first visit in 1979. It has still been rough sometimes – Hector Bencomo remembered chasing away three prisoners who surrounded Father Thomas, trying to steal his wallet – but mostly the prisoners are at least polite.

There's still not much follow-up, but some of the prisoners turn up to prayer meetings when they get out, and some of them have even joined the jail ministry. The jail officials are mostly friendly, too, and sometimes they actually welcome the volunteers and ask for their prayers.

Once, though, the volunteers did have to make their escape. When *Viva Cristo Rey* (Long live Christ the King) a video about the OLYC ministries, was being filmed in 1980, the cameraman went along on the regular jail ministry day, and the jail officials thought he was a news reporter. The supervisor was going to call the police and confiscate the film and $200,000 worth of camera equipment. The camera crew and Father Thomas were all called into the office. Father Thomas announced in a loud voice that he had to pray before anything else could happen, and commenced praying for all the officials present, for their families, and a long list of other intentions. "I prayed for everything I could think of. If I had the vocabulary, I prayed for it." As he recalled it, nothing more was said, and they were allowed to go, but as Sister Mary Virginia remembered, the officials wanted to confiscate the film. The photographer handed over blank film. Then an official asked about containers the photographer had; most of them were batteries, but one did have the recorded film. The official looked into one that really was batteries and told the visitors to get out; Father Thomas told them to load up and get across border as fast as they could.

One important part of the jail ministry was food. In 1981, around Easter time, the women of the ministry brought a traditional bread pudding for the men, along with tortillas and lemonade. They thought there would be about 75 prisoners, the number they had served in the jail at Christmas, so that's how much food they brought. But there were actually 250 men in the jail that day. It was Christmas 1972 all over again. There were seconds and thirds for everybody, enough extra for the administrators and guards, and the food didn't run out until everybody had enough. "You've never seen people praise God like they did that day," Father Thomas told *New Covenant* writer Jeff Hensley.

Giving food to a prisoner through the cell bars
in the Juárez city jail, 1999.

The jail visits sound dangerous, especially the part about getting locked in the cells, but Father Thomas just made a joke of it. On my first visit I noticed one of the guards counting us as we went in, and I made a point of not being last in line on the way out, in case he counted wrong and kept me inside. Father Thomas just laughed when I told him about it. "There was nothing to worry about," he said. "We would have brought you sandwiches next Wednesday."

The jail ministry was one of many areas in which Father Thomas did not behave like the boss. He knew when to take a back seat, said Hector Bencomo; he would respect local knowledge. At the jail, Aurora Villa, the Juárez resident who led the ministry until her death in 2007, knew more about many of the circumstances than he did. "He was very obedient," said Bencomo. "He was not in charge at the jail. Whatever Aurora told him, he did." Villa was also a key leader at the food bank, along with Pedro Ibarra.

Visits to the local mental hospital started around the same time as the jail ministry and are part of the same weekly trip to Juárez. In the hospital, some patients are free to roam the courtyard, and the volunteers invite them into the recreation room for praise music, preaching, prayer, sacramentals, and refreshments; volunteers and patients dance in a circle, clumsily but joyfully. "When we go, they call it happy Wednesday," Father Thomas said. "A lot of them know that holy water helps them." As for the dancing, "We hold hands in a big circle and shuffle around as best we can as our musicians play songs to praise the Lord. The movements are often stiff and uncoordinated because the patients are frequently sedated with drugs, and none of us are especially good at dancing," he wrote in a newsletter. "The mental patients have the same reluctance to dance that other people have: fear, embarrassment, wondering what others might think, etc. Once they break through their excuses and fear, dancing for the Lord is very liberating and healing."

In 1983, a team from OLYC began visiting a different kind of detention center: Alternative House, a motel contracted to the U.S. Immigration Service to house illegal refugees, mainly women and children, fleeing from violence in Latin America. "Some are economic refugees like two from Belize who came looking for jobs," Father Thomas wrote in a newsletter. "However, most are political refugees seeking safety from sudden death." Mrs. Tula led the team, which visited Mondays. "She brings love, peace, prayer and hope where there is fear and insecurity," Father Thomas said.

CHAPTER 45

Tending the Youth
in God's Gardens

In early February of 1981, the community found a new opportunity in Juárez: working with juvenile offenders. The group got an invitation to visit the juvenile detention home. It was the start of one of the more difficult and frustrating episodes in Father Thomas's life, as he and his friends looked for ways they could rescue these youngsters from the poverty and bad influences all around them.

The term "juvenile offender" was used loosely, as they soon found out. In an early newsletter Father Thomas wrote about two orphaned sisters, age 12 and 8, who were in the detention home simply because the middle-class aunt they lived with refused to pay a $10 fine to get them released after the police picked them up from wandering around one night. Other young people were in the detention home for offences like theft. The population of the home was between 70 and 80, mostly boys but with some girls too.

The volunteers started by modelling their weekly Monday visits to the detention home on the jail ministry. "First we encourage the children to sing hymns of praise to God. Then we tell them God loves them and wants to help them change their lives. Finally we take each child who is willing and show him how to pray. The children learn how to ask the Lord to come and change their hearts. Every week many have a profound experience with the Lord. This is the consoling part."

The not-so-consoling part was the feeling of helplessness the volunteers got when the children left the home. A lot of them were headed for El Paso and life as illegal immigrants. "We're searching for a way to take care of them once they get out, but we haven't found a practical way of doing it," Father Thomas wrote. "Many have no homes at all and live on the streets or under bridges."

In January 1982, government officials, happy with what they were seeing from the ministry to the detention home, offered OLYC some land next door to build a youth center. "We hope to start building as soon as possible," Father Thomas wrote. "We are very excited about what the Lord is going to do." The center was going to include a large dining room to feed hungry children, sleeping quarters for the homeless children of the area – some as young as 10 and as much as 400 miles from "home," if you could call it home – plus laundry and storage facilities and quarters for permanent staff.

Around the same time, Father Thomas began buying rural land about 100 miles west of Juárez for a ranch-based orphanage which would be named *Los Jardines de Dios* (God's Gardens). At one point he got pulled in by American immigration authorities as he wandered back and forth across the border, looking for available land with good water. From a real estate point of view, he did well. He bought one parcel from a doctor who lived in El Paso, had his practice in Juárez, and owned land on both sides of the border; due to the 1982 devaluation of the peso, he needed to sell his Mexican land to pay the mortgage on his American home, and Father Thomas gave him a fair price.

The operation started there, as a few children moved in under the care of Tocha and Alfredo Ibarra, who had been working at the food bank. But the first location had some problems. "When the river flooded, or there was heavy rain, it became evident that that wasn't suitable because you couldn't get in or out," Father Thomas said. "We were looking for another place that was livable all the time."

He found that place, at a bargain price: a nearby parcel owned by an old farmer whose children didn't want to follow him into farming. The man sold his beloved land for a handful of peso notes in a cigar box. "It was pitiful. He just said 'this is what I want for it,'" Father Thomas said later. "He was very happy. I gave him exactly what he wanted for it. But I said, man alive, this is like Manhattan Island or something." Eventually the property ended up as a group of disconnected parcels collectively known as *Los Jardines*. Father Thomas himself didn't know the total acreage.

Bringing a dairy cow so the children would have fresh milk.
Pictured here with Tocha Ibarra (in white shirt, waving), some of her children and some of the orphans at *Los Jardines de Dios,* Mexico, 1983.

Four houses were established, all in primitive conditions with no electricity; lanterns, a gas refrigerator, and bucket showers were the amenities. A series of volunteers cycled through. Father Thomas came weekly, said Mass, and stayed for a couple of days.

In all, about 15 young offenders lived there during the time of operation of *Jardines*, including killers, and Sergio Conde said 13 of them went on to live law-abiding lives.

But things turned difficult quickly. Tocha Ibarra died of cancer in 1985, an enormous blow to Father Thomas (see also chapter 50), and not long after, legal and cultural conflicts began to build up at *Jardines*, with the Mexican authorities and with neighbors who wanted the land. Uncharacteristically for someone who was normally ready to tackle any obstacle, Father Thomas asked the Condes to take the lead in managing the situation. "After some time he said 'you do it, I cannot do it,'" said Lucía Conde. Finally, in 1988, the legal problems came to a crisis, U.S.-based volunteers were forced to leave, and the operation shut down, although the property continued to be held by the community under the supervision of the Condes.

The failure of *Jardines* haunted Father Thomas all his life. During his final illness, he told Michael Reuter about his dream for the property: "The property is so vast, we could have rehabilitation of girls in this part, and boys over there, because the place is so big."

"I still think of it. I see somebody and I wonder if they'd dedicate themselves to that."

CHAPTER 46

Prayer and Politics

Most people who know a little bit about Mexico think of it as a Catholic country, and that's an easy conclusion to draw from all the beautiful colonial churches, the religious processions and holidays, and the strong devotion to Our Lady of Guadalupe.

But while that might be true demographically – more than 80 per cent of Mexicans call themselves Catholics – the political story of Mexico is mostly the story of efforts to shut the Church out of public life. Many of Mexico's greatest heroes, such as independence leader Benito Juárez and beloved 1930s president Lázaro Cárdenas, considered the Church an oppressive and backward influence in society; Plutarco Elías Calles, the founder of the PRI which has ruled Mexico most of the time since the 1920s, went even further, and actively persecuted the Church. The PRI, which returned to power after a 12-year break (2000-2012), isn't actually a persecutor nowadays, but even today there are many restrictions on Church activities, and Father Thomas needed formal government permission to function as a priest in Mexico.

Father Thomas didn't shy away from politics, on either side of the border, any more than he shied away from any other area where he believed God's will was calling him. One of his oldest friends and supporters, an influential Mexican-American El Paso businessman who didn't want his name mentioned, saw Father Thomas's entire ministry south of the Rio Grande as an effort to give the poor of Mexico back the Church that the PRI and the Freemasons had taken away from them. There's a strong anti-Church current among the elite of Mexico, the businessman said, and it had succeeded to the point where the poor were doing well if they could so much as get to Mass. When Father Thomas began stepping up his ministry in Juárez, with charismatic prayer meetings and later the dump ministry, the city had only 40 priests to serve half a million Catholics. (Today it's 95 priests for 2.3 million Catholics.)

Father Thomas got an early lesson in Mexican politics when a woman from Juárez, holder of a law degree from Stanford, came into OLYC to share her story with Father Thomas. She said she had been forced to work for the PRI stuffing ballot boxes; if she refused, the PRI told her, they'd take away her house. "She'd put so many PRI ballots in ahead of time," Father Thomas recalled. Even with the extra ballots, she told him, "they'd still lose. And they'd just change the results."

Father Thomas filed that information away in his head, and some years later, in 1983, another visitor came to see him at the food bank: Francisco Barrio, an active Catholic and member of the center-right opposition PAN. Barrio told Father Thomas he'd be running for mayor; at that time no PAN candidate had ever been mayor of Juárez, and non-PRI office holders had been few and far between anywhere in Mexico. "I told him the whole system that this woman [with the ballot box stuffing story] told me," Father Thomas said. "He had his people at the polls. He took steps to do everything that this woman indicated, and he won. I think it's because he took all these steps to keep them from cheating." PAN also won elections in eight other cities in the state of Chihuahua, where Juárez is located, including the capital, also named Chihuahua.

Barrio, reaching out across party lines, invited Sergio Conde to be city secretary – second in command – in his new government. Conde had held the same office in a previous PRI government, though he said by 1983 he didn't belong to any political party. Conde, also a lawyer and university rector, spent time praying with Father Thomas to find out what God wanted him to do. He ended up taking the job on the condition that he could still evangelize and would not be asked to do anything dishonest.

Barrio's election and Conde's move into government marked a sort of golden age of Juárez politics from Father Thomas's point of view. Conde took a number of constructive steps. He had tax revenues go into a public account instead of private accounts as before. He raised police salaries so the police wouldn't have to depend on the *mordida* (literally it means "little bite" but translated it means a bribe) system of government corruption. He also reformed the city jail. "They did away with the things in the city jail that they tortured people with," Father Thomas said. "They were just architecturally destroyed. They used to put them in little rooms where they couldn't stand up, and the roof was slanted, so they were just in a little cage. They did away with those cages."

"He [Conde] did a lot of stuff. He didn't mess with it – he just said that's the way it's going to be, and that's the way it was."

Barrio has been a controversial figure through a long political career – he has held a number of offices including governor of Chihuahua and ambassador to Canada – but he ran a clean civic government. "Barrio was very straight and honest in everything he did as mayor," Father Thomas said. "Some drug guys came in there and dumped a lot of money on his desk one day and he turned it all back. He lived on a real meager salary that he got by law."

As might be expected, Barrio's election produced a considerable backlash, and so did Conde's Catholic faith; it was no secret that he was a friend of Father Thomas. "Everything came against Sergio," said Lucía. A Juárez newspaper columnist called Conde a "fanatical religious preacher." A deputation of federal inspectors from Mexico City once came to Sergio and accused him and Father Thomas of having weapons in the food bank.

"I said, 'yes, we have two-edged swords,'" Sergio said. How many? "Seven hundred," he told them. They went and discovered 700 Bibles; "they left very angry."

For his part, Father Thomas fought back with spiritual weapons. "As soon as they [Barrio government] were installed, I went into the *presidencia* and said Mass. They locked all the doors and had Paco [Padilla] being a scout. We had Mass in there and we put holy water everywhere and blessed salt in the air conditioning vents. I used to go to Barrio's house and say Mass."

Father Thomas also sat outside Conde's office for hours, praying. He would arrive in a van with seven or eight people, parked outside city offices, and execute Scripture all morning (see chapter 28 on spiritual warfare).

"All the strongholds the devil had in the running of the government, Father came with a strong word against it," said Lucía.

The community's government-level work in Juárez ended in 1986, when the PRI recaptured the mayor's office, but many of the improvements endured, including the jail reforms.

With prayer team outside the Juárez city government building, 1983.

CHAPTER 47

On the Road

Father Thomas didn't spend all his time in El Paso or Juárez or on the Lord's Ranch. Starting in 1976, he became a popular – and totally unpredictable – guest speaker at charismatic conferences. The work took him all over the world, from his first speaking engagement in Dallas to places as far away as Ireland, Israel, Trinidad, and New Zealand. "That's been a big part of my life," he said shortly before his death. "I've always enjoyed it."

It was his friend Bobbie Cavnar who got him started. Cavnar invited Father Thomas to join an all-star lineup of speakers at a three-day conference at Southern Methodist University in Dallas in October 1976, entitled Drinking the Cup. The speaker right before him on the program was Bishop Warren Boudreaux of Beaumont, Texas. "He was well-organized. He was terrific all the way around. And I'm supposed to follow him.... I had no preparation, I had no idea what I was going to talk about.

"I got up there and the first thing I said was, 'I don't know what I'm going to talk about,' which was true. I didn't have the foggiest. I said, 'But I learned something from Bishop Boudreaux:

organize your speech in four parts.' They thought that was pretty funny.

"Then I started speaking and the Lord had mercy on me. It was pretty good."

Speaking at a charismatic conference in 1978,
Bobbie Cavnar in background.

Not knowing his message in advance became standard practice for Father Thomas over the years. While he would do a bit of preparation for his teachings at OLYC prayer meetings, at conferences he would wait to get his topic from God. He'd usually be waiting a long time.

"At these conferences, I'm waiting to see what the Lord wants to talk about. He usually gives me something about two minutes before the thing's to begin," he said. "God has always been merciful, but not till the last minute."

Almost always. Once, that approach failed, at least in an outward sense. God didn't give him a message. He couldn't remember the location ("somewhere up north"), possibly because it happened at a place he never went back to.

"I was supposed to speak after lunch," he said. "So the MC gets up there and gives a big introduction, what a great guy I am and all that kind of junk, and [says] I have a great message for the people. They clap. He leaves the stage and goes to the bathroom. I go up there, and I am totally blank, I mean blank.

"I have a choice, whether to go up there and BS, which I knew how to do and still can, or sit down. I said, 'well, if God hasn't given me anything, I'd just as well tell people I have nothing to say.'" He couldn't remember exactly how he explained himself to the audience. "I said 20 words and sat down." The musicians scrambled to get their instruments and started to play. "About this time the guy comes back who introduced me as the greatest thing on earth. Here I'm sitting down, and the music ministry is playing and he can't figure out what the heck happened.

"That's the only time I drew a blank. They didn't pay my ticket, which I can't blame them for. I've never been invited back." Whether this actually counts as a failure is open to discussion, though; Father Thomas saw it more as a test of obedience; would he rely on his own considerable preaching skills, or would he wait for the message the Lord wanted him to deliver, even at the cost of looking like a complete fool? He made the only choice he knew how to make: everybody who knew him, from his own brother to his co-workers to people who only saw him at conferences like this one, knew he was totally indifferent to what anybody thought of him, as long as he was convinced he was obeying God.

Anyway, God was apparently pleased with his choice, because he never drew a blank again. But there were plenty of other surprises for the people who organized the conferences. He almost always challenged his listeners more than they were expecting. In Toronto, for example, he organized an unplanned

youth march up the main downtown street at a time he deliberately picked so that participants would have to miss supper.

In Riverside, California, in 1987, he went a lot further than
that. The conference ran Saturday and Sunday, with Father
Thomas scheduled to speak Sunday morning. Saturday evening,
he felt led by the Holy Spirit to get the organizers to cancel the
talks that were supposed to come after his own and use the time
to evangelize and feed the poor. That message was a surprise to
him, but he checked with one of his traveling companions and
the message was confirmed. So in the morning he approached
the host pastor, Father Michael Barry, and they agreed to make
the changes. The other scheduled speakers didn't like having
their speeches canceled; "I wouldn't have, either," he said later.

During his own talk, Father Thomas passed the collection
plate twice. The first time, he asked everyone to put all the
money they had into the plate; the second time they were to take
back out what they really needed – less than they put in, for most
people, but if somebody actually needed to take more, that was
OK too. The surplus was $5,000. Organizers spent $2,500 on
food at Costco and the rest on paying past due utility bills for the
poor; some of the congregation stayed behind and prayed, and
others went out of the conference hall and into the neighbor-
hoods and parks to evangelize. The incident was the start of
Mary's Mercy Center, an outreach that continues to this day
under Father Barry's direction.

At another conference, in Long Beach, he even spent his talk
reaming out conference organizers for the way the event was set
up. It was a two-tier program. "If you wanted to eat and be at the
table, you'd pay so much, and they'd serve you a meal. If you
didn't want to eat or couldn't afford to eat, you'd sit in the chairs.
During this meal I'm supposed to tell them about the Christmas
at the dump and the dump ministry."

Before the meal, the volunteers gathered around the speakers
to pray. "They prayed over me and laid hands on me, and I began

to weep. They said 'are you going to be able to give your talk?' I said 'yes, but I don't know who's going to be able to hear it.' I kept weeping and weeping."

When his time to speak came, he told the crowd, "we have people here who can afford to sit down and eat, and we have people who can't afford it, but they want to hear me talk about the poor, and they have to sit out there without eating.' That's why I was crying ahead of time, because I knew this was just so terrible, so blatant. I talked about how terrible it was to charge people to hear the word of God. I really lowered the boom on them. I've never been invited back, but they changed. They never charge for anybody to come to the conference."

On a speaking tour of New Zealand in 1990 he visited a local bishop, who was annoyed with him because organizers had scheduled him to speak at a Baptist church without getting the bishop's permission. Father Thomas offered to cancel his talk or do anything else the bishop might direct. The bishop told him not to cancel, which might have caused scandal, but he assigned Father Thomas to say high Mass at the cathedral the next Sunday as a demonstration that Father Thomas was solidly Catholic.

The cathedral had a top-class choir and orchestra, which were planning a European tour, and Father Thomas wasn't in a position to measure up to that level in singing the Mass. "I don't think I'd said high Mass since my first [in Tampa in 1958]," he said. "I was the worst singer on earth. I came out like a frog that had emphysema. I said, 'God, you just humiliated me.' They never had anybody as bad as me. I know the people were in agony." Nobody complained, though, about his singing or about the tennis shoes he was wearing as usual. He didn't see the bishop there.

Father Thomas enjoyed the travel, and, showing the curiosity he had inherited from Wayne Sr., asked his hosts question after question about every new location. "He never, ever had an attitude of 'been there, done that,' nor was he ever jaded," said Ellen Hogarty. "There was always something new to be gleaned or learned from any experience. It was a child-like trait that he had throughout his life."

He could enjoy the special treats, too, up to a point — in New Zealand, where there are, literally, more sheep than people, he was looking forward to lamb, but New Zealanders take lamb for granted and served beef instead, intending to honor him. "I wanted lamb because I never get any lamb," he said later. "They were serving me beef." But he didn't like luxury on the road, any more than at home. Lucía and Sergio Conde remembered him fuming through a fancy dinner at a Fisherman's Wharf restaurant where conference organizers had taken him in San Francisco. Finally he exploded when the waiter brought a flaming dessert. "Are we disciples of Jesus or King Solomon?" he asked.

Celebrating Mass in Jerusalem with some
Missionaries of Charity present, 2000.

CHAPTER 48

Hard Sayings About Money

When it comes to material goods, nobody could have been less like King Solomon than Rick Thomas. On my very first visit to OLYC a saying paraphrased from a sermon by St. Basil the Great was staring me in the face from the bulletin board: "The second coat hanging in your closet is stolen from the poor."

Father Thomas had very definite ideas about what we should do with our coats – and with all the other material resources God gives us.

> "If we are piling things up for ourselves and hoarding something for the future, then we can't be obeying God's word clearly expressed by John the Baptist. The crowds asked John, "What ought we to do?" In reply he said, "Let the man with two coats give to him who has none. The man who has food should do the same." (Luke 3:10-11) One would not think that two coats are excessive, and they wouldn't be excessive if everyone in the world had two coats."

***

> "Some Christians think that tithing, giving ten percent of what they earn, is what the Bible commands. Tithing was something developed in the Old Testament as a rule of thumb for those people just beginning to understand revelation. In the New Testament where we have the fullness of Divine

teaching, neither Jesus nor his disciples, ever said anything about giving tithes or ten percent. It was always a much greater demand. John the Baptist did not tell the person with two coats to give one sleeve to the man who had none but to give one whole coat to the man who had none."

Those passages are from *God's Goods*, a book Father Thomas put together about 1973, and published by the OLYC community after his death. The title was intended to reflect his belief about who really owns everything we think is "ours": God.

Quoting constantly from Scripture, the 82-page book attacks pretty much everything most of us think of as the normal elements of modern economic life: the profit motive, saving for a "rainy day," insurance, and any other way that we rely on money or human effort when we ought to be relying on God. The book reminds readers that the Our Father asks God to provide our daily bread – "Jesus does not teach us to ask for the bread of tomorrow or the bread of six years from now" – and also that the Bible calls failure to give to the poor a mortal sin of omission: "The bread of charity is life itself for the needy; he who withholds it is a man of blood." (Sirach 34:21).

Father Thomas had no problem about what to do with his own coats – or his shoes, or anything else that came into his possession. Former OLYC secretary Helen Guajardo remembered people giving him money for a coat or shoes; that money always went to the poor. "I already have a coat," he said.

As a Jesuit, Father Thomas had a vow of poverty, and he took that vow seriously. But he also believed the Bible teaches everybody, in vows or not, to live as simply as they can, for as long as anybody else in the world is in need. He frequently quoted Matthew 25, Jesus' discourse on the judgement of the nations, in which those who have helped the poor are welcomed to eternal life and those who haven't get sent away for eternal punishment.

"We know the questions on the final exam," he said in a 1988 TV interview on Trinity Broadcasting Network's *Praise the Lord*.

"What did you do with your clothes? What did you do with your food? What did you do with your house? What did you do with your time?" Everything belongs to God, he said, so we simply need to drop any claim that anything at all belongs to us. That doesn't mean falling into helpless poverty – we can't help anyone else if we do that – but it does mean that meeting our own simple needs is a question of *using* God's material resources, not owning them, and using what's left over to help others who are in greater need than we are. "It really hurts me to see people in the United States washing their cars, and half a mile away [in Juárez] a baby is dying due to lack of water," he said on *Praise the Lord*.

To Father Thomas, reaching out to the poor is more than just an obligation for Christians. In a very real sense, it *is* the Christian life. It gives us "a special knowledge of Jesus that you're not going to have in prayer," he said in the same TV interview. "If you haven't dealt with the poor, you really haven't met Jesus, and Jesus hasn't met you. There's no substitute for meeting Jesus in the suffering."

"This is the work of Jesus, and it should be done by believers. You can't pay somebody to love. We have to incarnate with the suffering and the sinner and the sick and the miserable."

Jean Soto said that Father Thomas taught that dealing with poverty was not just a matter of giving people something to eat but of making friends with them and spending time with them. "That's why we didn't just organize yard sales and bake sales and donate the money to the poor," she said. "We went *to* them."

Father Thomas's "God's goods" theology didn't just mean all material resources *belong to* God and should be used for His purposes; it also means those resources all *come from* God in the first place, and so God is the only source of them that Christians should be looking to. "I'm always asking people to come to work for the Lord full-time," he told me around 2000. "They say 'who's going to pay the bills?' I say God will pay the bills, but they think that's ridiculous."

Holding a baby dying from malnutrition in a Juárez hospital, 1970.

"Suppose every Christian doctor did all his work *gratis*," Father Thomas said in a talk in Jerusalem in 2001. "Every Christian plumber, every beautician, every cook, every teacher gave it away. What a witness! Now that would get the attention of everybody. That would be the Gospel in action."

In his own life and ministry, he practiced what he preached. At OLYC, he had always trusted in God for funding, even when the till was empty and a deadline was looming, but for the first 12 years he also trusted in the United Way. That ended when OLYC quit the United Way in 1976 (see Chapter 42), and from then on, for as long as he lived, Father Thomas trusted God and God alone to give OLYC everything it needed.

He trusted God outside the OLYC operation as well. He was on his way to a massive ecumenical charismatic conference in Kansas City in 1977 when Frank Alarcón tracked him down at the El Paso airport and asked him for money for an emergency at the garbage dump. "I gave him all the money I had," Father Thomas recalled years later. "I said, 'I'll just trust God.'" He had his airplane ticket but nothing else. He went on to Kansas City and ended up attending all the events, getting rides from various people (including Ruth Carter Stapleton, sister of then-President Jimmy Carter), and sleeping on the floor of Bobbie Cavnar's hotel room.

In his own ministry, he didn't charge Mass stipends or speakers' fees (though he accepted airline fare and food and lodging for speaking engagements). He noted on *Praise the Lord* in 1990 that Jesus sent His disciples out on missions with no resources. "If we take care of ourselves, there's no room for a miracle." And if we leave it to God, he added, we usually have to wait a while for that miracle, but it will come: "God is a last-minute God."

Of course, a lot of God's goods come to us through other human beings, whether they send donations to OLYC or share their hotel rooms. Jean Soto said Father Thomas's conviction that God is the ultimate source of everything kept him from giving adequate credit to the human beings who are usually part of the process; he didn't have much to say about that, beyond minimum courtesy. "God is acting through many people," she said, but "all he would say was 'the Lord provided.'" She said his attitude reminded her of a comment by former Indian prime minister Jawaharlal Nehru to his mentor, the great Indian leader Mohandas Gandhi: "your poverty has cost me and my friends a lot of money."

Throughout his time in El Paso, Father Thomas lived his personal life by his convictions. He lived as simply as possible and passed any gifts he received on to the poor. (See especially chapters 20 and 22.) He mostly ate what people brought him, including a lot of fruit, and milk, which he loved, Soto recalled; "I was very struck by his habit of putting corn tortillas in a toaster and spreading them with peanut butter and eating them with milk." He didn't drink coffee, and only after his death did a few of his friends learn that he loved coffee but had deprived himself of it for most of his life. At an early stage he'd occasionally have a bit of port wine if he couldn't sleep, Helen Guajardo said, but no other alcohol; later, say his friends at the Lord's Ranch, he didn't drink any alcohol as a matter of principle, because some of the people he was helping were alcoholic.

For decades, Susan and Paul Vescovo, who owned the Las Cruces Toyota dealership, sold the OLYC community vehicles at a steep discount and serviced them for free. Father Thomas didn't want air conditioning in any of the cars, vans or trucks. Eventually it became almost impossible to get a vehicle without air conditioning. "You don't have to turn it on," Susan told him. "The luxuries we have here in life became unnecessary to him," she recalled later. "It's almost like they got in the way."

On the Lord's Ranch, he lived for many years in a concrete-floored room in Ezekiel House, the nearest building to the front gate; it was his bedroom and his office. He mostly used the outhouses rather than the flush toilets, and he had to walk to another building to the dining room. He usually wore a clerical shirt and collar when working on the ministries, T-shirts or button-down casual shirts at home on the ranch; plus black jeans and black high-topped basketball shoes which became his trademark and the subject of numerous jokes. The nearest thing to a luxury he enjoyed was riding the horses at the ranch, and he once said in a newsletter that he was grateful that God let him have dogs as a substitute for the television he never watched.

Still, the stories about his personal poverty tended to get out of hand. Even his friends, much as they admired his simplicity of life, got tired of the exaggerations, especially the ones that spread after his death. It was written somewhere that he owned only two shirts and fasted twice a week.

"He had lots of shirts," said Ellen Hogarty. And he didn't fast, in the usual sense – he would get weak and light-headed, so his health would not permit going without food for long. He ate enough, including meat if it was from a good and known source. But he did eat simply, and with great discipline. And he did have his own way of fasting: eating foods he didn't like. (He gave the same advice to other people, especially those who had to keep up their strength for manual work.)

When the OLYC community formed, Father Thomas's ideas about material goods were very much part of the program. Sometimes this worked well, sometimes not. Mike and Mary Ann Halloran lived cheerfully in two cramped rooms on the Lord's Ranch, with two children and a third on the way, until their modest home was built. On the other hand, his co-worker Martha Medrano remembered a time in the middle 70s when Father Thomas asked community members – even those living in their own homes – to give up their blankets, "because the poor deserve to have our blankets." As far as she knew, not many people went along with that idea. "He was not able to differentiate about how much people were able to give up," she said. "Not all of us were able to give up everything."

Father Bill McCann, who discerned his vocation to the priesthood as an OLYC community member in the late 80s, remembered a speaking trip to New Hampshire where Father Thomas got into a major row with a congregation at a wealthy parish. He made the people repeat over and over, "you cannot serve God and money" (Matthew 6:24) and "don't work for food that perishes." (John 6:27). "He hit them right between the eyes, so much so that people were actually yelling at him from the pews."

"He had a way of teaching that antagonized people," said Father McCann, who is now a Las Cruces diocesan priest, "and when they were antagonized they had to think about it."

The "think about it" part may have been more important to Father Thomas than the details. "He loved to preach in black and white," said Father Nathan O'Halloran, who grew up on the Lord's Ranch and is now a Jesuit priest. (He is the son of Mike and Mary Ann Halloran but has resumed using the "O" of his Irish ancestors.) "The more I went to school, the more I wanted him to relent on things, to explain how it was going to work out practically. I often thought he was preaching a message no one could live.

"He said 'I have to preach this way. It's what makes people listen.' He used superlatives to make a point, but not everyone understood."

"He was very insistent on the hard sayings about money," said Jean Soto. "Sell your possessions, give to the poor – now. What was not clear to any of us was just how much to sell. We were pretty much left to figure that out ourselves."

"In retrospect, I do not think that he had a clear plan of what such a community would look like. It was more a case of his waiting to see how the Spirit would lead people," Soto said. "Father Thomas respected what each needed to do, especially in private conversation. In fact, I think there was a dichotomy between what he would preach – give your life to God in service to the poor – and what he would counsel in private." On one occasion, Soto said, he even refused to let her increase her own financial contribution to the ministries, and Mary Ann Halloran said he actually told some people who were in need of stability to get jobs.

When Tommy and Ceci Barrientos joined the community in 1993, they were afraid to give up their downtown El Paso restaurant for fear they wouldn't be able to support their children. "Father said, 'don't worry about it,'" Tommy said. "'You have your ministry there. Just pray to the Lord about how you can serve him in that place.'" They continued to sell food, but they also gave out a lot of free meals, and they used the restaurant for evangelization, prayer sessions and Bible study.

Father O'Halloran notes that Father Thomas's poverty, like most things in his life, was based on the teachings of St. Ignatius Loyola, and unlike the better-known Franciscan poverty, it was not a goal to pursue for its own sake. "Jesuit poverty remains subsumed under the greatest Ignatian principle of AMDG [*Ad Maiorem Dei Gloriam*], the greater glory of God," Father O'Halloran said. "He was not opposed to using technology, starting a radio station, spending money on a new building. Poverty was not an end in itself. But it was a powerful means to the greater glory, and to underestimate its effectiveness would be costly to the mission."

Despite his preaching and his personal poverty, Father Thomas did not reject people, from the ministries or from his personal friendship, just because they continued to live middle class or even affluent lives. And by the time he got to be a priest, of course, his own family was wealthy. He visited his relatives in Tampa every year or two, and as his nephew Robert remembered it, they had a grand time. He'd ride horses, hike, and fish, and Robert would cook for him.

"We spoiled him while he was here, and he really enjoyed that," said Robert. "He had a great sense of humor. He was always cracking jokes. He would make a joke and I would make a joke. We would just howl. If you would say something, he would try to figure a way he could turn it around and make it funny. He was always laughing."

With Robert, at least, Father Thomas did raise the issue of wealth, but he brought it up as part of the sparring – kidding on the square. "Trappings are a trap," he admonished his nephew. "Don't get trapped."

"Lucky for you that we're trapped here so that we can send you money for all the things you do," Robert jibed in return.

"He just said, 'let's go fishing.'"

CHAPTER 49

On Top of the Mountain

B y the early 1980s, Father Thomas wasn't toiling in obscurity. His work and the OLYC ministries had been featured in *New Covenant*, which was the official magazine of the Catholic charismatic renewal at the time, and other publications. In 1980 he won the local and southwest district Sertoma Humanitarian Awards, presented by the Sertoma service club. And in 1983 he was given the Poverello Medal, awarded each year by Franciscan University of Steubenville, Ohio, to honor people for charity on the level of the beloved St. Francis of Assisi.

He had even moved the head of his order to tears of joy, though he wasn't present to see that honor. Bobbie Cavnar's Christian Community of God's Delight in Dallas had filmed *Viva Cristo Rey*, a video about Father Thomas's work in Juárez, in 1980 (see chapter 44), and in 1981 Cavnar, visiting Rome, showed the video to Father Pedro Arrupe, superior general of the Society of Jesus. "After he viewed the program, with tears streaming down his face, he reflected about Father Thomas for a moment," Cavnar wrote later. "As he tapped his right temple with his finger, he very humbly said, 'We Jesuits are so intellectual – it is nice to see there are some who are also spiritual.'"

Father Thomas did know about the Poverello, and it was big. Previous winners included Mother (now Saint) Teresa of Calcutta, Catholic social activist Dorothy Day, and Jonas Salk, inventor of the pioneering polio vaccine. The El Paso *Times* article on the award ran with a six-by-eight-inch photo of Father Thomas and a headline describing him as a "Modern-day St. Francis."

That story and an earlier *Times* article making the initial announcement also contained praise for Father Thomas from several prominent people, but there's not a word from Father Thomas himself. That would be no surprise to anybody who knew him – he didn't like recognition. He did go to Steubenville to accept the award, but he also used the trip to conduct an evangelistic crusade in low-income housing near the campus, and he never displayed the plaque; the OLYC community still has it, but only because his co-workers wouldn't let him throw it out.

The following year Father Thomas got an even bigger honor, at least physically. His friends parted the Rio Grande for him.

Actually, it was the U.S. Boundary and Water Commission that diverted the river into a canal for six days in October 1984 for an international prayer meeting called Jesus: Gather at the River. And to read the newsletter Father Thomas finally got around to writing about the event the following February, you'd never know he had anything to do with it except celebrate the occasion with everybody else. But as his friends will tell you, Jesus: Gather at the River actually began as a proposal by local Protestant pastors to honor Father Thomas's work. The only problem was, he wasn't about to be honored.

"If you do that I'll leave town," he said (as recalled by his friend Richard Munzinger). "Why don't we have a prayer meeting and honor Jesus instead?"

And that's what happened. From Oct. 30 to Nov. 4, the river was diverted, the boundary and water commission designated an area on the American side of the river for the purpose, near the Oñate crossing at the west end of El Paso, and the U.S. Immigration and Naturalization service recognized the area as a free zone, letting Mexicans cross over an earthen ramp, with no document checks; the area was fenced off, so it was easy for immigration officials to keep anyone from going farther into the country. Americans, too, thronged to the area for the celebration, under a 70-foot cross erected for the occasion. According to a newspaper account, about 60 churches participated.

"Eyes filled with tears and throats choked as those long excluded from the U.S. were welcomed openly for the first time," Father Thomas wrote. "Outward and inward 'borders' crumbled as Americans and Mexicans embraced each other. Brothers and sisters celebrated their joy in the Lord with singing and dancing."

On the final day, a Sunday, Americans and Mexicans shared food at a picnic, and then everyone assembled at the foot of the cross. "On bended knees hundreds of people asked God's forgiveness for the sins committed by both nations. All prayed for God's blessing on both countries and indeed for all nations of the world." The celebration was repeated in 1985, for two days, and 1986, for three.

If Father Thomas had been a man to think in terms of "career," by the early 80s he had pretty much reached the peak. But he didn't think like that. He knew perfectly well he was a celebrity, and he did everything he could to keep that from poisoning him spiritually.

Michael Reuter remembered going to a conference with him in Colorado Springs; he was just attending, not even speaking, but he was recognized and greeted by an admirer who praised him to his face. "Well, goodbye," Father Thomas said, and walked away abruptly. It was almost rude; Reuter was shocked and asked him why. "They were glorifying me, not God," he replied.

"Everybody deals with pride," Reuter said, "and that was Father's way of dealing with his."

But as the 80s wore on, God found some new ways to help him deal with pride, and for a few years there the peak of his "career" began to look like ancient history.

Site of "Jesus: Gather at the River" in the dry river bed of the Rio Grande, on the border of the United States and Mexico, 1984.

CHAPTER 50

Changes and Challenges

In the early 80s, the work of the OLYC community carried on pretty much the same as in the late 70s, with ministries in El Paso, in Juárez, and at the Lord's Ranch, staffed most of the time by three distinct groups of volunteers working at those locations. But the work didn't continue unchanged. Some of the original OLYC ministries had fallen away because of new circumstances. Youth sports teams, a major program since Father Rahm's day, had stopped when Tula died in 1976. The employment office closed about 1982. Social work kept going until Consuelo Martínez died in 1989. Meanwhile, new ministries started up, on both sides of the border.

While the ministries were changing, people were also changing, and some of them left – not only the paid employees when the paychecks stopped, but also some of the people who were willing to work for free. Sometimes it was because Father Thomas wasn't always the easiest person to get along with. Martha Medrano, the original manager of the Lord's Food Bank, left in 1978 because she was hurt by some roughly-worded criticism. There was never a grudge between them – Medrano said she came to see that the criticism was partly valid, and she and Father Thomas stayed on cordial terms if they happened to see each other, but the relationship was never the same again. But she also said it was time for her to go anyhow, and she has kept working with the poor, using principles she learned from Father Thomas. Over at the dump ministry, Father Thomas actually fired Frank Alarcón at least once, but brought him back after a while. "He would come down on me pretty hard," said Alarcón. "He was intimidating. They [volunteers] were afraid of him. But I wasn't intimidated."

Jean Soto, one of the original Juniors, left the community in the early 80s after a fight with aggressive breast cancer; she felt that Father Thomas disapproved of the cutting edge medical treatment she was getting in Houston and thought she should have just stayed around and trusted in prayer, although he never actually said that to her. "There was certainly the idea that if we had enough faith, we could be healed of anything." He didn't contact her while she was getting her treatment, and she couldn't relate to him any more when she got back to town, so she went in another direction. Like Medrano, she didn't hold a grudge, but when Father Thomas wrote her not one but two letters of apology years later, because their parting was so abrupt, she didn't answer. She didn't think she could deal with personal feelings in a letter and she didn't think Father Thomas was capable of discussing feelings one on one. "He was not comfortable talking about interpersonal relationships. He was wonderful as a leader of a group, as a minister to a group, in private spiritual direction. But all those things are very different from talking about my relationship with you and your relationship with me."

But the loss that shook Father Thomas the most was somebody he had no trouble at all getting along with: Tocha Ibarra, who was in charge of the orphans at *Los Jardines de Dios*. Tocha, her husband, Alfredo, and their four children had been at *Jardines* since late 1982, and Father Thomas believed she was absolutely essential to the operation; "I didn't think we could run the orphanage without her." She was also a close friend, and he said just chatting with her was a spiritual experience that led him into prayer.

Tocha fell ill in late 1984. She had a biopsy, and it showed breast cancer. She was pregnant at the time; "she was told you can't carry that baby and live," recalled Kim Curtis, who helped take care of her. She had a mastectomy but said no to an abortion, and the Ibarras moved to the Lord's Ranch. Tocha gave birth to a three-pound, three-ounce daughter by Caesarian section March 4, seven weeks premature, in the hope of starting chemotherapy, but she died in El Paso March 7. Father Thomas, who had believed God would heal her because she was so important to *Jardines*, was now convinced that God would raise her from the dead – on video, no less.

"I was not concerned about her dying, because I knew the Lord would resurrect her," he said. "I was very sure of it. I told everybody that she would come back to life." He even said that to the doctor.

"We had the video tape there to have it all on video when she did come back to life. We prayed with her for hours to come back to life. She didn't," he said.

"I told the Lord at that time I'd never be able to speak on faith again, because I really had faith," he said the first time he talked publicly about the incident, almost two years later. And other people in the community shared that faith with me, and it was a shattering experience."

In that talk, in early 1987, Father Thomas said the problem wasn't lack of faith but lack of discernment: he didn't look for God's will but believed God would raise Tocha because he – Rick Thomas as an individual – wanted her raised. He also said that faith does not mean expecting God to act in a predictable way, for our convenience. "We cannot put God in a box. We cannot control God. We cannot force God to do things, nor should we try. We think we have it all worked out, but you're going to find that God is going to jump out of your box as quick as you get Him in there."

The operation at *Jardines* did not collapse because of Tocha's death after all, and Father Thomas eventually felt able to talk about faith again. "I would pray again for somebody to come back to life," he said in the 1987 talk, "but I'd be a little more careful about my discernment."

Nearly a year after Tocha died, Father Thomas suffered another major loss, this time a long way from the OLYC community. Wayne Thomas Sr. died in February 1986, leaving Father Thomas several hundred thousand dollars' worth of stock, which he converted to cash and handed over to OLYC. The death of the man he always called "Daddy" rocked Father Thomas, and he was extremely emotional while conducting the funeral back home in Tampa.

"He was wound up pretty tight," said his nephew, Robert Thomas, Bob's son. Even though Wayne wasn't Catholic, he had a Catholic funeral, with more than a dozen priests on hand. Robert said Father Thomas wept during the funeral Mass. "It was obvious he was pretty torn up." Tensions ran high, in part because Wayne Sr. had told Father Thomas he wanted to be buried in a simple wooden box, and Father Thomas dug in his heels on the point over the objections of some family members.

Robert, who had been close to his grandfather, got into a loud argument with his uncle in Bob's living room afterwards. "You're not the only one who had a relationship with Wayne Thomas Senior," Robert said just before he walked out. But there was no lasting effect. Robert was worried about what their next meeting would be like, but when it came, a year or more later, "it was like we were best pals."

Father Rick showing his dad how he had trained this donkey
to ring the bell, the Lord's Ranch, 1981.

CHAPTER 51

Into Deep Waters

N ot all the challenges facing Father Thomas and the community in the 1980s were imposed from the outside. At least one was chosen deliberately.

Spiritual warfare had been part of the ministry of OLYC since the days of the first Cueva and Father Thomas's encounters with Bobbie Cavnar and "Mrs. V" (see chapter 28). But in the mid-80s, the community began to raise the stakes.

In August 1985, Father Thomas led a team from OLYC into the middle of a weekend witches' conference held at an El Paso motel. He rented a room in the motel, and used it to celebrate Mass, sing, pray, and execute the sentence (reciting Scripture passages out loud) against the scheduled event; they also scattered blessed salt in the conference room in the middle of the night. Team members witnessed to some participants, including the main attraction, a man known in Mexico as the *Brujo Mayor*, or Grand Warlock. They also reported that the lighting and microphones malfunctioned, participants were quarreling and dissatisfied, speakers were confused to the point of mixing up "yes" and "no," and no one could do hypnotisms and *limpias* ("cleansings" performed by Mexican *curanderas* or "healers") that had been planned. At one point. Sister Mary Virginia said, the hotel manager approached the team and threatened them with the police. "If there is any trouble at all that you cause, we will take you all to jail."

With the team in the hotel room who were praying while
the witches' conference was taking place downstairs, 1985.

The same year, the community began praying against rock concerts. Father Thomas regarded rock, and some other forms of popular music, as a tool of Satan, because the effect of the pounding sound and the questionable lyrics does the devil's work by keeping listeners from praying and focusing on God – "garbage in, garbage out." OLYC workers rented space in a building near the El Paso Coliseum, where most of the concerts were held, and prayed and executed the sentence during the events; the concerts had a lot of electrical and technical problems, and Father Thomas said, "word got around that El Paso wasn't a good place to play – something always goes wrong."

Also in 1985, Father Thomas decided to start a shortwave radio station at the Lord's Ranch to broadcast Scripture readings (see chapter 58). That was intended as spiritual warfare too: putting the word of God on the airwaves, not for teaching, but to execute the sentence. There were endless technical delays and other problems, and the station didn't start broadcasting until 1992, as station KJES (King Jesus).

The community took a much bigger step, both spiritually and geographically, in the 80s, reaching all the way to the Caribbean. In 1982 Father Thomas went to the island nation of St. Lucia to evangelize, and in November 1986 traveled to Trinidad, bringing community members with him on each trip. In Trinidad the team visited the president of the country and prayed with him; evangelized in public parks and at the local university, drawing huge numbers of Catholics, Protestants, Hindus, and even Muslims to Jesus; and ministered in a school and a mental hospital. Father Thomas was interviewed on television, even though religious programming was not normally permitted. He also blessed mounds of commercial salt he saw on the island.

The group had a scary confrontation in one park. As Father Thomas preached the gospel, he and one friend were accosted by members of a competing religious group, voicing death threats. Other team members couldn't see their friends over the heads of the crowd. So Mrs. Tula gathered children and led them around singing while Marie Heredia and Ellen Hogarty played guitars. The hostile gang left one by one. Some of the team were shaken up, said Hogarty, but "Father thought it was the funniest thing."

The results of the visit were complicated. In the short run it was a great success, with many conversions and displays of spiritual power and a big boost to the Trinidad charismatic community, said Hogarty, but the team found out later that spiritual problems had come back worse than ever on the island, like the unclean spirit that gets chased away and comes back with seven spirits worse than itself (Matthew 12:43 ff).

Back home, the results were complicated as well, and at least one community member saw it as a turning point. "They came back different," said Esther Padilla, Mrs. Tula's daughter, who was not on the trip. She said the difference wasn't anything bad in itself, but it was noticeable, and she implies that it led to some uneasiness in the community. Hogarty didn't see the change as quite that big, but she did say the trip led to a new focus on what God was doing.

CHAPTER 52

A Shakeup and a Breakdown

In 1987 the community began to receive disturbing prophecies. There were warnings about pride and sin. Around that same time, people started leaving. In 1987 and 1988, a population of more than 40 at the Lord's Ranch was reduced to single digits.

There was no single cause for all the departures, but there were underlying issues. The community was never a cult; people were never pressured to stay against their will. But for those who did stay, life was heavily regulated, with a long work week, permission needed for trips off the ranch, restrictions on romance, and many other rules.

Alan and Kim Curtis, who arrived separately and married in 1983, lived in OLYC buildings in El Paso and worked in Juárez, but they left in April 1987. "We loved the work, but the work was like trying to empty the ocean with a bucket," said Alan. "I didn't know whether I could balance that with the emerging responsibilities I had as a young husband and new father." They considered staying in El Paso and working part-time in the ministries but decided that would be too much like ignoring part of the need among the poor, and instead they left amicably to move back to Alan's native Pennsylvania.

Some people were asked to leave; some left because they were unhappy; some left due to personal circumstances not connected to the ranch. Even Sister Mary Virginia left: she was recalled by the Daughters of Charity in April 1988 and sent to work with homeless women in Amarillo. And finally, with so many people gone, the community was no longer what it had been in the past, so even more people decided to leave.

Those who stayed on at the ranch were devastated. "I cried for days about some people that left," said Mary Ann Halloran.

Nobody was more devastated than Father Thomas himself, especially as one person after another left the community. Towards the end of the period, he literally headed for the hills. Ellen Hogarty calls it an "emotional breakdown." He spent about six weeks camped in a tiny trailer near the town of Ruidoso, NM, on an undeveloped parcel of land that some realtor friends were trying to sell. It was about 100 miles northeast of the Lord's Ranch. While he was gone, Father Rosales handled Mass at the prayer meeting and performed other priestly duties for the community. Hogarty and Michael Reuter brought Father Thomas supplies.

Father Thomas also asked Hogarty to pray with him for inner healing. She had never prayed with anyone for "healing of memories" as it was often called, so she headed to the ranch library to look for books on the subject. Father Thomas saw her with those and shook his head. "You're not going to need those," he said. "The Holy Spirit is going to guide you."

Those prayers for his emotional healing went on through many sessions over several weeks. They started with his childhood and went all the way through his adult life to the present. He cried as he brought up past hurts long-buried. He also began reading the book of Job; he identified with Job. He also read Isaiah 43:1, "I have called you by name." "I think my name is 'rejection'," he said. And Hogarty could see why he felt that way, having just prayed with him about so many instances of rejection in his life. "God really moved," recalled Hogarty. "After all that prayer and healing, he became a different person."

As the process went on, Hogarty had two visions. In the first, Father Thomas was wearing a double yoke, but the other half was empty and dragging on the ground; it was a desperate battle to pull the plow. In the second, she saw a yoke with five slots, all filled, and the plowing went much more smoothly. Understanding the message of this vision, the community reorganized, with less of the burden of leadership on Father Thomas and more on four people who hadn't left the ranch: Hogarty, Reuter, and Mike and Mary Ann Halloran. Father Thomas nicknamed the group the Navigators. They remained the leaders of the community, with Father Thomas, until his death in 2006, and they are still the core of the leadership today.

Meanwhile, farming at the ranch pretty much came to an end. There were not enough volunteers to keep the dairy operation going, so that stopped too. In an interview for *Our Sunday Visitor* in 1989, Father Thomas stressed that OLYC and the ranch were not covenant communities and there was no official process for becoming a member. "We have no formal covenant," he said. In an interview with me in 1999, he calmly described the community as like a school of fish, with some joining and some leaving as time goes on.

But the wounds of all the people leaving the community stayed with Father Thomas for a long time.

CHAPTER 53

God's Buddy

What was it like to live around a man like Rick Thomas? Well, for much of the time it was a lot of fun. For one thing, he was a world-class wise guy, and just as uninhibited about that as he was about everything else. His jokes were never off-color, but other than that, the sky was the limit, and as usual, he didn't care about how it made him look. He laughed at his own jokes, and he loved corny puns. Once, he made a pun that I proceeded to top. He laughed with delight and repeated mine.

"He loved to make people laugh," said Evy Nelson, who knew him when she was a pre-teen in El Paso. "He used to have fun playing with people's names: 'Hello Bill, I hope you're not ill,'" said his protégé Father Bill McCann. A successful businessman who has supported the OLYC ministries but preferred not to have his name mentioned recalled the time he asked Father Thomas to remember him in his prayers. "Remember me when you're counting your money," Father Thomas quipped.

He was also unabashedly enthusiastic about what he was doing. "I loved how eager he was," said Frietze-Lewis. "I loved that he didn't mind showing that he was eager. I wanted somebody in the Church to be eager."

The negative side that comes up most was brusqueness. He didn't have much time for social niceties or small talk; he wasn't the nurturing father figure people might expect to find in a church leader. Jim Gallagher, a new community member who got a lot of Father Thomas's time when he was preparing to convert to Catholicism, had a surprise coming after he joined the Church and volunteered for the ministries. "I thought, 'I'll spend all the time in the world with Fr. Thomas.' It was anything but that. He'd be there for any questions you had, but he'd be busy with the guy that was where you were five years ago." Sometimes, when people insisted on a moment of his time, "he'd say 'walk with me to the *baño* [outhouse],'" Mike Halloran recalled. Still, "he never said 'no,'" said Tencha Tapia, who volunteered in the ministries for many years.

At the same time, he could show great affection. He was particularly good with young people, said Evy Nelson. Carmen Molina, who started work in the ministries at age 20 and stayed for 20 years, said "he was always happy to see me. I would be so happy to see him, and the way he received me." Once, walking to the car with him after Mass at the food bank, she accidentally called him "Dad." "I was so embarrassed, but he didn't laugh at me – he just smiled."

He had a knack for teaching from the very beginning. "He was very intelligent, but he talked like a common guy," said Father McCann. "He had an incredible talent for making complex things as simple as possible. His goal was to have you learn, not impress you with his abilities." His friend Richard Munzinger, though, thought that he sometimes took the simplification too far. "I felt that he repeated himself too often. A teaching that could have been done in 25 minutes was done in an hour, and nothing new was said."

A minor flaw, but hard to miss, was Father Thomas's lack of organization. Part of it came just because he was always open to changing plans if he thought God wanted him to; nobody can organize the Holy Spirit. But part of it was his general approach to his work. "We can't keep track of anything," he once told me, and while that's an exaggeration – I was pleasantly surprised by all the documentation I found for this biography – his keeping track certainly wasn't very systematic. His personal calendar, for example, is a wonderful source of information, but it's a long way from helpfully prioritized: in 1972, it lists a visit from his Jesuit friend Father Cohen in April but does not mention the Christmas Day visit to the Juárez dump, which would have been a big deal even without the multiplication of food.

"I'd say he was disorganized," said Ellen Hogarty. "He could never finish anything. He left piles and piles of things to be done. The urgent pushed out the important." "I'm a good squirrel," he once told Hogarty, and he would clean up messes if they got further out of hand, usually with Hogarty's help. "It's certainly not that he liked to live with a mess."

Father Thomas's daily life wasn't organized the same way as most people's, either. He often got up at 5 or 6 a.m. to pray, then went back to bed for a nap; he once complained because Hector Bencomo woke him with a phone call at 9:30 a.m; that time he had been up praying at 3 a.m. The morning nap was sporadic, but he took an afternoon nap no matter what, anywhere from 30 to 60 minutes. He went for a slow morning jog most days for as long as his health permitted, and he rode horses on the Lord's Ranch – his favorite recreation – whenever time permitted. He preferred to ride with companions; while he was no party animal, he wasn't really an introvert either, and he needed human company to unwind.

His most treasured companion, though, was always God. The closeness of the relationship could be breathtaking, and it wasn't always a comfortable closeness. Munzinger, who had plenty of challenges in his own life around the time he joined the community, once complained to Father Thomas, "God sure is tough!" "He sure is," Father Thomas agreed. Munzinger said he doesn't know exactly what personal cross Father Thomas was carrying, but there's no question there was one. "It was more than, 'yes, I've seen that happen to other people.' It was 'yes, it happens to me.'"

But there was a lighter side to that closeness with God, as well. Munzinger recalled a time when his vehicle was stalling repeatedly on the freeway west of Las Cruces, speed dropping off from 70 to 45, while Father Thomas sat oblivious in the passenger seat, reading. Finally the vehicle refused to restart at all. Munzinger coasted to the side of the road and Father Thomas finally looked up; Munzinger explained the problem.

"Father said, 'Jesus, I need to be at Loretto [in El Paso] at 3 o'clock this afternoon,'" said Munzinger. "The car started right up" and didn't stall again.

"This was early when I knew him. It made my hair stand up. I knew I was in the presence of a holy man."

Later, the two men took a trip to Wyoming. They were sitting in the car by the roadside eating lunch. "He said, 'Jesus, send a buffalo over here so I can see one up close,'" Munzinger said. "Out of the trees comes a great big female buffalo, all by herself." She walked up to Father Thomas's side of the car, six inches from the window, showed herself from every angle, and then wandered away again."

"Let me tell you something," Munzinger said. "This is God's buddy."

CHAPTER 54

Operation Rescue

The loss of so many workers in the late 80s may have steamrollered Father Thomas on a personal level, but it didn't keep him from carrying on with his ministry.

Even while the dust was settling, he was finding a new way to stick his neck out for the Lord, a way that would take him all the way to jail cells where he wasn't just visiting: Operation Rescue, a protest where demonstrators physically blockaded abortion clinics.

Father Thomas had been fighting abortion for years. Ellen Hogarty said that back in 1984, when she was a 19-year-old newcomer to the ranch, he had sent her and another volunteer into an abortion clinic in Akron, Ohio as a "truth team" to ask the clients whether they knew their pregnancy was an actual baby. (They got asked to leave very quickly.) The community also held pro-life marches and celebrated Mass outside abortion clinics in the 80s. But no matter how much he was doing, he always felt he should be doing more. By 1989, he had decided "more" meant being willing to go to jail.

Father Thomas first heard about Operation Rescue in July 1988, when activist Randall Terry put on a rescue in Atlanta during the Democratic national convention. Not long after, another

Operation Rescue leader, Rex Moses, came to speak at a meeting in El Paso. Father Thomas bought right into the program. By early 1989 he was having visitors to the ranch listen to how-to tapes by Randall Terry.

Father Thomas traveled to Austin in April 1989 for a statewide rescue organized by Moses, planning to read pro-life Scripture at the clinics. "I had told Rex, man, we'll freeze those guys [with the Scripture readings]." The rescue was scheduled for Saturday, but one of the clinics decided to get its abortions done Friday evening to dodge the protest, so rescuers went there Friday too, and Father Thomas wanted to join them. Moses said OK, but don't get arrested – he wanted Father Thomas on hand for the main event the next day. Moses dropped him off at the clinic; he was the last protester to arrive, and there were already 10 or 11 rescuers in the waiting room, facing off against the clients. "There's one guy, a big guy, and he was standing in the door [to the procedure room] so nobody could get in there to get an abortion. He had his two feet placed up against each side of the bottom of the door, then his body, and he had his hand up on the doorjamb. He was going to block anybody going into the procedure room."

The atmosphere was so overwhelming that Father Thomas couldn't bring to mind the Scriptures he had planned to read aloud. "I was so scared, all I could say was 'our help is in the name of the Lord, who made heaven and earth.' I was sitting on the floor with my back against the wall. I forgot every other prayer, all my great plans."

"Somehow I got a message the police were coming. So I said 'it's time for me to leave, because I'm not supposed to be arrested.'" Out he went, and back down the walkway to the street. "I saw this officer coming in. He was scared. You could just tell. He was scared, he was nervous, he didn't know what he was going to do. I said 'God bless you, officer,' and kept on going."

Father Thomas came back for the main rescue the next day, but he didn't get arrested then either, and he returned to Austin several times for more rescues; he never did get arrested in that city. He did have a creepy experience, though, when one rescue was so successful the clinic shut down for the day and he went with two of the other rescuers to see what else they could accomplish with their time.

"We went to the office of the guy who does abortions" he said. "We park outside the office, and we can see in there [from the car window], and there's X [the abortionist], and he had a big needle, and there's a woman in there. We're discussing – can we go in and do anything to stop him? Now whether he was doing abortions at that moment, I have no idea. Anyway, we left without doing anything, because we weren't sure what we could do."

In El Paso, though, he did get arrested. On Aug. 26, 1989, Father Thomas and other protesters staged the first local rescue under the auspices of Rescue El Paso, and 77 of them, including Father Thomas and at least 20 other OLYC workers, got arrested on a misdemeanor charge of blocking a passageway.

The group blocked the doorways and passageways at Reproductive Services on Gateway East. According to front-page newspaper coverage, the demonstration began at 5 a.m. with about 125 people participating, although not all of them blocked the way. The police said the demonstration was peaceful, with no violence, but it took 25 police officers to lift the protesters one by one and take them away. Clinic officials said the demonstration delayed abortions by four hours, and organizer Bernadette Gartner of Rescue El Paso said two women were talked out of abortions altogether.

Hogarty said Father Thomas sat on the steps blocking the door, praying and admonishing the police. "Do you want that on your conscience?" he asked them. "You're sworn to protect life." When they said they were just doing their job, he shot back "that's what they said at the Nuremberg trials" [of Nazi war criminals]. He started songs to keep the protesters' morale up. Police identified him quickly as a ringleader.

"They separated him out really quick," said Michael Reuter, who was also taken to jail but was not put in the same cell as Father Thomas. "The next time I saw him, I'm in the cell and he's on the nightly news." The head jail official on duty was a former Camp Juan Diego counselor who let TV reporters in to see him.

This first of several jailings taught Father Thomas a lot about life behind bars. At age 61, he had to drag his own mattress into his cell, where he was immediately met by an aggressive prisoner who told him where to put the mattress and which of two toilets to use for which function.

"Like a dang fool I said, 'who are you?'" he recalled years later. "I don't know what his answer was. I laid down and went to sleep." In the morning, though, "I found out pretty quick, this guy is the boss [of the cell]. That could have been the dumbest thing [to say]. He could have floored me right there." Still, he was generally treated with respect when the prisoners found out he was a priest and a pro-lifer, and the jail boss's rules weren't necessarily unreasonable. For example, the boss made every prisoner take a bath every day, "because you stink otherwise. He enforced that. He enforced everything."

His fellow prisoners weren't the only company he had. Pretty soon he had a guest: Bishop Ricardo Ramírez of Las Cruces, his bishop at the Lord's Ranch. "He came roaring down from Las Cruces to see me. I was so touched, because he came all the way down to see me." He thanked Bishop Ramírez more than once over the coming years. "I so much appreciated it, I cried." The visit stayed with Bishop Ramírez, too; in his eulogy at Father Thomas's funeral 17 years later, he remembered it as his most memorable encounter with Father Thomas, who wept openly in the visiting room. The bishop said he believes Father Thomas was emotional over getting unexpected support from the

Church hierarchy "at a time that he may have felt very abandoned by us."

Arrested on a Saturday, Father Thomas spent the next couple of days jockeying in the media with the legal system over bond. Bond was set at $200; he and some others wouldn't pay it. A local bail bondsman offered to pay it for him; he turned down the offer. Bond was lowered to $1. Still he refused; the only bail he was prepared to accept was a personal promise to appear in court. "I'll stay in here forever if it will save lives," he said in one newspaper interview. "I feel I'm guilty of murder for not doing anything." In another interview, he said he'd rather spend the dollar fighting abortion.

Monday afternoon the jail officials got sick of him and threw him out, apparently without even the promise. "I had to go out the side door in a hurry. I don't think I signed any paper. They just took off my uniform, gave me my black clothes, and said 'get out.'" He found a reporter from Juárez waiting to interview him. "They were trying to put him off and get me out," he said. Later, most of the protesters, including Father Thomas and the whole OLYC group, had their charges dropped because the police couldn't identify which protesters they had warned to move before arresting them.

The second rescue took place Sept. 16 at Reproductive Services. Fifty-one protesters were arrested this time, including some OLYC people but not Father Thomas, who did not personally block the door. He was present and told the police to warn each individual before arrest; he was stalling, of course, to keep the door blocked longer.

Rescues continued in El Paso for about two years, half a dozen or more – it's difficult to give an exact count because tactics varied so much that it isn't always clear what counts as a rescue. Sometimes protesters would block the door but move away when ordered. Some of these are listed in Father Thomas's calendars as "spook" or "fake" rescues. Father Thomas and his friends also took part in rescues in other cities, notably Dallas and San Antonio.

Perhaps the most spectacular and controversial rescue of all was the "kids' rescue" of March 9, 1991, at Reproductive Services in El Paso. The protest started out with both adults and children blocking the door. When the police came and issued the usual warning, the adults moved out of the way; the children, including 11-year-old Rachel Halloran, her nine-year-old brother Nathan, and Joshua, age 8, decided to stay on the steps and pray the rosary, as their parents watched from the sidewalk 20 feet away. The police couldn't touch the children and had to call the juvenile detention squad. The juvenile officers warned the parents to remove their children, and Father Thomas made sure there were plenty of lengthy discussions and plenty of questions asked.

"It dragged on and on," said Hogarty. "Father just loved it. It was a David vs. Goliath type situation, where the whole abortion operation was shut down temporarily because of some children sitting peacefully and courageously in front of the door. It was one of the highlights of his life." Eventually the children quietly left the door and returned to the sidewalk.

CHAPTER 55

Needling the Judge

In all, Father Thomas went to jail five times for protesting abortion: two arrests and one jail sentence in El Paso, and one arrest each in Dallas and San Antonio.

He was arrested in Dallas in January 1990 as part of a rescue staged by Bobbie Cavnar's charismatic Community of God's Delight, and spent several hours in jail, getting out at 3:30 a.m. In April 1991, defended by his lawyer friend Richard Munzinger, he was found not guilty of criminal trespass in that case, because a juror spotted a discrepancy in the evidence.

In March 1992 Father Thomas, Ellen Hogarty, Michael Reuter and others, including at least two other priests and several Protestant pastors, were arrested in a rescue in San Antonio. They spent the next five days in jail. Hogarty and the other women had it rough – she and two others were squeezed into a cell designed for one and had to wear masks because they refused to be tested for tuberculosis. Father Thomas saw them wearing their masks at one point and was moved to tears.

His own experience in the men's section in the San Antonio jail was more pleasant. The male rescuers had the basement to themselves, and there were so many of them that they got most of what they wanted from the jailers. They all refused to take the TB test, but they got away without wearing masks. The head of the jail was kind to the protesters, and best of all, the priests were allowed to celebrate Mass daily. There was plenty of prayer, preaching, singing, and mutual encouragement – "it was like a week's retreat," said Reuter. When the court case came up, Father Thomas was sentenced to time served and didn't have to go back to jail.

In June 1992 Father Thomas spent two days at the center of a spectacular courtroom drama in El Paso. He was charged, along with 21 others, including many OLYC people, with obstructing a passageway at Reproductive Services, in a rescue held Feb. 23, 1991. The judge ruled that only the issue of obstructing the passageway could be raised; he gave Father Thomas a list of 50 words, starting with "abortion," that he could not use in court – the opposite of the ruling a different judge had made in the case of the 1989 rescue, before that trial fell apart. A lawyer told him he had no chance at all of winning the case and might as well represent himself. That way, he could get away with saying and doing things no lawyer would dare to do, because lawyers are supposed to know better and need to keep making a living in court.

"I did all kinds of things you're not supposed to do," he said. "I gave them a fit all the time." The judge didn't like it and offered many times to appoint a real lawyer to defend him; "I said no, your honor, you're my defense lawyer, I voted for you." Whenever the judge asked him if he would accept a lawyer, he replied by asking the judge if he would dismiss the case, which of course wasn't going to happen. He quoted Latin legal sayings "just to be cantankerous. Nobody in the courtroom knew what the heck I was saying." He handed out his business card to the jury until the judge caught him and made him stop. None of his lawyer friends would visit him – they were afraid they would be appointed to defend him.

"I was needling [the judge] every time I got a chance. I don't know whether he knew I was needling him or not. I guess he did, but what could he do about it? He had to be a judge and fair. I'm just a dumb guy that doesn't know anything about the law or courts or anything. I'm just like a bull in a china shop, doing all kind of things I shouldn't do."

At the end of his life, Father Thomas seems to have had mixed feelings about the way he treated the judge. On the one hand, he told Reuter all the stories with every sign of relish. But on the other hand, he said he realized that a lawyer's job is to help educate the judge on the facts of the case and the law that applies to it, each lawyer presenting both law and facts slanted to the lawyer's own side of the case, so that the judge can decide between them. "I wasn't helping [the judge] at all. I'm sorry that happened."

The case did not go well, even though 10 witnesses testified that Father Thomas was not on the steps blocking the doorway at the clinic. The problem was the police report. Apparently it accused him of blocking the door, but he couldn't get his hands on it; the judge said the police had to give him the report, but that never happened. "I was accused of blocking that entrance, and I had all those witnesses and they testified one after another, 'he did not block that entrance.' I was standing 15 feet away from the entrance. That was the accusation, but I could never get it in writing. [The judge] said they have to give it to you, but that didn't do any good because I didn't have it." The assistant county attorney argued that he was the ringleader and responsible for the actions of those who did block the door. Father Thomas wasn't impressed with that. "Her final sum-up was, this guy was arrested, so he's guilty," he said later. "By all rights I won the case."

When the jury convicted him, the judge asked him whether he wanted to be sentenced by the jury or by the judge. "I said 'I want you to sentence me. I voted for you.' The judge wanted the jury to do it, because he didn't want to be saddled with it. I wanted him to be saddled with it." The judge gave him five days in jail.

After his conviction, Father Thomas asked to address the court. The judge said he was leaving but Father Thomas was welcome to use the courtroom. He told his supporters he was happy with the verdict because it put the evils of abortion on the front page of the local newspapers. Quoting Romans 8:28, he said "I'm not worried about the guilty verdict. For those who love God, everything works out for the best." Then his supporters began praying, singing and dancing in the courtroom; the newspaper headline read "Revival breaks out after jury's verdict."

Later, on a Christian TV show, he said his jail time wasn't comfortable. He was just convicted of a misdemeanor, but he had to share space with multiple murderers, and he was only allowed to flush the toilet during TV commercials. But he was welcomed as a priest, asked to hold "services" and counsel the prisoners; he prayed for one prisoner for deliverance. He couldn't say Mass because he didn't have his sacramentary, hosts, or wine with him in the jail, but he did lead a Bible study. So all in all, it was a good experience.

"I recommend it," he said. "I think it's part of your education."

"The question is not why Christians are in jail," he told another TV interviewer. "The question is why they're not in jail. If we conform to a sinful society, then we're left alone, but if we oppose it we're going to end up in jail. Most of the early [Christian] folks were jailbirds, and we have to remember that."

In a 1990 interview with Lisa Ferguson of *New Covenant*, Father Thomas said he saw Operation Rescue as God's next step in the Catholic charismatic renewal.

"There is a great outpouring of the Holy Spirit going on at this moment," he said, "but it is not widely recognized as such because it is not in the form it was 10 or 20 years ago. The Lord is purifying His church and pouring out the grace of martyrdom for those who are open to receive it. The lollipop stage of the renewal is the outgoing tide, and the martyrdom stage is the incoming tide. What I have experienced in the Operation Rescue movement is a new outpouring of the Holy Spirit for those able to embrace it."

CHAPTER 56

The Creative Pro-lifer

J ail or no jail, Father Thomas's war against abortion went way, way back – and also way, way out. "That was constantly burning in him," said Ellen Hogarty. "A lot of creative juices went into finding ways to fight abortion." "I am responsible for these innocent children being killed in this country," Father Thomas said on a Christian TV interview. "There's blood on my hands if I don't do anything about it."

No non-violent tactic was too extreme for him. One really unpopular project was picketing abortionists' homes. A couple of years the volunteers went picketing the homes on Christmas Day and Thanksgiving; that move was based on chapter 2 of the Old Testament (Catholic only) book of Tobit, in which Tobit leaves a holiday meal sitting on the table and goes out, at great danger to himself, to bury a murder victim. On one of the Christmas visits the doctor came out and called Father Thomas a terrorist. "Maybe so," he replied, "but I never killed anybody." "Neither have I," said the doctor. "Well, then," Father Thomas asked, "what would happen to that child if you didn't intervene?" The doctor went back into his house.

Sometimes the picketing took place on the doctors' birthdays; sometimes on a regular weekly schedule; sometimes new picketers arrived shortly after an earlier group of picketers had left.

"It makes them quit," Father Thomas said. Obviously it didn't make all of them quit; some of the abortionists settled down resignedly to a mild state of siege, with family members coming and going and ignoring the picketers, while the picketers in turn left the family members alone and followed police rules about where they could walk. Owners of the buildings where clinics were housed were also picketed.

Father Thomas and his friends carried picket signs in a lot of other settings, too. A 1986 newspaper photograph shows two-year-old Josh Halloran holding an anti-abortion sign in a rally, part of a nationwide protest on the 13th anniversary of the Roe vs. Wade Supreme Court decision legalizing abortion in the United States. A 1990 clipping shows food bank worker Francisca Terrazas holding up a sign that says "Hispanic Mothers Against Murder" at the Fort Worth Democratic convention that nominated pro-choice candidate (and eventual winner) Ann Richards for governor; Terrazas was among half a dozen protesters who held up their signs during Richards' victory speech. Father Thomas, a lifelong Democrat, was a pro-life delegate himself at a party convention in 2002; somebody tore his sign in half, and a group of bikers crowded around to protect the 74-year-old priest.

The OLYC community picketed hospitals, held marches on the Cordova Street bridge from El Paso to Juárez protesting abortion, and picketed orientation of interns at a Texas Tech medical school because the doctors there were being offered work as abortionists, and Father Thomas wanted the interns to know right away that if they were tempted to moonlight as abortionists, they could look forward to being picketed. For several years the group went to a city park a block from Reproductive Services, every Saturday during abortion hours (7:30 a.m. onward) to pray, sing, pray in tongues and recite Scripture. They would then celebrate Mass at La Cueva for the souls of aborted babies.

Another ministry is "sidewalk counseling" in front of abortion clinics, which isn't illegal if the women aren't physically prevented from getting to the clinic. That work continues today, and the community estimates it has saved more than 1,000 babies. Father Thomas and others also arranged for a few adoptions of children who were originally scheduled for abortion.

On a completely different level, lawyer and OLYC volunteer Richard Munzinger was the author of a proposed city ordinance, put forward in October 1989 by a pro-life council member, that would have placed substantial restrictions on abortions within El Paso. There was some argument about whether the municipal government had any power to restrict abortion, and the ordinance was defeated 4-2.

Pro-life work doesn't stop with trying to prevent abortion. OLYC volunteers offer support to pregnant women who change their minds and turn down abortion, making sure their needs are met. One group used to hold baby showers, and still gives mothers baby supplies. The community also has a support group for women who are suffering after having an abortion. Meanwhile, every visiting youth group gets a pro-life presentation, usually featuring a speaker who has had an abortion.

Rescues, though, are a thing of the past. The group refocused its work after the February 1991 rescue where Father Thomas was tried and sentenced. The situation had reached a point where heavier and heavier sentences – trespassing at a clinic is now a felony, not a misdemeanor – and a shortage of volunteers threatened the entire OLYC operation.

"There were so few of us to run the ranch and the community and the ministries," said Hogarty. She said the availability of workers is a key sign for discerning God's will: "if God doesn't send you the necessary help, it might be a sign that He doesn't want you to do it."

CHAPTER 57

Trouble at the Food Bank

ardships and heartaches inside the OLYC community did not end with the exodus of many of its members. In the early 90s Father Thomas lost three important co-workers, two to death and one to a Jesuit transfer, and also suffered a traumatic blow of a different kind.

In September 1991 Guillermina Valdes-Villalva, aged just 51, was killed in a plane crash near Houston. Besides her work with Father Thomas, Villalva, a sociologist, had an international reputation for both academic and political service to Mexican workers, especially women. In August 1992 Father Sam Rosales, the only Jesuit priest ever to work with Father Thomas for such a lengthy period, was sent away by his superiors, to attend Loyola University in Chicago, and then to parish work in San Antonio.

Next came a very different, but devastating, setback both to Father Thomas and to the OLYC ministries. The food bank in Juárez had carried on under the leadership of the apostles, and in the early 90s was feeding about 900 families a week. But in 1993 seven of the apostles sued Father Thomas under Mexico's strong employee protection law. They claimed that Father Thomas paid them a salary and that they had the rights of employees. The apostles were awarded damages – very minor, because while workers are always legally right in such cases under Mexican law, the judge thought they were morally wrong. "The whole experience was very demoralizing to Father Rick," said Ellen Hogarty. "It was a great heartache to him and a very difficult time."

With the ruling in place, the remaining leaders, loyal to Father Thomas, couldn't ask anybody to work, which meant they couldn't physically operate the food distribution. So the operation had to be cut back drastically. The regular Monday food distribution shut down, although the Friday delivery to the homebound continued, and the clinic stayed open. Only a handful of the 50 men and women who had operated the food bank stayed on, among them major leaders like Aurora Villa, Pedro Ibarra, and Maria Luisa Domínguez. Another was Carmen Molina, who was saddened by the loss of fellowship. "It was just like a mother when all the children leave the home," she said.

Father kept celebrating Mass at the food bank on Mondays, though, with about 20 to 30 attending. Some of the families even brought their own meager food to share with those worse off than themselves. Gradually services were restored, but on a smaller scale, with only about 100 families getting food. (The number has since grown to about 350.) The work-for-food policy was gone forever, although full-time volunteers still get a large basket of food and some other benefits.

Finally came one more devastating death: Manny Basurto. He died in February 1994, age 74, following a long battle with diabetes. Basurto had been converted in 1974 following years of prayer by his wife. He had been one of the Juniors, he and Father Thomas were close friends, and Father Thomas had looked to him many times over the years for advice.

Early photo of eating a meal at the Lord's Ranch. Pictured: Sister Mary
Virginia, Bill Halloran, Father Rick and Manny Basurto, 1976.

CHAPTER 58

King Jesus on the Airwaves

The early 90s also brought the launch of a project that had been dear to Father Thomas's heart for almost a decade: radio station KJES, a 50-kilowatt shortwave radio station, located at the Lord's Ranch, that for many years broadcast Scripture readings 7½ hours a day. (The ministry has recently been transferred to the Internet.) The call letters stand for King Jesus.

The Bible readings, in both English and Spanish, were almost the entire content; there was a little praise music, and the law required station identification, but there was no preaching, no commentary, and no requests for money. Readers (frequently children) were never identified.

The broadcast Bible readings were yet another example of "executing the sentence" by reading Scripture aloud. "There's all kinds of garbage in the atmosphere," Father Thomas said. "We're putting out something that's pure. We're putting out the Word of God to take effect in creation." The broadcasts were pointed toward various parts of the world, based on a schedule. Listeners have contacted the station from as far away as Siberia and New Zealand.

KJES originated in the mid-1980s when Father Thomas was talking to some evangelical Christian friends who were involved in Christian radio and wondered aloud what would happen if Scripture were broadcast. They offered to help him, but technical, administrative, legal and financial problems dragged on for years, and the station never seemed to get any closer to reality. Finally Father Thomas asked Bill Halloran, Mike's father, to take over the job. "I don't know anything about radio and I don't want to know anything about radio," Bill responded, but after prayer he decided he couldn't say no to Father Thomas. Bill, and then John and Ruth Stanley, Methodist missionaries who do technical work for Christian stations of many denominations, were eventually able to overcome seemingly endless obstacles to get the station running.

Bill Halloran wasn't the only community member who was less than enthusiastic about the idea. Most of Father Thomas's closest friends were against it too, so much so that ordinarily it would have been enough to get him to back down. Not this time; he played the authority card and went ahead. It was that big to him.

After a number of false starts, the first broadcast was made June 22, 1992, in English and aimed at western Canada. The second, in Spanish, was aimed at Mexico.

The radio ministry was based on Isaiah 55:10-11, Jeremiah 1:9-10, Jeremiah 23:22 and other Scriptures, all relating to the power of the word of God. Broadcasters went to the station two or three times a day, depending on the season.

Working at the station wasn't just a technical job; volunteer broadcasters prayed for direction as they picked out each session's tapes, and there's a chapel in the station with the Blessed Sacrament. John Stanley, the Methodist, said KJES was the only station where he has ever seen a sign on the transmitter saying "do not sprinkle holy water on the plate." But Stanley was well impressed – he also said he has never seen transmitter operators chosen on such a spiritual basis; even Christian stations often pick employees solely for their technical qualifications. At KJES, "it's an absolute ministry for them."

The station continued to break down from time to time; Father Thomas's orders were to broadcast anyway, play the tapes, and ask the angels to take the program wherever God wanted. The operators did that, and sometimes they got back reports of people hearing broadcasts at just those times.

Many listeners have written in to the station, saying thanks for the encouragement – Father Thomas's favorite letters were from listeners in Communist Cuba – or simply expressing gratitude that there was at least one Christian station in the world that never asks for money. Sometimes people have had more than that to be thankful for, though. Sergio and Lucía Conde were listening to KJES at their home one Holy Thursday with a friend who was suffering from serious pain due to a prostate or kidney problem (they weren't sure which). The man felt a surge of heat from his feet to his head, and after 20 minutes he got up and said "the pain is gone! The pain is gone!"

Shortwave radio station KJES at the Lord's Ranch, 1995.

Sitting in the broadcasting room at KJES radio station.

CHAPTER 59

A New Headquarters

By the mid-1990s, the community had outgrown the old OLYC building on Kansas Street. It was too small, and there was no place for the children's activities that had become part of the ministry. There were gas leaks and other repair problems stretching back to Sister Mary Virginia's time and before. The community prayed about the problems and began looking for something that would meet the ministries' growing needs: easy accessibility, good location, and 6,000 square feet of floor space, with open space for meetings and room for classes, offices, storage, and parking. Ellen Hogarty received a prophecy: God would provide the perfect place.

Father Thomas spent two years looking around and came up with a few less-than-perfect places. In March 1996, notwithstanding the prophecy, the community decided to buy one of them. They were tired of looking, and ready to settle for sort-of-OK: a commercial building on Piedras Street. Father Thomas decided to overlook the fact that it was well short of the necessary space, had too few rooms, and needed a lot of work, not to mention that it was a mile and a half from the existing OLYC building. He talked the rest of the leaders into settling for it, too, and for three days they prayed outside the building. Then they put in an offer, meeting the asking price in full.

Apparently, though, God hadn't forgotten the prophecy. The offer was ignored; it turned out the owner had sold the property to a friend, for less money. So, the group went back to looking for the perfect place. "We got the message, loud and clear," said Hogarty. "Clearly God blocked this purchase and wanted us to get back to work on looking, waiting and trusting."

Years earlier, Father Thomas had had his eye caught by a downtown retail operation, a modern building that took up almost a full city block on the north side of Paisano Drive, two blocks north of the old OLYC and just the width of the street away from South El Paso. The building measured 100 by 200 feet, with an enormous open area, two floors of smaller rooms and offices, and a large basement; the rest of the block was a fenced parking lot. He drove by the building and claimed it in God's name as he prayed.

Father Thomas asked a realtor about the building. "Forget it," was the answer. "That building is out of reach." But in September, soon after the Piedras deal fell through, the Paisano building came on the market. The North American Free Trade Agreement had dug a deep hole in the owner's sales, and he had to sell the building and move to a more affordable location to keep the operation above water. The bank set a November 1st deadline for the sale, and OLYC joined the bidding. But the property still looked to be out of reach. The bid OLYC could afford was a long way under market value ("pitiful" was Father Thomas's actual word). Meanwhile, three major public bodies – the State of Texas, County of El Paso, and El Paso Independent School District – were in the bidding too, with real money.

And then, suddenly, all the rivals were out. The school district was offered another building, free, and dropped out of the race. The bid from the county was disqualified because the state attorney general enforced a requirement that usually gets ignored: the bid required an appraisal which could not be completed by Nov. 1. And the State of Texas bid fell through by sheer mistake. The state was planning to renovate the existing building, but somebody put a condition into the official offer that the building had to be demolished by the vendor before the sale; it wasn't possible to get the offer rewritten in time for the bank deadline. The bank had no choice: only the OLYC offer was left on the table.

The deal closed December 3, 1996. The OLYC team moved in in March to clean up the building, and the first prayer meeting was held March 26, 1997: Wednesday of Holy Week that year. Father Thomas picked the building's name: *Las Alas*, Spanish for "the wings. The name alludes to many biblical images of God protecting His people "under His wings."

Meanwhile, the OLYC community tried to give the old youth center away, to the diocese or to Catholic charities, but nobody wanted to take on the liabilities and insurance costs. Then a businessman turned up with an offer of almost three times the market value of the property. Father Thomas's jaw dropped, but the man assured him he knew what the building was worth, and he still wanted to pay the offered price.

Father Thomas never stopped working hard, but after the shrinking of the ranch population, his pro-life work and other duties actually left him time to do a fair bit of gardening, for the first time in his adult life – a real treat for a man who was always a country boy at heart. Meanwhile, the prayer meetings had been carrying on as usual at the old OLYC building. But when the meetings moved Las Alas, life changed again, and the gardening had to go by the boards.

"I need to make myself available at Las Alas," Father Thomas said, and started offering spiritual counseling. He never announced it at the prayer meeting, but all the same his friends were nervous. "When word gets out, he's going to be inundated," Ellen Hogarty thought at the time. Word got out slowly, but by the time a year had passed, "the line was enormous."

Mondays and Wednesdays were counseling days, but they weren't just counseling days by a long shot. Both days he went to Juárez in the morning. Mondays he had Masses at two different food banks, complete with confessions; Wednesdays it was the jail and mental hospital ministries. Then it was time for lunch and a nap. On Mondays he would work on phone calls and correspondence until 3 or 3:30, then counsel and give spiritual direction until anywhere from 7 to 9 p.m. Wednesdays he was in the confessional until 7; he would then give a teaching at the prayer meeting, and then vest for Mass, complete with homily. The crowd wasn't finished with him when Mass was over, either – "as he was going back to unvest, people would be still going to him," said Hogarty – so eventually he began unvesting in the bathroom, the opposite direction from what people expected, and ducking out the nearby back door while his helpers took his vestments to the sacristy. Hogarty would hand him something to eat – often a tortilla with peanut butter and honey. "He would be exhausted. When he finally reached the car and got in, he would be silent." But nothing stopped him from counseling; for one stretch of several weeks, when the building was closed for asbestos removal, the prayer meeting moved to the parking lot, and he did confessions and counseling in a van.

In front of the newly acquired building that was "out of reach" and which he should have never been able to purchase, 1997.

CHAPTER 60

Counseling by the Book

People who went to Father Thomas for counseling at Las Alas could count on getting a prescription, but it wouldn't be for tranquilizers. Or drugs of any sort.

He'd meet with them, anywhere from 10 minutes to an hour; hear their confession and send them away with homework. He had a pre-printed list, and would check off the appropriate assignment, in English or Spanish as necessary, for each visitor. They might have to read the lengthy Psalm 68 ("Let God rise up, let his enemies be scattered...") for half an hour a day; or eat blessed salt every hour; or drink two quarts of holy water a day; or read Deuteronomy, chapters 4 to 34, and mark every verse related to the First Commandment ("you shall have no other gods before me"); or read certain verses from the Bible for half an hour daily; 1 Peter 5:7, Sirach 2, Ephesians 5:20 and Philippians 4:4-8 were the most frequent prescriptions. He'd also give them tapes or CDs on the dangers of the occult, and on the use of sacramentals like holy water and blessed salt.

When the person came back, which most of them did, he would ask to see the sheet: "show me what homework I gave you." If they didn't have the sheet, he'd give them another one, but that would be their last chance. The prescription was more than therapy. It was a test of seriousness.

"He'd give them a good fair try," said Hogarty. "There are some people who are so wounded they can't do what you tell them to, and he would make allowances for them, but there are others who have no intention of changing their lives. They just want a blessing. He was really going to invest more time in working with the people who were serious."

Confession was an important part of the process, and his work as a confessor was as unusual as his prescriptions. He often knew people's sins before they confessed them, said Hogarty; he never told her that himself, but she heard about it second-hand, from people who had that experience. (I heard the same thing from one OLYC community member who did know about it first-hand.) If penitents didn't mention the sin he discerned, he wouldn't confront them directly, but he'd find a way to bring the conversation around to it. Sometimes, especially if he suspected abortion, he would ask "what's the worst thing you've ever done?" "Ever" might be 30 or 40 years ago, but it would need to be confessed to start the healing process. "He was a doctor of the soul," said Hogarty. In ordinary daily life, though, he would ignore this gift as much as he could, rather than pry into people's private lives or waste time pursuing problems with people who had no desire to change.

Jim Gallagher, who joined the OLYC community in the 90s, said he was astonished at how much Father Thomas could see into people's souls; "he had the ability to spiritually look at someone and say a word or have a visual image and just bowl them over like a pin." Often, said Gallagher, Father Thomas's insight would be what the person needed to address and open the door to the spiritual progress they needed to make.

As time went on, Father Thomas found ways of spreading the work around so that he could help more people without stretching himself past the breaking point. He put teams together and had Hogarty train them to pray for some people for inner healing during the same time he was counseling others in the confessional. He also taught self-deliverance prayers so that people could do part of their spiritual work to free themselves from demonic infestation or harassment.

"Father Thomas said that the longer he was in the deliverance ministry, the more he realized that rarely did he need to get involved in a head-on, combative confrontation with the demons," said Hogarty. "Instead, he could and should have the person do the majority of work on their own. This proved to be highly effective in that not only was he able to help a lot more people, but the individual was able to grow in their spiritual life, learn discipline, how to pray, and how to keep themselves spiritually strong."

CHAPTER 61

The Land War

"**F**ederal lawyers who in the past have taken on such heavyweights as Al Capone and Richard Nixon may finally have met their match," reporter Eric Enders wrote in an August 1997 article in the El Paso *Herald-Post*.

And who might this super-heavyweight be? Why, none other than Richard M. Thomas SJ. Father Thomas had just weighed in for a three-year battle that would make the federal Bureau of Land Management wish it had never heard his name.

In 1975, the BLM had leased 320 acres of land to the Lord's Ranch. The land sits next to the 160 acres OLYC already owned, to create an L-shaped parcel totaling 480 acres. A BLM official had typed in a provision over Father Thomas's signature on the agreement allowing the ranch to buy the BLM land after completing improvements on the property. Over the years, the ranchers had dug a three-acre lake and built two campsites with outhouses, plus some other improvements; they also fenced the property.

But in June 1997, three years from the lease expiration date, the BLM served notice that it was canceling the lease. The notice said the improvements did not meet the original agreement and were more of a detraction than an improvement. BLM officials came across as reasonable in newspaper interviews; they said the ranch had a right to appeal, and even if it lost, it would still be able to use the land along with the rest of the general public. Up close, though, the BLM people weren't quite so friendly, said Jim Gallagher, the OLYC community member who handled the case as a lawyer; "they made some pretty harsh comments."

Michael Reuter said the ranchers gave the officials a tour of the land in good faith and happened to mention that they used one particular spot for prayer; later, he overheard one official tell another "this is where they pray" in a sneering tone of voice. "Boy, that was a spiritual battle, I don't mind telling you," said Gallagher. "I told them 'you're making a real mistake. This isn't going to go away.'"

Father Thomas declared war. He called in the media, and the news coverage was sympathetic to the ranch, with lots of pictures of happy children. Father Thomas had T-shirts made, displaying a map that showed graphically how small the disputed lands were compared to the BLM's total holdings in the area; "70 sq mi of BLM land – BLM please give back the ½ sq mi of the needy children's land and lake," the adjoining wording read. He wrote a song; a clip of the song ("BLM, for goodness sake, don't dry up the children's lake") ended up on the TV news. And biggest of all, he called on OLYC community members, their friends, and Anything-a-Month newsletter subscribers to mount a letter-writing campaign to the media, to politicians, to BLM officials at the local, state and national levels, and to Interior Secretary Bruce Babbitt. The result was a flood of letters. *The 700 Club*, a Christian TV program, paid a visit; the song clip ended up on that show too.

In newspaper interviews, Father Thomas described the Lord's Ranch as "a poor kid's Ruidoso" (a popular resort in southern New Mexico, a place the poor of El Paso could never afford to go.) He also said the new fence protected the children from dangerous and even illegal activities, including gunfire, which were pretty much all the surrounding BLM lands were used for. "Is there any mother who would let her kids camp on BLM land at night?" He also said the BLM land had agreed long ago that the improvements were satisfactory, then changed its story completely when it wanted to cancel the lease.

But by 1998, following a flood of letters of protest from outraged ranch supporters and a steady diet of negative media coverage, BLM officials changed their tone and seemed ready to negotiate a settlement. An agreement for sale was reached in April 2000, and the land was transferred to the Lord's Ranch, complete with an official ceremony on October 17.

In December of the same year, the ranch expanded to a full square mile (640 acres), as Father Thomas's nephew Robert, Bob's son and a successful Florida businessman in his own right, bought the missing quarter-section (160 acres) in the northeast corner of the property and donated it to the ranch. One of the toughest battles of Father Thomas's life had ended in victory.

Some of the youth who have visited the Lord's Ranch.

Father Rick and Mike Reuter giving some children a ride on a cart at Las Alas, with Father's brown Lab named Cocoa, 2000.

CHAPTER 62

Later Years and Unwanted Honors

A s the dairy animals, the food production, and many of the full-time residents left the Lord's Ranch, visitors kept coming – young and old, short-term and long-term. In particular, the ranch drew high school and college groups from all over the United States during the last 15 years of Father Thomas's life; fittingly, visiting teenagers in Catholic youth group t-shirts were highly visible in the congregation at his funeral Mass. These groups, of all ages, were usually taken across the river to work in the ministries in Juárez.

The Navigators, and some others, continued to live full-time at the ranch. As time passed, Father Thomas himself lived on the ranch more and more. At first he stayed in his tiny single room in Ezekiel House. But Ezekiel is the first building visitors see on the way into the ranch from the main gate, so he was flooded with people needing help, and in 2001 the ranchers convinced him to move into a small house several buildings away from the entrance to have more time to study and pray. The small house was Bethany House, a simple 600-square-foot house with one bedroom and one bathroom, which he thought was too large a home for one man. "That was a death to self for him to move in there," said Mike Halloran.

A newsletter from 1998 described a March Saturday at the ranch, starting with the cooks fixing breakfast in the Noah House kitchen at 6:30 a.m., and ending with lights out at 10:30 p.m. On hand for the day were 15 teenage girls in the final day of a girls' retreat and 10 teenage boys arriving for the first day of a boys' retreat. The boys weren't expected for lunch, but they hadn't eaten, so the cooks fed them, along with a couple with a small child who arrived unexpectedly. Also on hand was a TV camera crew covering the BLM dispute, and all the retreatants spent time on the BLM land. Meanwhile, the ranchers were working on meeting the needs of a pregnant Las Cruces woman who had been talked out of an abortion and needed food, and a pregnant woman from Mexico who needed a place to stay before her father found out about the pregnancy. Mass was at 6 p.m., with a lot of singing.

"One of our mottoes is 'flexibility,'" Father Thomas began the newsletter. "In other words, expect the unexpected and get ready to be stretched." And at the end: "Thank you, Lord, for this day, for the surprises it held, the lives that were touched, the work that was accomplished. Bless us all with a good night's sleep so we can arise and serve you well tomorrow. Amen."

Father Thomas had some more personal losses during this period. Mrs. Tula died of cancer in December 1998, and two more his friends died not long after: Father Harold Cohen of New Orleans in January 2001 and Bobbie Cavnar of Dallas in February 2002. Bill Halloran died at the Lord's Ranch in 2004, age 94, and was buried in a small cemetery on the far side of the property.

In 1999 came an announcement that would probably have been good news to anybody except Rick Thomas. He was named the first-ever recipient of El Paso Bishop Armando Ochoa's Option for the Poor award, to be awarded along with other honors at the diocese's first Peace and Justice banquet. He immediately headed for the door – the words "banquet" and "award" weren't high on his list of favorites, and he did his level best to get out of the whole business. He said he didn't like awards; he said he might be out of town on the night of the banquet; he said his controversial reputation might cause problems for the Church. But Bishop Ochoa made it clear that he wanted Father Thomas there; he also agreed to a request from Father Thomas that actual poor people – 10 of them, sponsored by a benefactor – be invited to this banquet about poverty. Seating was open, with no head table; Bishop Ochoa and Bishop Ricardo Ramírez of Las Cruces, the featured speaker, sat at different tables mingling with the audience. So, reluctantly, Father Thomas turned up to his own banquet, and even smiled for the cameras. But he told the *Rio Grande Catholic*, the diocesan newspaper, "I'd be a fool to take credit for my ministry. It's all God's doing."

In 2004 Father Thomas and another priest were given the René Mascareñas Medal, a similar award on the other side of the border, named in honor of a former Juárez mayor and philanthropist. At that ceremony he asked the other priest, who was sitting next to him, whether it would be OK to slip out quietly during the lengthy musical entertainment. "The priest told him no, that would be very rude, so Father resigned himself to staying," Hogarty recalled, who was also there. "He made an aside to me, 'If Jesus hung on the cross for three hours in agony, I can sit here for two.'"

Father Thomas kept busy on other social issues, too, not just poverty and abortion. He protested against the Gulf Wars of both 1991 and 2003, not an easy position to take in a city with an army base (Fort Bliss) as one of its biggest employers. Community members visited two African-American churches in 1997 to ask forgiveness for the oppression of black people. And he spent the last eight years of his life working toward the regulation of sexually-oriented businesses such as strip clubs. He and his friends picketed some of the businesses, and some women volunteers went into the strip clubs to pray. He teamed up with other clergy and civic activists, notably Model Cities El Paso, an anti-pornography organization led by his Baptist friend Roger O'Dell, to press for the adoption of an ordinance which would require licenses for owners and employees of these businesses, enact a six-foot distance between customers and performers, and require open floor plans with no private viewing rooms. He told a city council meeting it was time for "sin city" to put residents ahead of the "almighty dollar." The ordinance was formally introduced in July 2003, and finally passed May 8, 2007 – the one-year anniversary of his death.

Near the beginning of his final illness, a successful businessman who had just started hanging out with the OLYC community came to see him and asked how he could help. "You can build us an event center and you can pay for it," Father Thomas replied in what he called "one of the shortest and most significant conversations I've ever had." The man agreed. The building was tied up in approvals for a long time and didn't open until three years after Father Thomas's death, but he did get to tour the structurally complete but unfinished building in a wheelchair, and celebrated Mass where the chapel would eventually be. The 140-by-65-foot building is now the center of activity at the Lord's Ranch. It was named Bellarmine Hall after St. Robert Bellarmine, a 16th century Jesuit cardinal and leader of Church reform.

First Mass celebrated in Bellarmine Hall chapel
while still under construction, 2006.

CHAPTER 63

Expansion in Juárez

T he ministries in Juárez continued to change and develop in the later years of Father Thomas's life. He kept up his usual work until his final illness, with Mass at the food bank, visits to the jail, and other activities. A newsletter from 2000 describes his weekly visits to what he called "a truly wonderful group of old widows" living at the *Arroyo de las Víboras* (roughly, "Rattlesnake Gulch). "These women are extremely poor," he wrote. "Some of them have no groceries to eat other than what we bring them each week.... One of the ladies always wears a threadbare bath towel as a shawl covering her head and shoulders. One can barely walk as she shuffles along to greet the other women with an embrace. One is very shy and embarrassed because she has never learned to read. I suspect some of the others don't know how to read either. One of the ladies pictured [in the newsletter] is embarrassed because she has no left hand. Another has no right hand."

What made the women "truly wonderful," he said, was their generosity. "Their motto is what Jesus said, 'It is more blessed to give than to receive.' ... If any one of them has something like tortillas or soup they will bring it for all to share at a common meal.... If they have a few pesos they collect them and pay for bus fare or medicine for the others that are in need." Some of the women even offered him money to pay his bridge toll from El Paso.

"It is a privilege for me to be with these people each week and see how God has moved them to love each other so deeply and so practically," he said.

Enjoying a meal and conversation in the kitchen
at the Lord's Food Bank, Juárez, 2002.

In 2003, the community began a new ministry in another part of Juárez. Crossing the bridge into Mexico one day to be picked up by one of the volunteers on the Juárez side, Father Thomas asked to be taken to a place where the people are even poorer than the people who live around the food bank. This isn't as hard as it sounds, because squatters' settlements tend to improve over time as residents gather better materials and stabilize their lives; the food bank neighborhood, as desperate as it looks from an American perspective, is much better off than it was in the 70s and 80s, while new settlements tend to be much poorer. The volunteer took Father Thomas to Loma Blanca in southeast Juárez, a newly-settled area with very few houses, no water or electricity, and extremely poor people. Homes are made of cardboard boxes, old wooden pallets, or cinder blocks. Father Thomas was delighted to be brought there. "God wants to do wonders here," he said.

OLYC workers were the first Catholic group working in an area that already had eight Protestant churches. The local land-owner was happy to see the newcomers. They started out doing food distribution in the streets, under a shade; the owner lent them an office to hold meetings and gave them land for a church in front of the lots purchased by the other denominations. The OLYC group co-operates with one of the Protestant churches on home construction, and has built a meeting hall called *Las Alitas*, "the little wings," to show it was a sort of little sister to Las Alas. There's also a small soccer field, basketball court, playground area and community garden. Workers teach catechism and Bible classes to youngsters and their parents, and also run soccer teams to help keep the youngsters out of gangs.

Visiting a family in one of the homes near Las Alitas, 2003.

CHAPTER 64

Young Shepherds

I n the fall of 2002, Father Thomas started another new
ministry: Young Shepherds, a group of high school and
college women whom he trained for ministry to their own
age group.

It was only partly his own idea; he said it came to him when
he saw that "a number of young people were having extraordi-
nary spiritual experiences and sincere desires to serve God in an
outstanding way." He started with four or five of them, driving
to El Paso from the Lord's Ranch once a week to train them in
one-on-one ministry to other young people, evangelism, and
Christian witness in the schools. He also gave them intensive
spiritual training, based on the Ignatian principles he had learned
as a Jesuit. The group grew to 10 or so; there were a few young
men in the beginning, but over time only young women stayed
involved.

One of the first Young Shepherds was Daisy Pérez, who was
16 when her mother dragged her to a prayer meeting at Las Alas
in the spring of 2002. Pérez, who described herself as "a bit of a
rebellious teen," wasn't happy about it. "I always go every Sunday," she told her mother. "Why do I have to go another day of
the week?" Her mother doubled down, insisting she go to confession. To Father Thomas.

Pérez was even more upset about confession than she was about the prayer meeting, but in she went. In the confessional, "I lost it," she said. "I can't explain it to this day. Something supernatural happened. I started bawling like a baby. I wanted to change my life. Those words were not coming from me – I didn't go in with that intention. I really felt like I had a conversion in that confession." Later, she cried all through the prayer meeting and the Mass that followed.

Father Thomas became her regular confessor, and they stayed in contact. He told her he wanted to start a youth movement; she told him she wanted to be part of it. "It's not going to be easy," he warned her. "You're a teenager and you're probably going to lose a lot of friends because you want to follow the Lord." He was right – she did lose friends. But she made a lot of new friends, too, and she started volunteering in the Juárez ministries.

In the fall, the Young Shepherds began meeting, an hour and a half to two hours every Saturday with Father Thomas. "He'd drive in just for us," Pérez said. "He believed that we were like the good soil that needed to produce a hundredfold."

The meetings began with teaching, and Father Thomas left the subject matter wide open. "He would just get there and tell us to ask away," Pérez said. "We felt so comfortable asking him a question. It was a safe space." She remembered asking him about things she thought she would need as she prepared for college: about God's existence, why God allows evil, how to know you're making the right decision. "He was very patient with us," said Gaby Federico, who joined the group in 2004. "We had all sorts of questions."

But there was more than teaching for the Young Shepherds. There was action – especially pro-life work and evangelism. Some of it was pretty far out, like one escapade Pérez remembered in downtown El Paso.

"He had us march, on a random day, dressed up as clowns, with pro-life signs," she said. "I don't even know why – sometimes he had the most random ideas. We'd just go with it, because we trusted him. He wanted us to get out of our element and just be fools for the Lord."

He asked Federico to do some research on judges who were giving "judicial bypass" on abortion – using their power to waive the requirement under Texas law that parents had to be notified if a girl under 18 had an abortion. She found out one judge's address, picketed his house carrying a sign that said "who decides abortion for minors – parents or Judge X?" and talked to the judge's neighbors if they happened to come out.

Pérez did sidewalk counseling in front of an abortion clinic. "I saw a couple of friends go in there, and had to talk to them," she said. "That was not fun."

But not all the far-out ideas originated with Father Thomas. The women had some of their own. One of them, Federico said, was praying outside a Girls Gone Wild event, in which female partygoers are encouraged to expose their bodies to camera crews. Father Thomas was taken by surprise by that one.

Father Thomas admired the Young Shepherds as much as they admired him. "They're tough and they're effective," he said in an interview a few months after the group started. "They can do in a few minutes what an adult can't do at all. And they're highly self-motivated. They come up with a lot of stuff on their own, and I hear about it later."

Like Pérez, many of the women wanted help with making decisions, and Father Thomas taught them Ignatian discernment. One point Pérez especially remembered is that discernment requires a neutral state of desire. In other words, if you are asking God to help you choose between two possibilities, such as marriage or religious life, and you prefer one, you should pray for the other; if you want to marry, pray to desire the religious life. "If you're biased, you're not really asking God," she said.

"He would never say 'you need to do this' or 'you need to do that.' He would just provide me with the tools to make the decision."

He did offer advice about living as a Christian high school or college student – especially about the company you keep. It's good to be a Christian influence among your friends, but you need to ask yourself whether you really are influencing them, or whether they're influencing you. If they're influencing you, and the influence isn't Christian, you need to back away (while still remaining kind and friendly).

"The Holy Spirit inspired him to say something that the person needed to hear at that moment," said Federico. "Someone would say 'that was for me,' and others would say the same."

Some of the women asked him what to do if they were getting lukewarm in their Christian life. He told them lukewarmness is a spiritual disease, not at all the same as dryness, which is a struggle sent by God to strengthen us. We need to fight dryness, but we aren't falling off the Lord's path; in lukewarmness, we are. He called lukewarmness "a slow death" which leads to justifying our own sins and the sins of others. The cure is spiritual food: Scripture, examination of conscience, and the Eucharist. "You need to ask for the grace to become hot," said Pérez.

Father Thomas also taught the women how to recognize and resist temptation and showed them different forms of vocal and mental prayer.

There was a lot of mutual affection at those Young Shepherds meetings. They trusted him. "It was a friendship we had, and very trustworthy," said Federico. "Whenever we needed him, he was there. We never put him at the level of Jesus or anything. He was human, and we knew he would learn from us too."

"I felt like he was so wise," said Pérez. "I never felt he was an old priest. He was so full of life – you wanted what he had. I could see the joy in his whole life."

"When I got to Las Alas, I was just a cradle Catholic," Pérez said. "He made God alive for me again. God is everywhere, I get it, but he just made it so tangible for me. He will always stay with me in that sense.

"He invested so much in all of us. I know that after hearing all those teachings from Father Thomas, I will never turn away. I will never fall off that holy highway. I just can't."

CHAPTER 65

Here is Your God

For most of his life, Rick Thomas was a healthy man. His brother Bob remembered him as a child who hardly ever got sick, and as he passed through his 70s he was still dancing at prayer meetings and riding his beloved horses. In between he walked, jogged, and of course kept up a schedule that would have ground a weaker man into dust.

Not that he never had a problem. A lot of the seminarians at St. Mary's in Kansas were allergic to the pollen in the area, but Father Thomas was so allergic that he had to be transferred away from the men he had spent seven years with, to complete his studies in California (see chapter 7). He also had to be careful what he ate; he had an especially bad reaction to preservatives. But while some of his friends remember various illnesses over the years, health problems don't start showing up in his diaries until April 1996, a few weeks after his 68th birthday. That month he had a bout of shingles, and also problems with urination.

By the fall of 1996 he had major prostate problems, ending up in surgery in October, with three days in the hospital. It wasn't cancer. The calendar shows him carrying on with most of his activities apart from the hospitalization, including the crucial days of the purchase of Las Alas.

It's fair to say Father Thomas wasn't a model patient. He was queasy of needles and blood and called the catheter from his prostate surgery "my ball and chain." What's more, he was convinced that most Christians rely too much on doctors. His own policy was to follow Sirach 38:9-12 and turn to the doctor only after prayer and other spiritual remedies.

In 2000, though, he definitely needed a doctor. A biopsy showed malignant melanoma in his arm, so he let the doctor operate. But when no cancer turned up in the surgery, he was convinced he was healed. He wouldn't let the doctor take any lymph to be checked for cancer, and he turned down radiation and chemotherapy. He had cataract surgery in December, but apart from that he carried on as normal, working his usual schedule, still riding horses and dancing at prayer meetings.

His calendar reports a "very sick stomach" at the end of 2004. In August 2005 he went on vacation to Colorado with Michael Reuter. Ellen Hogarty remembered having a bad feeling about his health when they left, and on the trip he got seriously ill, with digestive problems and other symptoms. At first he thought it might be altitude sickness, but it didn't get better when he came home.

He stopped attending the Wednesday prayer meeting, permanently as it turned out, and stayed mostly on the Lord's Ranch, cared for by the ranchers. Aurora Alvarado, the El Paso nurse who ran the clinic at the food bank, gave him a physical in September; a blood test showed no sign of cancer, and Hogarty told him "you're a healthy dude." "You can put 'healthy dude' on my tombstone," he retorted. His local Jesuit superior visited him at the beginning of October, and they talked about his condition. He consulted several doctors but wasn't willing to go through any experimental treatment.

The doctors were convinced that his melanoma from 2000 had metastasized, and a CT scan in late November showed "probable metastatic deposits" in four locations in his abdomen and pelvis. His weight dropped, to 95 pounds by January from his normal 165 or 170 on a six-foot frame. He received sacramental anointing in November from a local parish priest.

At this point Father Thomas and the ranchers believed he was dying. He was anointed again in December, and the ranchers cried, thanked him, and said their goodbyes. Many years before, around the time of his ordination, Father Thomas had asked the Blessed Virgin Mary to keep him from going to purgatory; he asked that he be purified in this life so he could go straight to heaven when he died. Now, he cried out, over and over, "Mother, come get me."

In the middle of all this, Hogarty went to Mass and came away with a different message from God: Father Thomas should change his attitude and focus on living. She told him that, and he responded immediately: he got up, went back to eating, and began a period of recovery. In late January 2006, he resumed saying both Sunday and weekday Mass at the ranch, preaching in a loud voice, but seated at the altar and obviously still sick and weak. Around the same time he managed to meet with the Young Shepherds, for the first time in months.

"He had a good week, and he asked for us," said Daisy Pérez. "We went to the ranch instead of Las Alas. He was so fragile. It was beautiful." There was more fellowship to the visit than teaching, and with his birthday coming up in March, the young people gave him an early celebration. "He was just so happy," Pérez said.

Meanwhile, he spent long periods of time praying for everybody he could think of. He also came to believe that his illness had a spiritual origin, and that it was his job to unite his sufferings with the sufferings of Jesus. He offered his suffering for the community and for the Jesuits, especially those in his own province.

During this period, Father Thomas, who had never been a man to talk about himself if he could help it, started to tell his friends on the ranch stories he had never brought up before, like his call to the priesthood, his relationship with his father, his seminary education, and many incidents over his years as priest in New Orleans and in El Paso. This hadn't been going on for long before the ranchers saw that they needed to record the stories, so they got his permission and started taping him; the result is a shoebox-size collection of first-person CDs that has been the primary source for many parts of this biography, especially the early chapters.

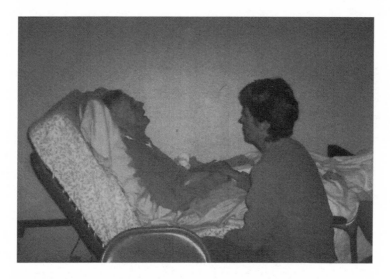

Ellen Hogarty with Father Thomas during his final illness, 2006.

At this point he believed he would eventually make a full re-covery. On March 6, he dictated a two-page letter to Hogarty, addressed to me and answering a long list of questions I had sent as I completed work on an earlier book on the OLYC ministries.

"My health has not returned to normal," he wrote. "However, the good news is that I gain strength every day and am able to do a lot more as I do my physical therapy and so forth."

"I fully expect to be vigorous and strong one of these days....
Everybody is going to see that God did it since I was so bad off
before. I get stronger every day, but I'm not up to normal. I
haven't left the ranch for months."

He had to be driven the short distance between buildings for
weekday Mass and helped from the vehicle to the building and
back, so leaving the ranch for the prayer meeting was out of the
question. As spring came on, his voice dropped to a whisper, and
he could barely eat. He received some visitors, but on a heavily
restricted basis.

I was one of those visitors, and I'll never forget the experience. I arrived on Easter Monday, April 17. Reuter picked me up
at the airport and told me Father Thomas's recovery seemed to
have plateaued. We got to the ranch at suppertime, just after
Mass finished, and Mike Halloran was helping him out of Noah
House and into the van for the ride back to his house. He looked
terrible. I greeted him in the briefest words I could find, and he
barely noticed me. I wondered how I could possibly ask for an
interview with a man who was obviously so sick. I told myself
he would probably feel better in the morning.

But then, to my shock, Hogarty sent word that Father Thomas
wanted to see me after dinner. I was horrified. I made my way
to his house, clumsy and distracted; I even knocked at the wrong
door before I found the right building. By the time I got there
and saw him, sitting slumped at the table with a half-eaten meal
in front of him, my brain and my tongue were totally paralyzed
with nervousness and confusion.

He looked up at me. "So tell me, Richard!" he said. I stood
there in silence, like a shirt dummy, for a good 30 seconds. I
knew I was acting like an idiot, but I couldn't think of a single
appropriate thing to say.

"Well, that was interesting," he finally said, with a slight
smile. "Tell me more!"

Same old Father Thomas. I relaxed a little, slid into a chair across from him and asked him my questions, keeping one eye on my wristwatch. But he ignored the time. On and on the interview went; he could barely whisper, but what he had to say was the same mixture of wisecracks and passion it had always been. Finally he let me escape and leave him in peace.

I had three or four more interviews with him over the next week; they lasted as long as two hours. Hogarty and I squirmed and watched the clock, well aware that I was exhausting a desperately sick 78-year-old man, but he said everything he was determined to say, and made sure I got all the answers I needed.

On Divine Mercy Sunday, April 23, he said Mass for an overflow crowd in the radio station building. He opened that Mass with a sly grin on his face. "A lot of people here think I'm going to die," he said. "Well, I am." Pause. "And you are too." The congregation laughed. "But I'm not going to die yet." The people burst into applause.

The sermon was pure Rick Thomas, based on Acts 4:32-37, where the first Christians shared all things in common so that no one would be in want. "We don't do that," he said. "The Church doesn't do it. We're disobedient. We need God's mercy... That's why there's needy people in Juárez. There was no needy person among them, but we have thousands and thousands of needy people among us. We can give ourselves all kinds of excuses, but it comes down to 'we are disobedient.'"

That evening, I dropped by his house for a last greeting, and he prayed a blessing over me and my work. That was the last time I saw him alive, and that was his last Sunday Mass, and his last sermon. He said Mass at Noah House the next day, but he didn't preach, and after that he was so weak he had to give it up. Finally he was bedridden, but he was still mentally sharp and still had the same sense of humor as always.

On May 8, near the end of one of his better days, he came up short of breath. Hogarty, who was with him, ran to get Reuter, and the two of them were present. "Scripture!" he called out. Hogarty started reading Psalm 23. "No!" he corrected. "Isaiah 35." As Hogarty began reading ("Here is your God... He will come and save you"), he stared off to one side. Hogarty asked if he saw someone coming for him; he smiled, and laughed the soundless, open-mouthed laugh he always used. Hogarty started CPR – "pro-life to the end," she said later – and he laughed again and died. It was 6:25 p.m.

An El Paso doctor issued the death certificate. It mentioned a full list of what was known or believed to be wrong with him – cardio-respiratory arrest (a matter of minutes), multi-organ failure (two or three days), metastatic melanoma (the last few months), skin melanoma (going back to 2000).

The day of his rosary and wake, May 11, the body lay in state all day at Las Alas in a coffin made by Reuter out of three-quarter-inch plywood. The vigil service itself turned into a prayer meeting for 800 people, complete with praise music, dancing, and testimony after testimony about what Father Thomas had done in people's lives.

The funeral the following day was at Sacred Heart, with Bishop Armando Ochoa of El Paso as chief celebrant, and Bishop Ricardo Ramírez of Las Cruces (the local bishop for the Lord's Ranch) and 17 priests con-celebrating. More than 1,000 attending, rich and poor, prominent and obscure. Bishop Ramírez drew a standing ovation when he said that "if there is anyone I have ever known who in our lives exemplifies the life of the Church as expressed in the Acts of the Apostles, it was Father Rick Thomas."

Father Thomas, the bishop added in Spanish, was not some hippie out on the margins of society. "He was at the center, in the heart of the Church – in the heart of Jesus."

Father Thomas wanted to be buried on the Lord's Ranch, like Bill Halloran, but members of religious orders don't get to make decisions like that, and Father Thomas was the same obedient maverick in death that he was in life. As directed by his superiors, he was buried in the Jesuit section of El Paso's Concordia Cemetery. Members of the community stood in the sun and the dust to help fill the grave, and someone raised the cry *"viva Cristo Rey!"*

A headline over his obituary in the El Paso *Times* read "Miracle worker: A chance at sainthood."

ACKNOWLEDGEMENTS

So many people have helped me with this biography that thanking them all is almost like writing another book. I have been truly blessed by all the people I have met, in person or by phone or email.

Ellen Hogarty has been an outstanding editor, cheerleader, and friend throughout the process, and she, Michael Reuter, Mary Ann and Mike Halloran and Father Nathan O'Halloran SJ have contributed so much information and guidance that they really deserve credit as co-authors. Michael Reuter gets an extra mention for recording Father Thomas's sickbed reminiscences, which have been my single most important source of information.

All those people have also offered me warm friendship and/or generous hospitality, along with Norma Reuter, Jim and Keith Gallagher, Mary Bencomo, Josh and Rebekah O'Halloran, Ceci and Tommy Barrientos, Blasa Corona, Richard Munzinger, Sergio and Lucía Conde, Father Sam Rosales SJ, Father Dick McGowan SJ, Father Rafael García SJ, Al and Betty Mills, Evy Nelson, Sister Mary Virginia Clark and Joe Lodder.

An even longer list of people have sat patiently for interviews, or provided other forms of help, guidance and encouragement (which they may or may not remember), and I am terrified that I might have left somebody out. But here's the list I have: Rosanne Allen, Aurora Alvarado, Nestor and Nellie Baca, Ann Ball, Father Michael Barry, Cande Basurto, Isabel Beltrán, Pastor Jim Bevis, Mary Bradfield, Paul and Laurie Bross, Judy Brown, Yolanda and Luis Carrasco, Cindy Cavnar, Father Bernard Charles SJ, Alan and Kim Curtis, Mario D'Amato, Pat Delgado, Gaby Federico, Colleen Finlon, Rev. Mike Flynn, Bishop Bill Frey, Aida Frietze-Lewis, Cecilia García, Rubén García, Helen Guajardo, Margarita Guerrero; Peter, Caleb, Justin, Rebekah and

Isaac Halloran; Bert Hernández, Grace Hernández, Vicki Hernández, Pochie Heredia, Father Patrick Hough SJ, Pedro Ibarra, Ralph and Marie Irróbali, Rudy and Blanca Irróbali, Joanne Ivey, Denise and Craig Jamieson, Sister Pat Joyce, Mary Leary, Lorenza Ledesma, Katherine Lee, Father Mark Lewis SJ, Ralph Martin, Father Bill McCann, Kathleen McCarthy, Martha Medrano, Victor Montes, Marcos and Celia Nieblas, Father Armand Nigro SJ, Roger O'Dell, Esther and Ernest Padilla, Margaret Paton, Alicia Pedroza, Daisy Pérez, Delia Ramos, Father Harold Rahm SJ, Bishop Ricardo Ramírez, Mike Ridley, Sylvia Rivas,   Laura and Pablo Rocha, Father Edmundo Rodríguez SJ, Deacon Juan Rodríguez, David Scott, Frances Shaw, John Sherrill, Ramona and Armando Solano, Rachel and Ralph Solis, Jean Ponder Soto, John and Ruth Stanley, Tencha Tapia, Joan Thibault, Anne Thomas, Richard Thomas (nephew of Father Thomas), Robert Thomas, Steve Thomas, Susan Thomas, Susan Vescovo, Carol Thomas Wilbert and Father Neal Wilson.

Many who have offered me help and friendship have gone on to the heavenly banquet, where I look forward to seeing them again: Hector Bencomo, who was always a special friend to me; Francisca Terrazas, Bill and Marion Halloran, Father Jack Vessels SJ, Aurora Villa, Ron Webster, Neto Heredia, George Roberts, Rickie Feuille, Maria Luisa Domínguez, Father Jack Deeves SJ, Father Louis Lambert SJ, Carmen Molina, Herminia Montes, and Very Rev. David Collins, plus Bob Thomas, with whom I never dealt directly but who was extremely co-operative with this project, and especially, of course, Father Thomas himself. It's hard to picture such a self-effacing man co-operating with his own biography, but he was a magnificent help with my previous book on the work of the OLYC community, and a friend and mentor in my own spiritual and personal life.

I also want to thank my children, Rachel Muller, Matthew Dunstan, and Beth Smit, and their families; they have been wonderfully loving and supportive. And above all I want to honor both my late first wife, Mary, who encouraged me through endless research, and my new wife, Lynn, who has spent our entire relationship watching me type. No man has ever been more blessed.

NOTES ON SOURCES

As much as possible, this biography has been taken from Father Rick Thomas himself. His own account of his life has come from my own interviews with him, at various times from 1989 until his death in 2006; from a personal history he wrote about 1980; from his monthly Anything-A-Month Club newsletters, published from 1964 until near the end of his life; from his office calendars and diary; from recorded testimonies and talks; from various other documents; and especially from his reminiscences as recorded by Michael Reuter during his final illness. Except for his one posthumously-published book, these sources are not listed in detail in the chapter notes below; whenever it has seemed important to single out a specific source, it is mentioned in the text of the biography.

In addition, I have relied extensively on four of Father Thomas's closest co-workers: Ellen Hogarty, Mary Ann Halloran, Mike Halloran and Michael Reuter, all of whom knew him for more than 20 years (30 for Mary Ann); on documents in Our Lady's Youth Center archives; and on my own personal observations over the years. These sources are also not listed below in most cases but are mentioned in the text as necessary.

The detailed list of sources below covers the many additional people interviewed for this biography, as well as published or other written sources from outside the OLYC files, and a few OLYC documents that seem to me to require more formal citation. I conducted all interviews myself, in person, by phone, or by email, except for Bob Thomas (conducted by Joan Thibault), Carmen Molina (conducted by Mike and Mary Ann Halloran), and Sister Mary Virginia Clark (conducted in part by the Hallorans and in part by myself.)

INTRODUCTION – 100 PERCENT FOR JESUS

Interviews with Father Jack Deeves, Father Richard McGowan, Rickie Feuille, Bob Thomas
Father Jack Deeves, printed recollections, 2006
The Sooner Catholic, Oklahoma City, June 21, 1981

CHAPTER 1 – A CHILDHOOD FREE TO WANDER
Interviews with Bob Thomas, Robert Thomas, Steve Thomas, Richard Thomas (nephew of Father Thomas), Father Harold Rahm
Robert M. Thomas, *A Message from Two Rivers*, as told to Richard D. R. Hoffman, page 9
Bob Thomas, 1990 letter to a family member
Wayne Thomas Sr., partial autobiography from family papers
Biographies of Wayne Thomas Sr., no author given, from family papers
Tampa Morning Tribune, obituary of Dorothy Thomas, Jan. 19, 1953
The Tiger (yearbook of Jesuit High School, Tampa), 1944

CHAPTER 2 – HORSES AT HOME
Interviews with Bob Thomas

CHAPTER 3 – "I WANT YOU TO BE A PRIEST"
Interview with Father Jack Deeves
Heart to Heart with Sheila Walsh, Christian Broadcasting Network, Sept. 9, 1992

CHAPTER 4 – JESUIT IN TRAINING
Interviews with Father Jack Vessels, Father Jack Deeves
Father Jack Deeves, printed recollections, 2006

CHAPTER 5 – A POINT OF CONVERSION
Interviews with Father Jack Vessels, Father Richard McGowan

CHAPTER 6 – REGENCY: TRAINING FOR THE OUTSIDE WORLD
Interviews with Father Jack Vessels, Bob Thomas
Jesuit High School yearbook, Dallas, TX, 1953
Tampa Morning Tribune, Obituary of Dorothy Thomas, Jan. 19, 1953

CHAPTER 7 – ENCOUNTER WITH THEOLOGY
Interview with Father Jack Deeves

CHAPTER 8 – CALIFORNIA AND ORDINATION
Interviews with Father Armand Nigro, Father Louis Lambert, Steve Thomas

CHAPTER 9 – A BRAND NEW PRIEST
Interviews with Father Armand Nigro, Father Jack Vessels

CHAPTER 10 – REACHING BEYOND THE CLASSROOM
Interviews with Father Jack Deeves, Father Louis Lambert
The Blue Jay, yearbook of Jesuit High School, New Orleans, LA, 1964

CHAPTER 11 – THE CALL TO EL PASO
Interviews with Father Harold Rahm, Father Sam Rosales
"History of Our Lady's Youth Center" (part of United Way funding application), 1974

CHAPTER 12—TAKING ON THE TASK
Interviews with Esther Padilla, Lorenza Ledesma Gil, Hector Bencomo, Helen Guajardo

CHAPTER 13 – IN A VERY LONG SHADOW

Interviews with Father Harold Rahm, Father Sam Rosales, Father Jack Deeves, Father Jack Vessels, Mary Bencomo, Evy Nelson, Helen Guajardo, Susan Vescovo
El Paso Times, "Happy Anniversary, Father Rahm," Guadalupe Silva, July 21, 2000

CHAPTER 14 – SO MUCH WITH SO LITTLE
Interview with Helen Guajardo
Father Harold Rahm and J. Robert Weber, *Office in the Alley: Report on a Project with Gang Youngsters*, 1958, page 19.

CHAPTER 15 – CHANGES FOR THE KINGDOM
Interviews with Father Harold Rahm, Father Sam Rosales, Pochie and Neto Heredia, Esther and Ernest Padilla, Ralph and Marie Irróbali, Rudy and Blanca Irróbali.

CHAPTER 16 – A HEART FOR A HIGH SCHOOL
Interviews with Helen Guajardo, Grace Hernández, Father Edmundo Rodríguez

CHAPTER 17 – A BREAK FROM THE SLUMS
Interviews with Evy Nelson, Joanne Ivey, Al Mills, Sister Mary Virginia Clark
El Paso Times, "It Takes Hard Workers To Counsel Here," Glenn Mueller, SJ, July 29, 1967
"History of Our Lady's Youth Center" (part of United Way funding application), 1974

CHAPTER 18 – THE WAR ON POVERTY
Robert Glasgow, *Arizona Republic*, Phoenix, "Unusual Poverty Battle Conducted By Slum Priest," May 5, 1966
Robert Glasgow, *Arizona Republic*, "El Paso Poverty Program Doesn't Follow The Book," May 8, 1966
El Paso Times, "Urges Workers To Stay Here," 1965 (date not preserved on clipping)
El Paso Herald-Post, "Plan Set Up To Aid Poor," Cliff Sherrill, Oct. 7, 1965
El Paso Times, "OK Funds For Migrant Program," Times Washington Bureau, Oct. 6, 1965
El Paso Times, "Disagree On Migrant Workers Being In EP," Hugh Morgan, Oct. 6, 1965
El Paso Times, "Asks Food For El Paso's Poor," Sarah McClendon, Oct. 6, 1965
El Paso Times, "Poverty Stand Stirs Resentment," Art Leibson, Oct. 7, 1965
El Paso Herald-Post, "Why The Sniping?" (editorial), Oct. 12, 1965
Southwest Catholic Register, El Paso, "Migrant Worker Project Gets Ready," late 1965 (exact date not preserved)
Southwest Catholic Register, "Community Action Project Grows," Jan. 14, 1966
El Paso Herald-Post, "E.P Gets $450,000 More For Poor," June 1966 (exact date not preserved)
El Paso Times, "85 Dropped From EP Program," Tom Bryan, July 29, 1966
El Paso Times, "To Renew EP Migrant Project," August 1966 (exact date not preserved)

El Paso Times, "Bad Publicity Blamed For Project Troubles," Tom Bryan, Nov. 4, 1966

El Paso Herald-Post, "Community Program On Probation," Dec. 30, 1966

New York Times (United Press International), obituary of Bishop Sidney Metzger, April 14, 1986 (accessed online)

CHAPTER 19 – OTHER BATTLEFIELDS

Interview with Rubén García

Gisella O'Neil, "Operation—We Care," *The Jesuit*, undated clipping

El Paso Herald-Post, "Five Directors Named To El Paso Chapter Of NCCJ," Nov. 18, 1964

El Paso Herald-Post, "Dirty Reading Object Of Group's Ire," undated clipping

El Paso Herald-Post, "Mystery in Tax Office Over Boxful of Forms, 1966 (exact date not preserved)

CHAPTER 20 – A MINISTRY IN CRISIS

Interviews with Father Richard McGowan, Helen Guajardo, Rickie Feuille, Father Edmundo Rodríguez

El Paso Herald-Post, "South E.P. Slums Likely to Blow Up," Feb. 7, 1967

El Paso Herald-Post, "Illegal Heater Cause of Fire," Frank Ahlgren Jr. Jan. 5, 1967

CHAPTER 21 – ALWAYS A JESUIT

Interviews with Father Mark Lewis, Father Richard McGowan, Father Nathan O'Halloran

CHAPTER 22 – MOVING OUT OF THE RECTORY

Interviews with Father Richard McGowan, Evy Nelson, Bert Hernández, Al Mills, Helen Guajardo, Frank Alarcón

CHAPTER 23 – BAPTIZED IN THE HOLY SPIRIT

Interviews with Jean Soto, Aida Frietze-Lewis, Father Edmundo Rodríguez, Sister Mary Virginia Clark

CHAPTER 24 – TRYING IT AT HOME

Interviews with Isabel Beltrán, Jean Soto, Aida Frietze-Lewis

CHAPTER 25 – LEARNING ON THE JOB

Interviews with Paul and Laurie Bross, Joanne Ivey, Frank Alarcón

El Fronterizo, Ciudad Juárez, Chihuahua, Mexico, "¿Es Usted Carismático?" June 11, 1972

CHAPTER 26 – PRAYER MEETINGS AT OLYC

Interviews with Aida Frietze-Lewis, Jean Soto, Rachel and Ralph Solis, Pochie and Neto Heredia, Evy Nelson.

CHAPTER 27 – MOTHER SUPERIOR

Interviews with Sister Mary Virginia Clark

CHAPTER 28 – TAKING THE BATTLE SERIOUSLY

Interviews with Sister Mary Virginia Clark, Jean Soto

Bobbie Cavnar, recorded testimony, 1983

Communication from Father Nathan O'Halloran

CHAPTER 29 – THE RENEWAL CROSSES THE RIVER

Interviews with Sister Mary Virginia Clark
Guillermina Valdes-Villalva, written testimony 1980

CHAPTER 30 – A BOOK TO BE OBEYED
Interviews with Sister Mary Virginia Clark, Rachel Solis, Jean Soto
Viva Cristo Rey (video), Catholic Charismatic Services of Dallas, 1981

CHAPTER 31 –1972: THE GREAT MULTIPLICATION
Father Rick Thomas, "Christmas at the Dump," *New Covenant*, Ann Arbor,
MI July 1981
Interviews with Frank Alarcón, Jean Soto, Sister Mary Virginia Clark
Guillermina Valdes-Villalva, written history of dump ministry, 1981
Praise the Lord, Trinity Broadcasting Network, Jan. 11, 1988
Viva Cristo Rey

CHAPTER 32 – "WE'VE GOT TO DO SOMETHING"
Father Rick Thomas, "Christmas at the Dump," *New Covenant*, Ann Arbor,
MI July 1981
Frank Alarcón, "A Miracle," *New Covenant* July 1981
Jean Soto, "A Personal Reflection," *New Covenant* July 1981
Interviews with Evy Nelson, Jean Soto

CHAPTER 33 – JUÁREZ MAN
Interviews with Frank Alarcón, Hector Bencomo, Sister Mary Virginia
Clark, and a Mexican-American El Paso businessman who does not wish his
name used.

CHAPTER 34 – A NEW LIFE BUILT ON GARBAGE
Father Rick Thomas, "Christmas at the Dump," *New Covenant* July 1981
Interviews with Frank Alarcón, Sergio Conde, Lucía Conde, Sister Mary
Virginia Clark
Sergio Conde Varela, "More Than Enough," *Guideposts*, New York, October
1997
Irma Padilla, written account of healing of brain-damaged children, c. 1980
Jean Soto, written account of healing of brain-damaged children, 1980
Guillermina Valdes-Villalva, written account of dump ministry, 1981

CHAPTER 35 – THE LORD'S RANCH
"History of Our Lady's Youth Center" (part of United Way funding applica-
tion), 1974
Interviews with Father Harold Rahm, Father Jack Deeves, Joanne Ivey, Jean
Soto, Rickie Feuille
Bill Halloran, "Streams Will Burst Forth in the Desert," Providence, RI *Visi-
tor*, 1977

CHAPTER 36 – BUILDING FOR THE LORD
Interviews with Sister Mary Virginia Clark, Pochie and Neto Heredia, Mary
Ann Halloran, Lorenza Ledesma Gil

CHAPTER 37 – THE LORD'S FOOD BANK
Interviews with Sister Mary Virginia Clark, Carmen Molina, Martha
Medrano, Aurora Alvarado

CHAPTER 38 – MAKING IT WORK IN JUÁREZ
Interviews with Sergio and Lucía Conde

CHAPTER 39 – A COMMUNITY IN THE DESERT
Interviews with Father Jack Deeves, Ralph and Marie Irróbali

CHAPTER 40 – REACHING OUT TO THE POOR
Interviews with Jean Soto, Sergio and Lucía Conde
Father James McCown, "The Lord's Food Bank," *The Jesuit*, Fall 1979
Sister Briege McKenna, workshop talk, Church of St. Ignatius, Rome, June 1, 2017
Henry Libersat, "Sister Briege McKenna, Healer," *The Evangelist*, reprinted in The Catholic Digest, St. Paul, MN, December 1986
Father Thaddeus Doyle, "Sr. Briege & the Eucharist," *The Curate's Diary*, Arklow, Ireland, June 2009 (accessed online)

CHAPTER 41 – "SPIRIT OF DEATH, I CAST YOU OUT"
Father Rick Thomas and a nurse, written testimony in Our Lady's Youth Center archives.
"The Wonders of Juárez," *New Covenant*, by Father Rick Thomas with editor's introduction, November 1978
Fr. René Laurentin, *Miracles in El Paso?*, Servant Books, 1982

CHAPTER 42 – LETTING GOD PAY THE BILLS
Interviews with Sister Mary Virginia Clark, Carmen Molina, Rickie Feuille
New Covenant, "Communities that Serve," Fred Lilly, March 1985
El Paso Times, "United Fund Looks Onward To Future," Jan. 31, 1968

CHAPTER 43 – NEW TIMES IN TOWN
Interviews with Father Sam Rosales, Esther and Ernest Padilla, Victor Montes, Rudy and Blanca Irróbali, Sister Mary Virginia Clark

CHAPTER 44 – GOD'S POWER IN THE JAILHOUSE
Interviews with Sister Mary Virginia Clark, Hector Bencomo, Sergio Conde
Jeff Hensley, "The Multiplication of the Bread Pudding," *New Covenant* July-August 1982

CHAPTER 45 – TENDING THE YOUTH IN GOD'S GARDENS
Interviews with Sergio and Lucía Conde

CHAPTER 46 – PRAYER AND POLITICS
Interviews with Sergio and Lucía Conde, and businessman who does not wish his name used
El Paso Herald-Post, "Mayor-Elect Wants City Audit," Ken Flynn (United Press International), July 12, 1983
El Paso Times, "Juárez mayor-elect announces Cabinet," Matt Pritchard, Oct. 4, 1983
Diario de Juárez, Ciudad Juárez, Chihuahua, Mexico, Sept. 18, 1983 (author's name and article headline not preserved)
Toronto Star, Ontario, Canada, "Controversy greets new Mexican ambassador," Feb. 26, 2009 (accessed online)

CHAPTER 47 – ON THE ROAD
Interviews with Father Michael Barry, Mary Bradfield, Sergio and Lucía Conde

CHAPTER 48 – HARD SAYINGS ABOUT MONEY

Father Rick Thomas, *God's Goods*, Vado, NM: The Lord's Ranch Press, 2008 (quotations taken from pages 13, 23 and 25)
Interviews with Father Bill McCann, Father Nathan O'Halloran, Helen Guajardo, Jean Soto, Susan Vescovo, Martha Medrano, Tommy and Ceci Barrientos, Robert Thomas
Good NewsLetter, Narkis Street Congregation, Jerusalem, "Good News for the poor, bad news for the greedy," March 2001
Praise the Lord, Jan. 11, 1988; Sept. 25, 1990

CHAPTER 49 – ON TOP OF THE MOUNTAIN
Interviews with Father Sam Rosales, Richard Munzinger, Susan Vescovo
El Paso Times, "'Modern-day St. Francis' honored," Pat Henry, March 19, 1983
El Paso Times, "Abortion protesters refuse to post bond" (with reference to Sertoma prize), Janet Pérez, Aug. 29, 1989
Bobbie Cavnar, *Praise the Lord* (newsletter of Christian Community of God's Delight), December 1981

CHAPTER 50 – CHANGES AND CHALLENGES
Interviews with Martha Medrano, Frank Alarcón, Jean Soto, Robert Thomas, Alan Curtis

CHAPTER 51 – INTO DEEP WATERS
Interviews with Esther and Ernest Padilla, Marie Heredia Irróbali
Written testimonies from OLYC volunteers praying against witches' conference, September 1985

CHAPTER 52 – A SHAKEUP AND A BREAKDOWN
Interviews with Sister Mary Virginia Clark, Alan and Kim Curtis

CHAPTER 53 – GOD'S BUDDY
Interviews with Father Bill McCann, Richard Munzinger, Evy Nelson, Aida Frietze-Lewis, Jim Gallagher, Carmen Molina, Tencha Tapia, Hector and Mary Bencomo, and El Paso businessman who does not wish his name used

CHAPTER 54 – OPERATION RESCUE
Interviews with Bishop Ricardo Ramírez, Sister Mary Virginia Clark
El Paso Times, "77 jailed at El Paso Abortion Protest," Joe Olvera, Aug. 27, 1989
El Paso Times, "Abortion protesters refuse to post bond," Janet Pérez, Aug. 29, 1989

CHAPTER 55 – NEEDLING THE JUDGE
El Paso Times, "Revival breaks out after jury's verdict," Benjamin Keck, June 10, 1992
New Covenant, "A Chance to Meet Jesus," by Lisa Ferguson, April 1990
Heart to Heart with Sheila Walsh, Sept. 9, 1992
Praise the Lord, Sept. 25, 1990

CHAPTER 56 – THE CREATIVE PRO-LIFER
Heart to Heart with Sheila Walsh, Sept. 9, 1992
El Paso Herald-Post, "Council slaps down abortion law," Terrence Poppa, Oct. 24, 1989
Dallas Morning News, photo by Michael Pruitt, June 10, 1990

El Paso Herald-Post, photo by Michael Levy, Jan. 22, 1986

CHAPTER 57 – TROUBLE AT THE FOOD BANK
Interviews with Father Sam Rosales, Sergio Conde, Rudy Irróbali, Pedro Ibarra, Carmen Molina
El Paso Herald-Post, "Think tank chief dies in air crash," Alfredo Corchado Sept.13, 1991

CHAPTER 58 – KING JESUS ON THE AIRWAVES
Interviews with John and Ruth Stanley
Bill Halloran, written account of the history of KJES

CHAPTER 59 – A NEW HEADQUARTERS
Interviews with Sister Mary Virginia Clark, Michael Ridley
Michael Ridley, written report on OLYC's acquisition of Las Alas

CHAPTER 60 – COUNSELING BY THE BOOK
Interview with Jim Gallagher

CHAPTER 61 – THE LAND WAR
El Paso Herald-Post, "Lord's Ranch: Local site offers recreation and relaxation to people of all ages," Eric Enders, July 12, 1997
El Paso Herald-Post, "Lord's Ranch appeals BLM eviction," Eric Enders, Aug. 21, 1997

CHAPTER 62 – LATER YEARS AND UNWANTED HONORS
Interview with Roger O'Dell
Voz en el Desierto (Peace and Justice Ministry, Diocese of El Paso), "Father Rick Thomas to get Option for the Poor Award," fall 1999
Rio Grande Catholic, El Paso, "Honoree Gives Credit to Lord," Mary Ann Herman, October 1999
Rio Grande Catholic, "If you seek peace, work for justice," Mary Ann Herman, October 1999
El Paso Times, "Strip club ordinance introduced," Charles K. Wilson, July 23, 2003 (Father Thomas misidentified as "Father Victor Thomas")
City of El Paso Ordinance 016624, May 8, 2007 (online)

CHAPTER 63 – EXPANSION IN JUÁREZ
Interviews with Marcos and Celia Nieblas

CHAPTER 64 – YOUNG SHEPHERDS
Interviews with Daisy Pérez, Gaby Federico

CHAPTER 65 – HERE IS YOUR GOD
Bishop Ricardo Ramírez, funeral address for Father Rick Thomas, as delivered and from transcript, May 12, 2006
Interviews with Bob Thomas, Daisy Pérez
El Paso Times, "Funeral Mass for Rev. Thomas is today," Diana Washington Valdez, May 12, 2006

ABOUT THE AUTHOR

Photo credit: Roy MacIntyre

Richard Dunstan is a former newspaper reporter and editor, now retired from teaching journalism and religious studies at Vancouver Island University in British Columbia, Canada. He has been part of the Catholic charismatic renewal since 1982 and is a member and former chair of Catholic Charismatic Renewal Services of British Columbia. He is the author of *Fire in the North: A History of the Catholic Charismatic Renewal in Canada*. He has three children, nine grandchildren, and three great-grandchildren. He and his wife, Lynn, live in Victoria, B.C.

He first visited Father Rick Thomas and the OLYC community in El Paso and Ciudad Juárez in 1989; while there, he had a life-changing encounter with Jesus during a visit to the prisoners in the cells at the Juárez municipal jail. He has returned to the community frequently since then and is the author of *The Bible on the Border*, an account of the OLYC ministries published in

2009 and based on extensive interviews with Father Thomas prior to his death in 2006. Since then he has been working on this biography at the request of the OLYC community, drawing on interviews with numerous community members, documentary research, and extensive reminiscences which Father Thomas recorded at the request of his friends during his final illness.

21265276R00228

Made in the USA
Columbia, SC
16 July 2018